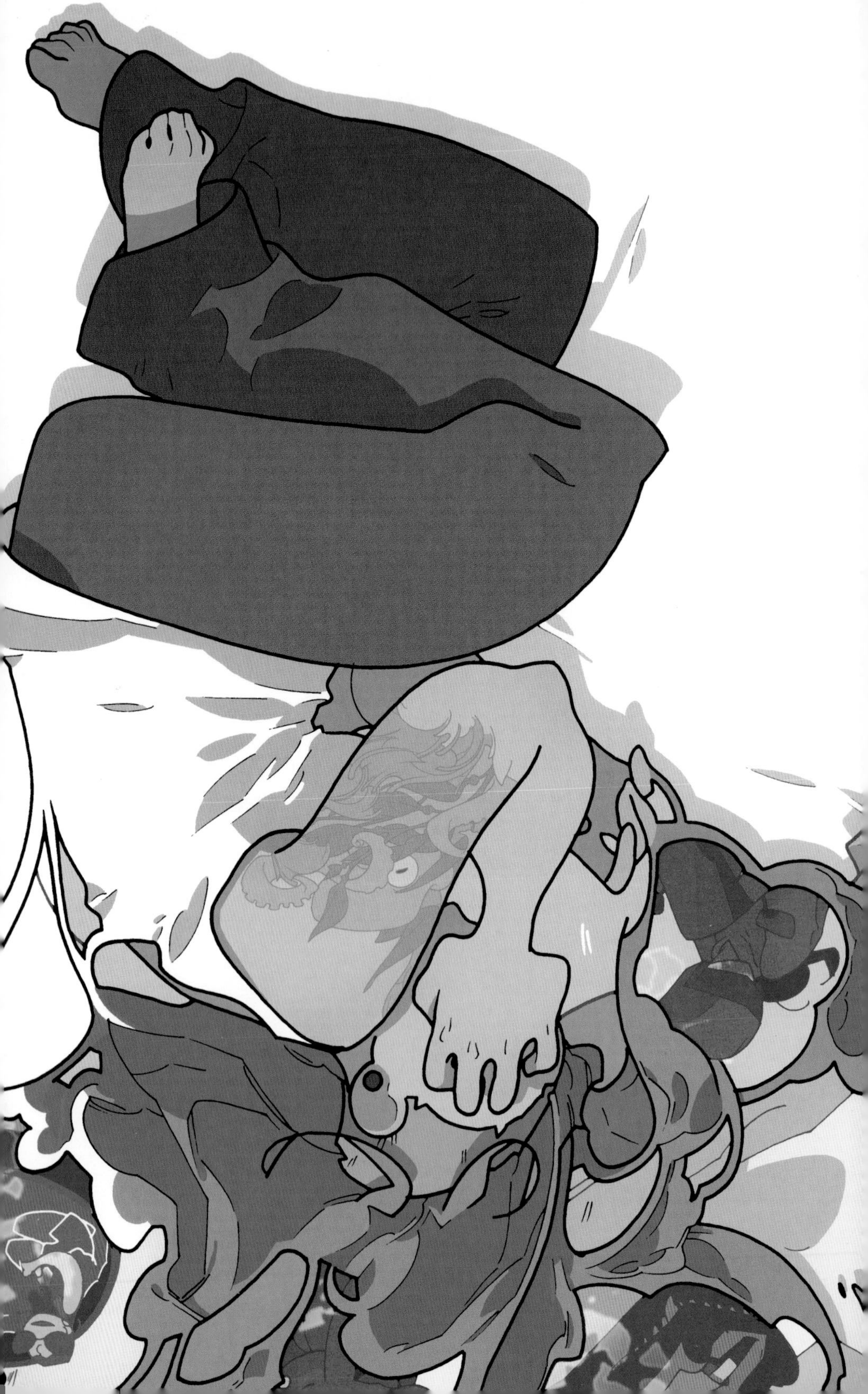

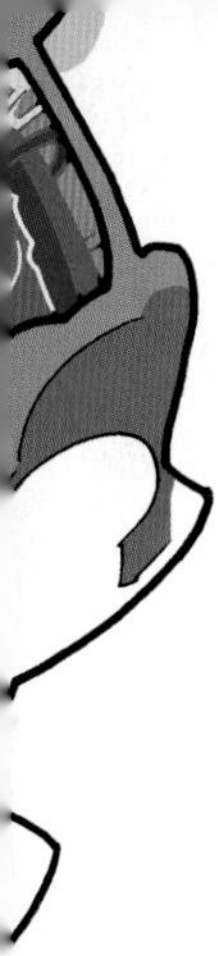

heart in a box

written by
KELLY THOMPSON

art by
MEREDITH McCLAREN

DARK HORSE BOOKS

president and publisher
MIKE RICHARDSON

editor
BRENDAN WRIGHT

designer
SANDY TANAKA

digital art technician
CHRISTINA McKENZIE

Published by Dark Horse Books
A division of Dark Horse Comics, Inc.
10956 SE Main Street
Milwaukie, OR 97222

DarkHorse.com

To find a comics shop in your area, call the Comic Shop Locator Service toll-free at
(888) 266-4226.
International Licensing: (503) 905-2377

First edition: September 2015
ISBN 978-1-61655-694-5

Library of Congress Cataloging in Publication data is available.

1 3 5 7 9 10 8 6 4 2
Printed in China

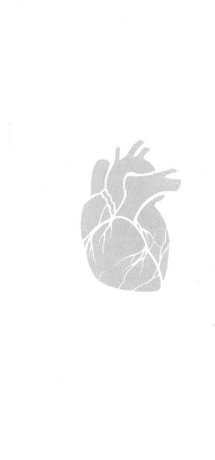

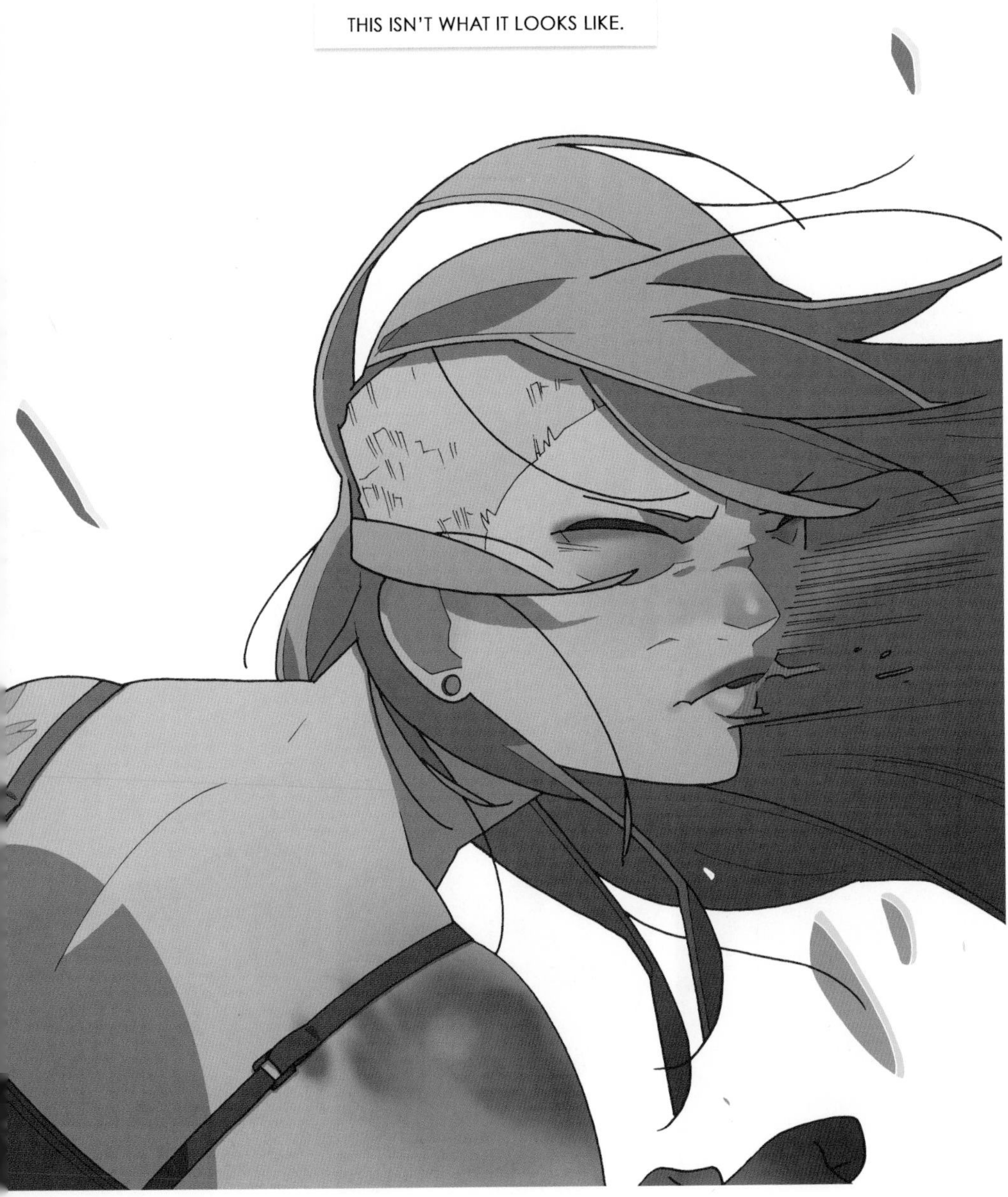
THIS ISN'T WHAT IT LOOKS LIKE.

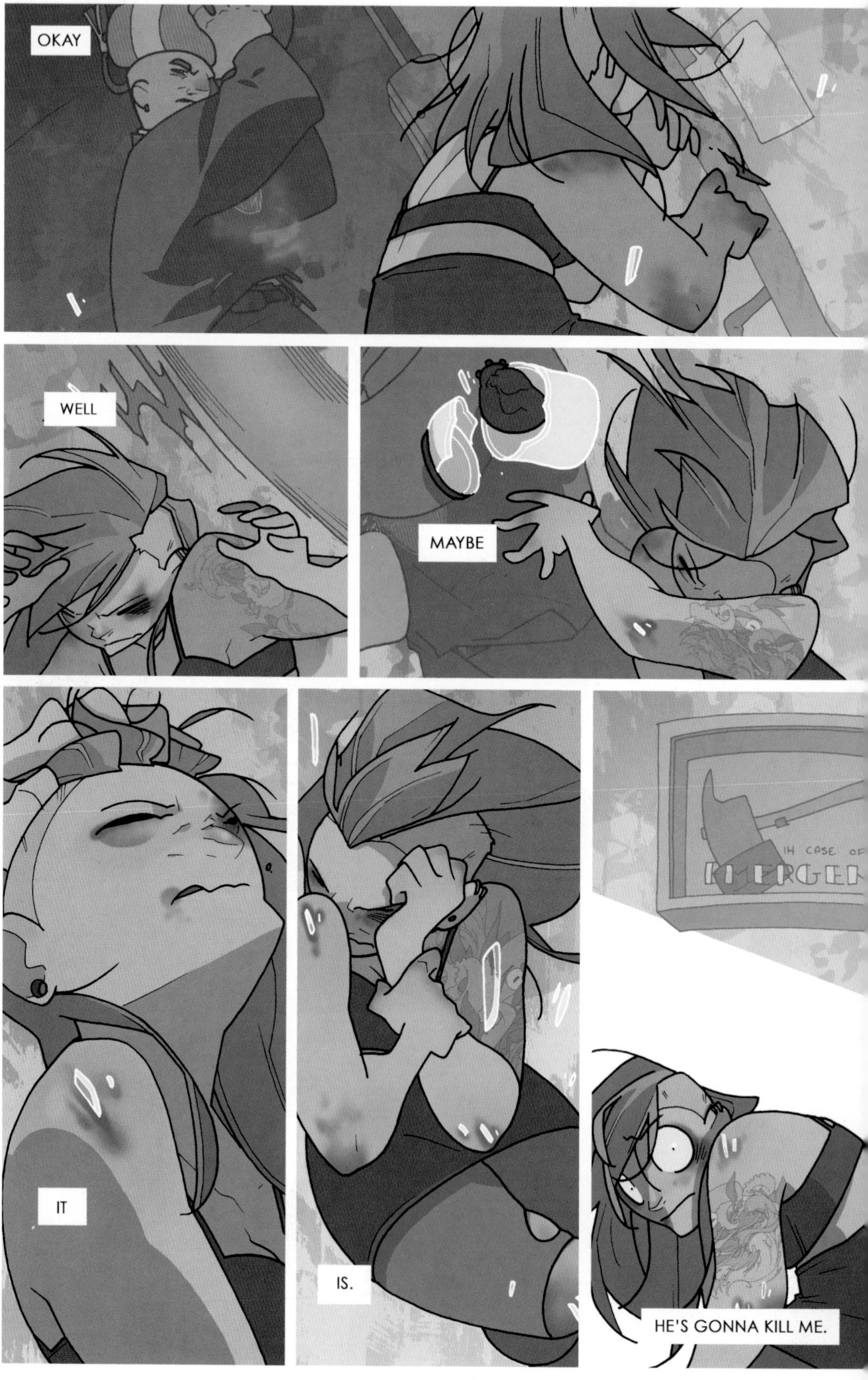
OKAY
WELL
MAYBE
IT
IS.
HE'S GONNA KILL ME.

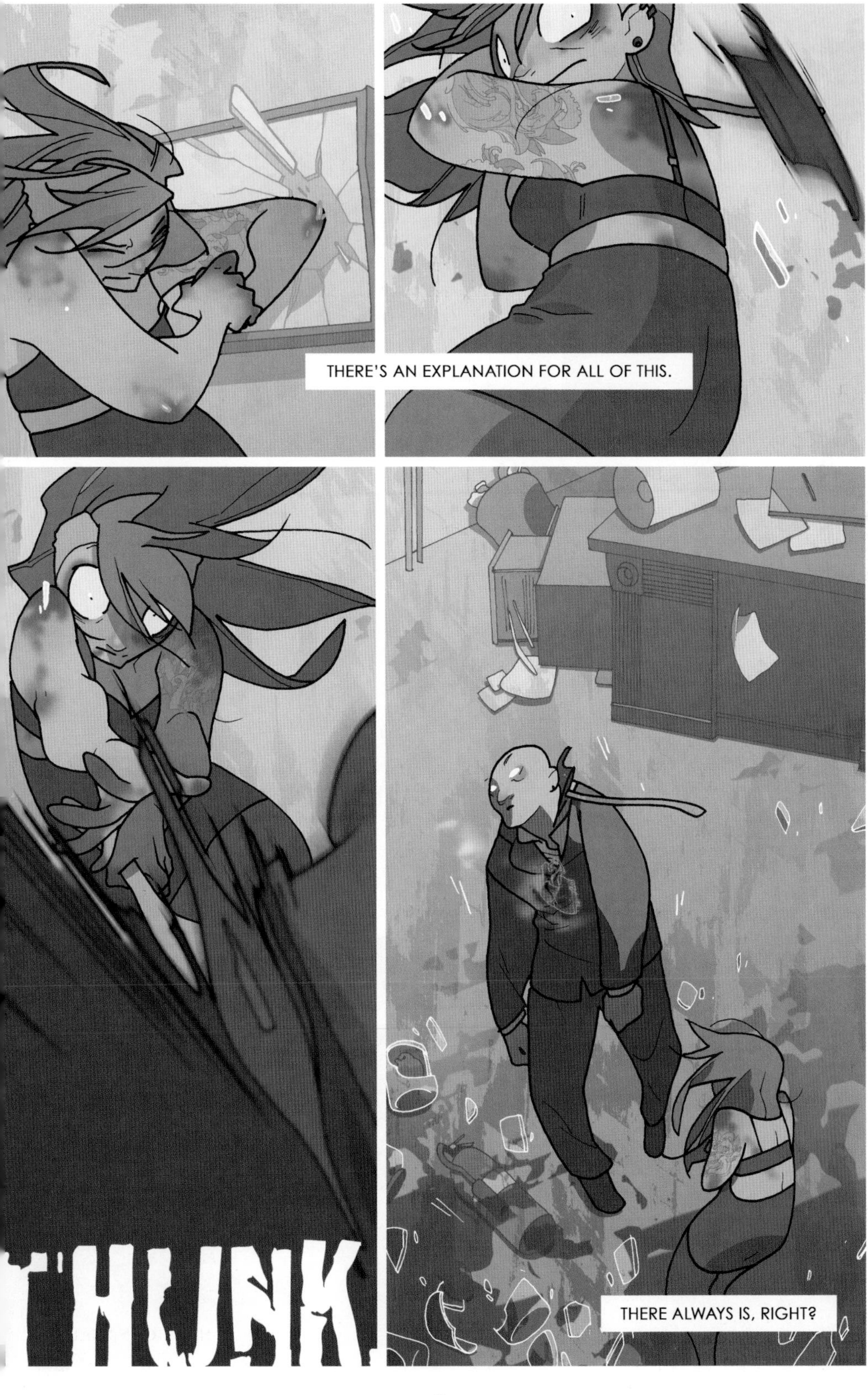
THERE'S AN EXPLANATION FOR ALL OF THIS.
THUNK
THERE ALWAYS IS, RIGHT?

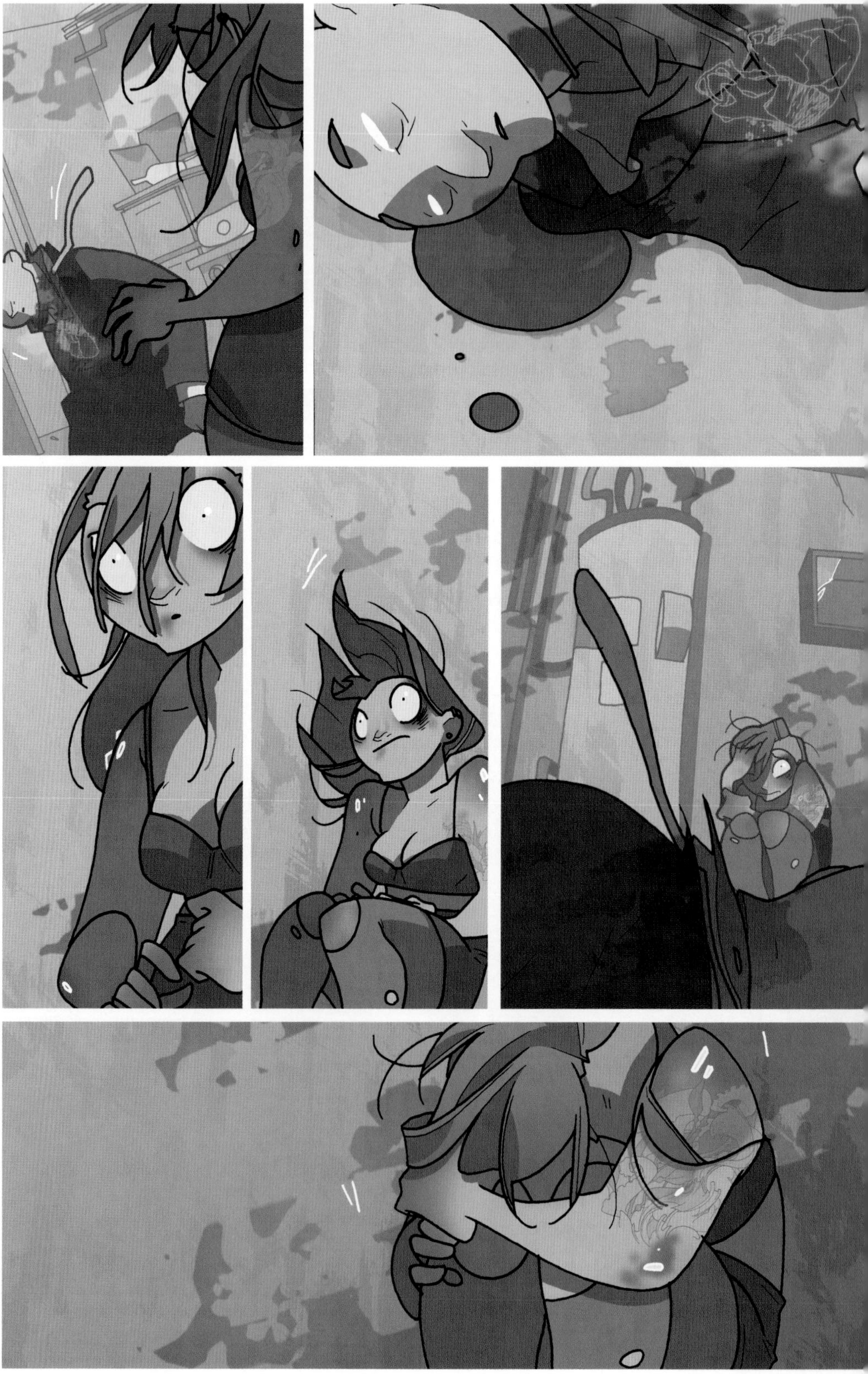

EMMA!

EMMM MMMMM AAAAA!

THIS IS RIDICULOUS...

EMMA! YOU'VE BEEN IN HERE FOR TWO WEEKS!

YOU HAVE TO COME OUT!!

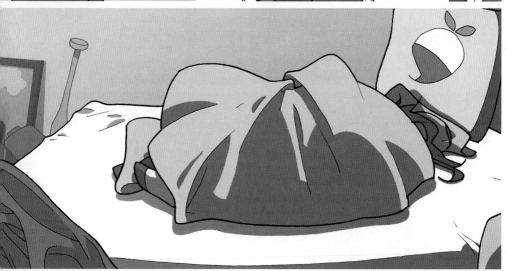

YOU ARE SHOWERING AND WE'RE LEAVING THE HOUSE!

YOU CANNOT HAVE BEEN LUCKY ENOUGH TO ACTUALLY DIE UNDER THERE.

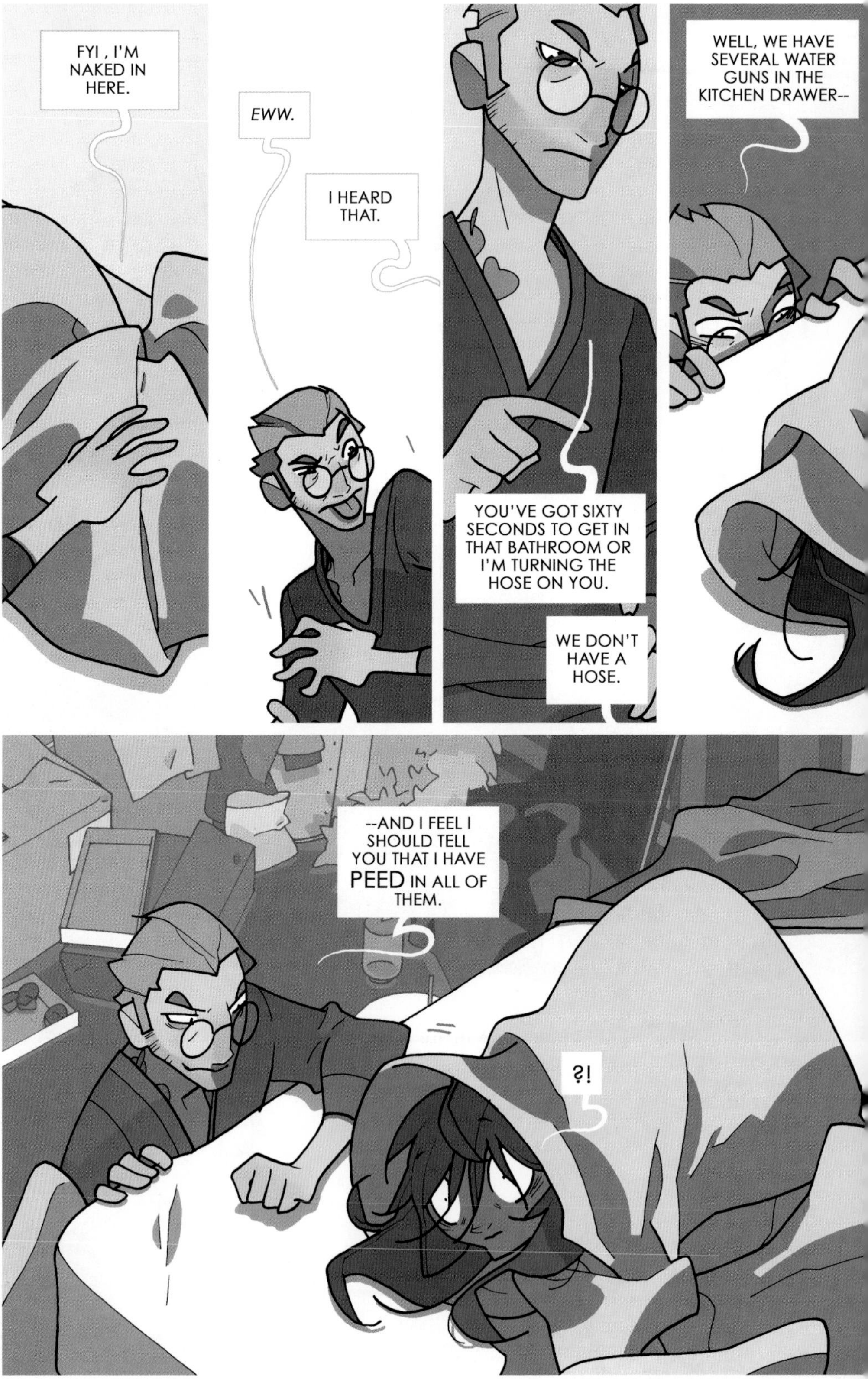
FYI , I'M NAKED IN HERE.
EWW.
I HEARD THAT.
YOU'VE GOT SIXTY SECONDS TO GET IN THAT BATHROOM OR I'M TURNING THE HOSE ON YOU.
WE DON'T HAVE A HOSE.
WELL, WE HAVE SEVERAL WATER GUNS IN THE KITCHEN DRAWER--
--AND I FEEL I SHOULD TELL YOU THAT I HAVE PEED IN ALL OF THEM.
?!

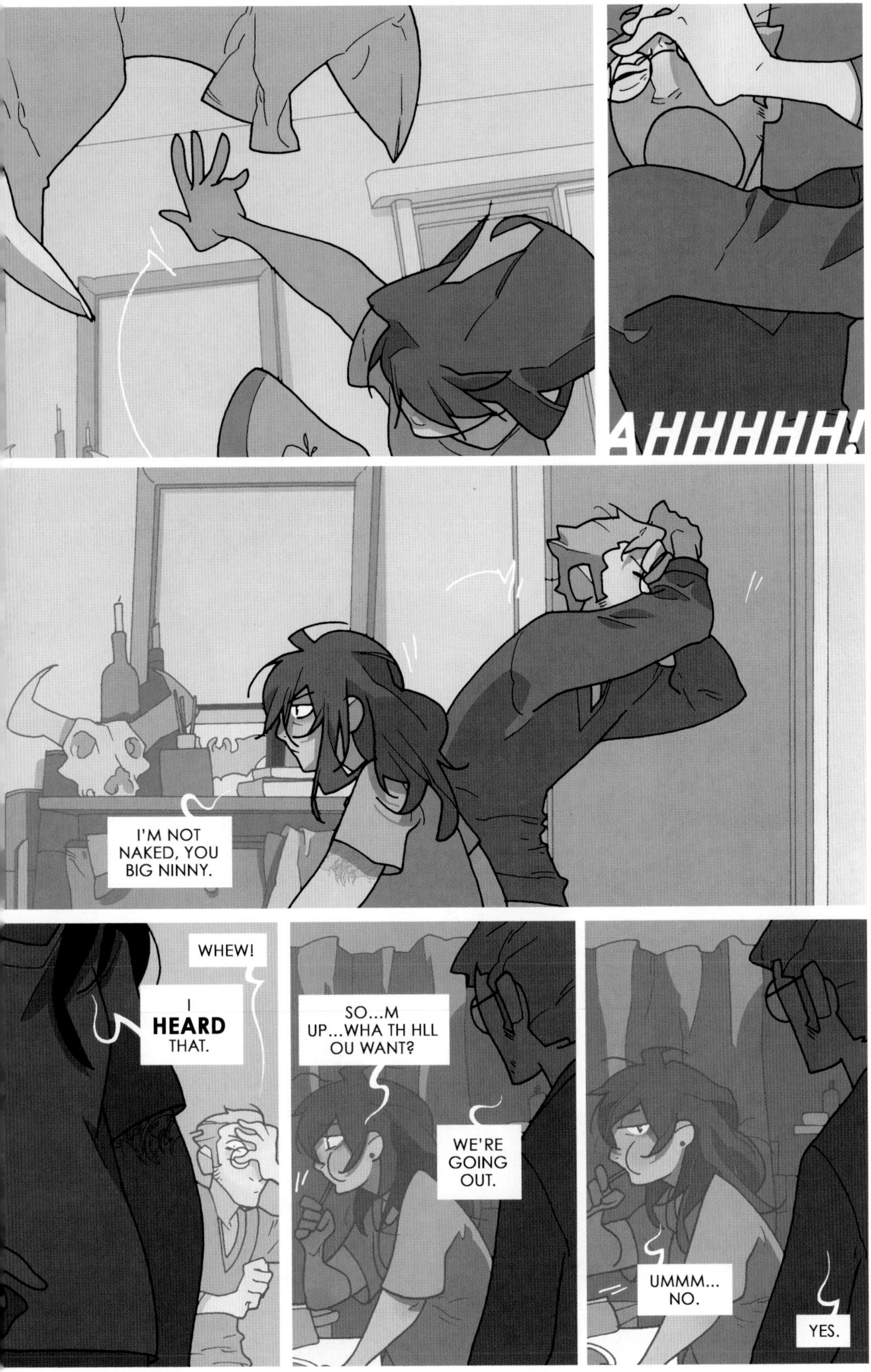
AHHHHHH!
I'M NOT NAKED, YOU BIG NINNY.
WHEW!
I **HEARD** THAT.
SO...M UP...WHA TH HLL OU WANT?
WE'RE GOING OUT.
UMMM... NO.
YES.

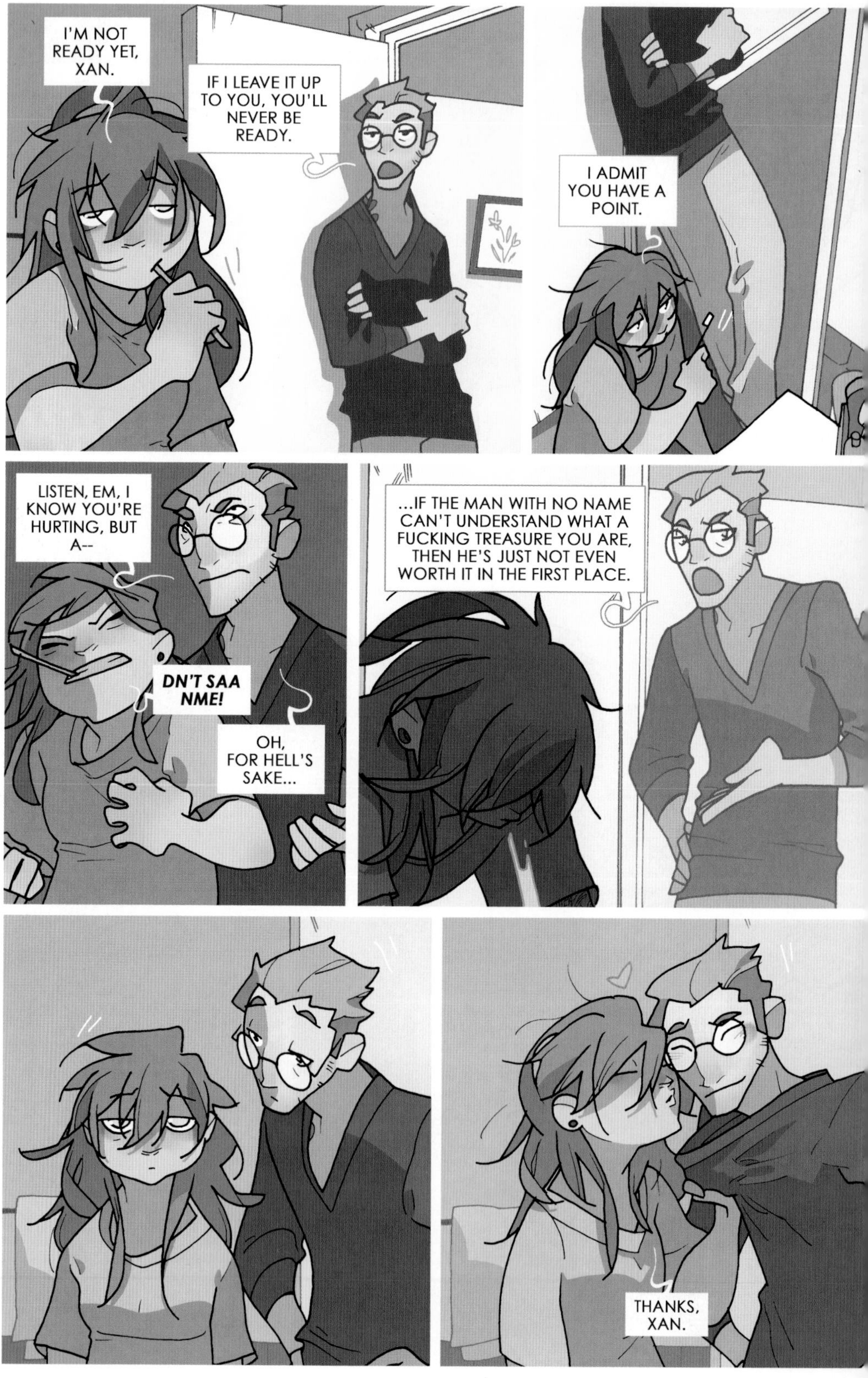
I'M NOT READY YET, XAN.
IF I LEAVE IT UP TO YOU, YOU'LL NEVER BE READY.
I ADMIT YOU HAVE A POINT.
LISTEN, EM, I KNOW YOU'RE HURTING, BUT A--
DN'T SAA NME!
OH, FOR HELL'S SAKE...
...IF THE MAN WITH NO NAME CAN'T UNDERSTAND WHAT A FUCKING TREASURE YOU ARE, THEN HE'S JUST NOT EVEN WORTH IT IN THE FIRST PLACE.
THANKS, XAN.

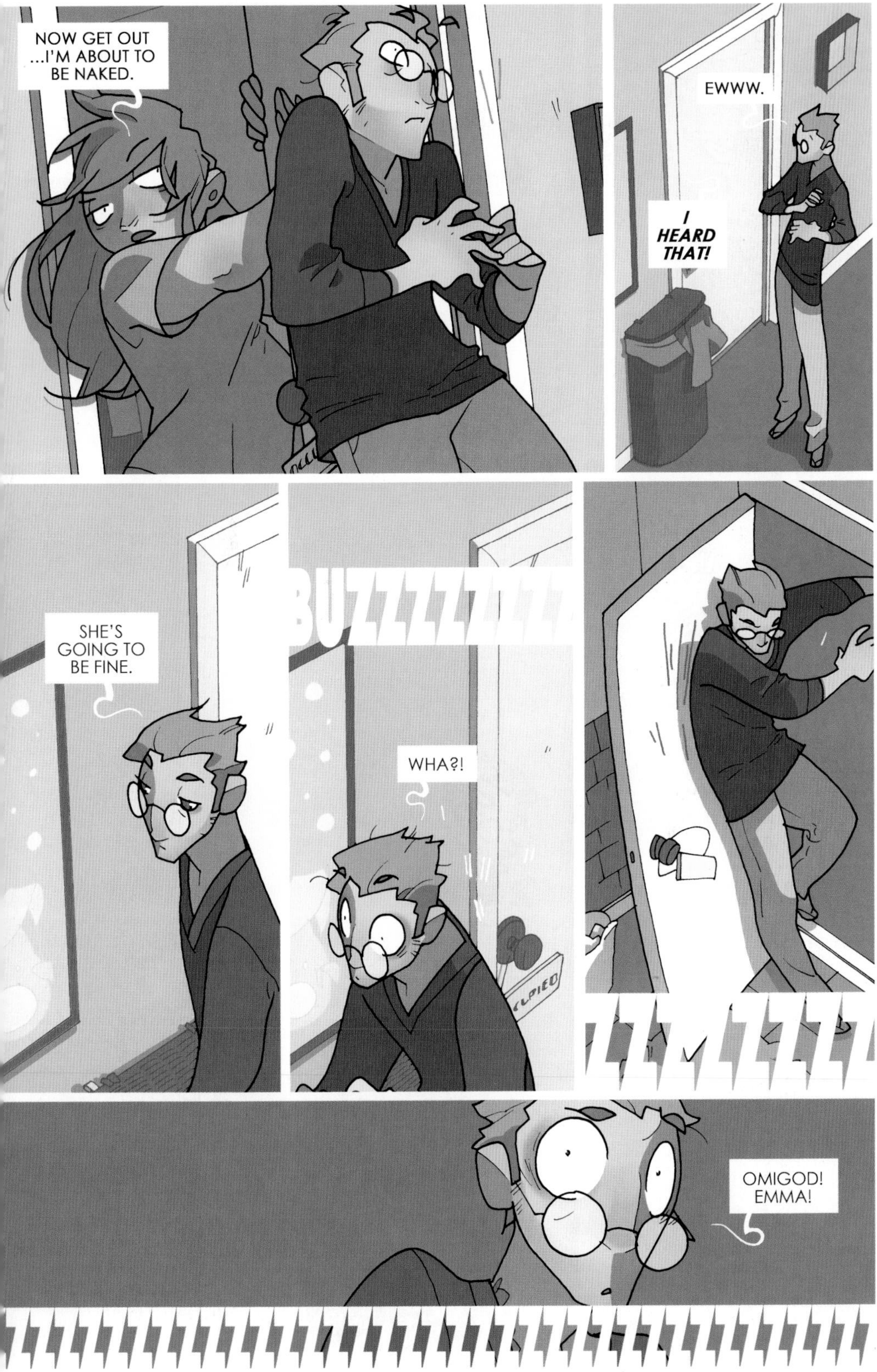
NOW GET OUT ...I'M ABOUT TO BE NAKED.
EWWW.
I HEARD THAT!
SHE'S GOING TO BE FINE.
BUZZZZZZZZ
WHA?!
OMIGOD! EMMA!

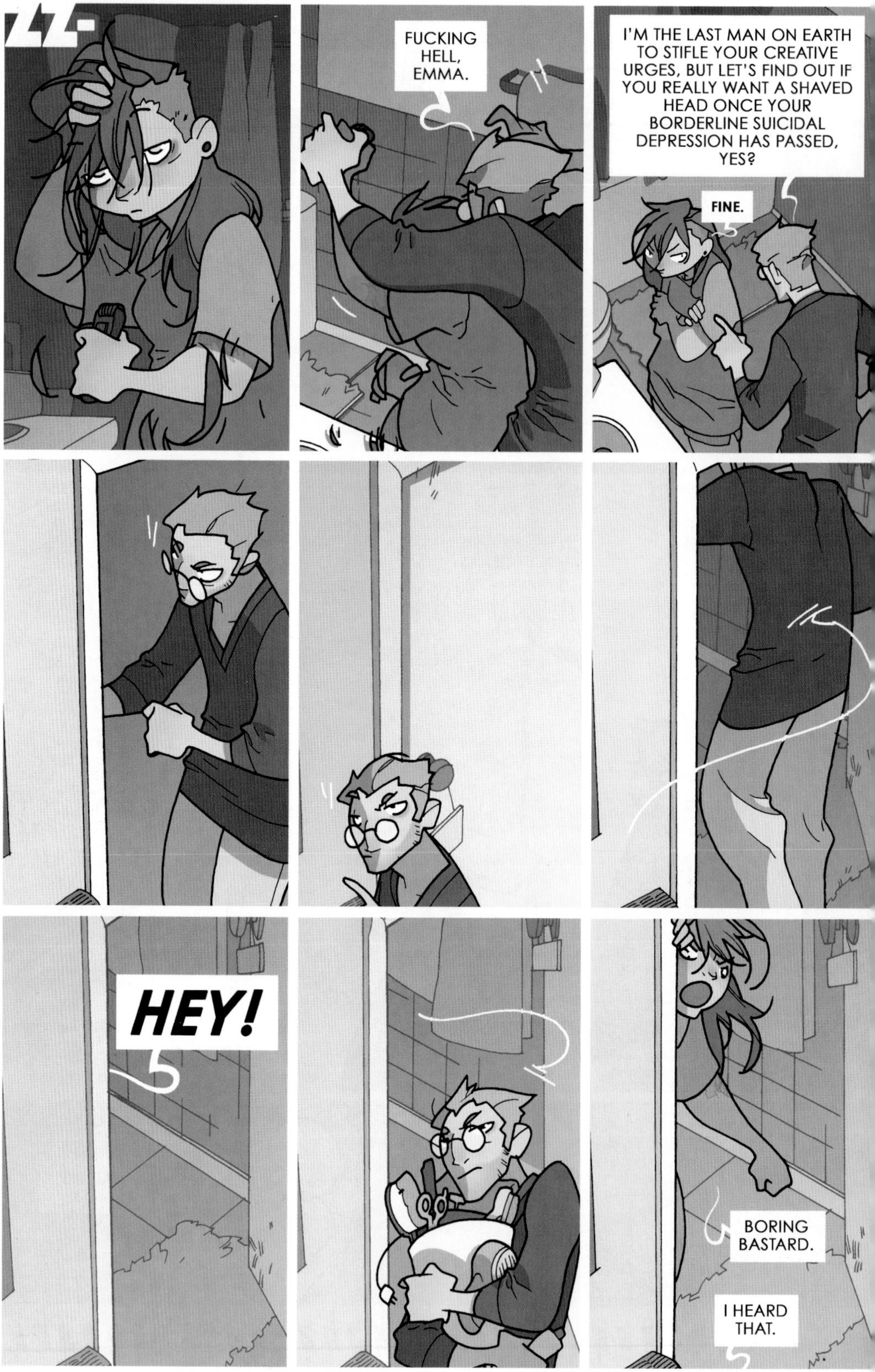
ZZ-
FUCKING HELL, EMMA.
I'M THE LAST MAN ON EARTH TO STIFLE YOUR CREATIVE URGES, BUT LET'S FIND OUT IF YOU REALLY WANT A SHAVED HEAD ONCE YOUR BORDERLINE SUICIDAL DEPRESSION HAS PASSED, YES?
FINE.
HEY!
BORING BASTARD.
I HEARD THAT.

WENTY-SIX MINUTES LATER.

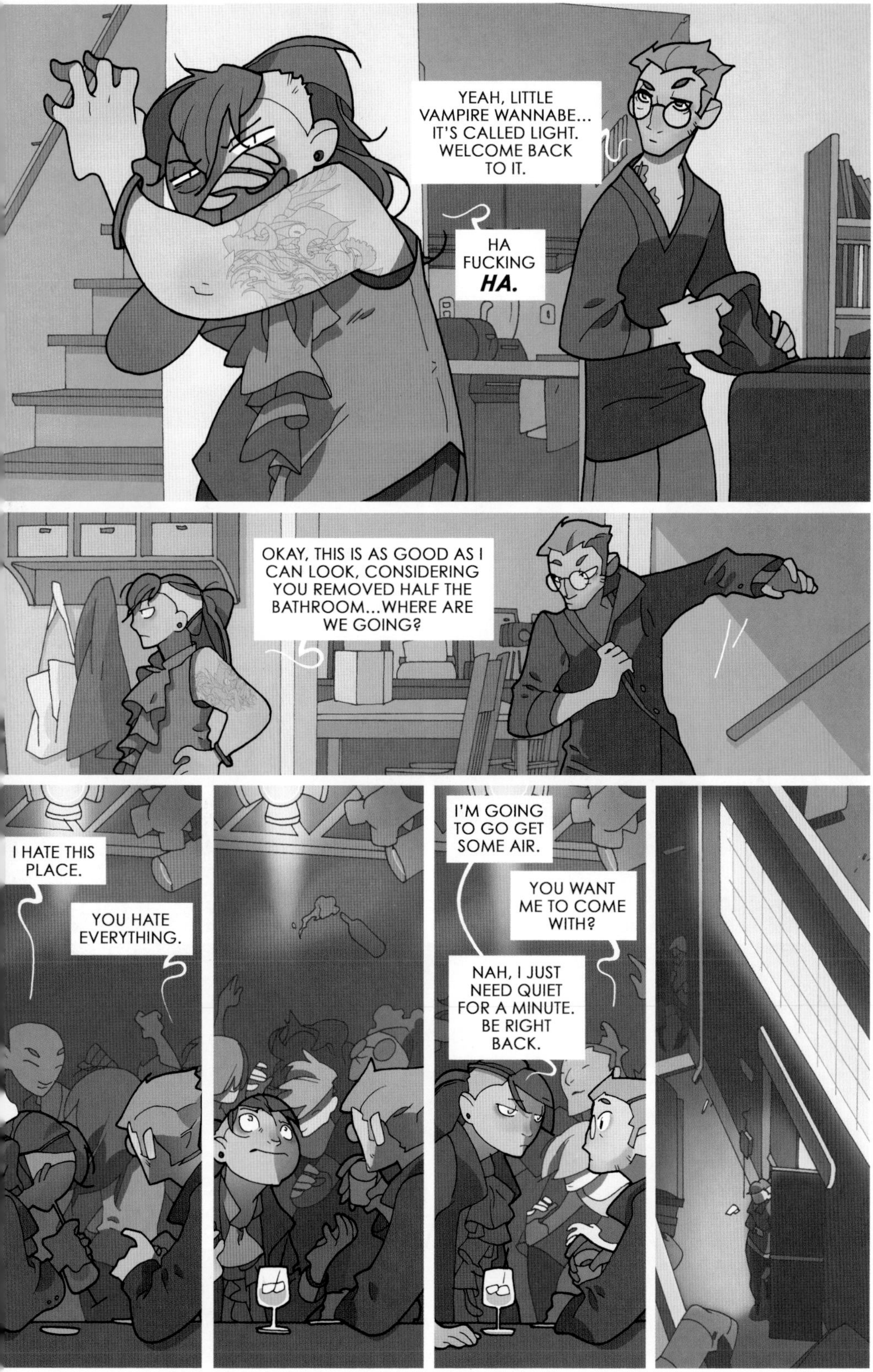

YEAH, LITTLE VAMPIRE WANNABE... IT'S CALLED LIGHT. WELCOME BACK TO IT.
HA FUCKING ***HA.***
OKAY, THIS IS AS GOOD AS I CAN LOOK, CONSIDERING YOU REMOVED HALF THE BATHROOM...WHERE ARE WE GOING?
I HATE THIS PLACE.
YOU HATE EVERYTHING.
I'M GOING TO GO GET SOME AIR.
YOU WANT ME TO COME WITH?
NAH, I JUST NEED QUIET FOR A MINUTE. BE RIGHT BACK.

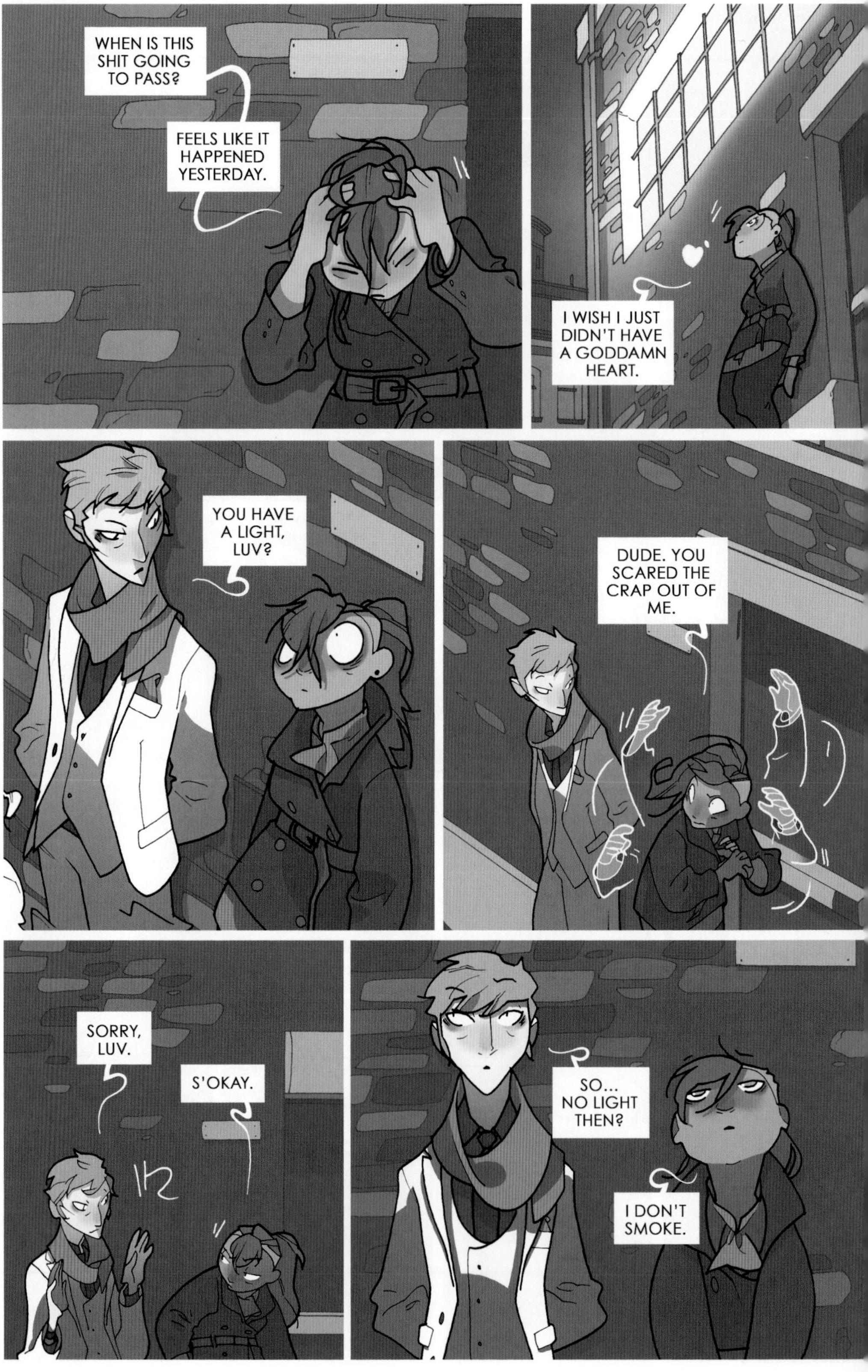
WHEN IS THIS SHIT GOING TO PASS?
FEELS LIKE IT HAPPENED YESTERDAY.
I WISH I JUST DIDN'T HAVE A GODDAMN HEART.
YOU HAVE A LIGHT, LUV?
DUDE. YOU SCARED THE CRAP OUT OF ME.
SORRY, LUV.
S'OKAY.
SO... NO LIGHT THEN?
I DON'T SMOKE.

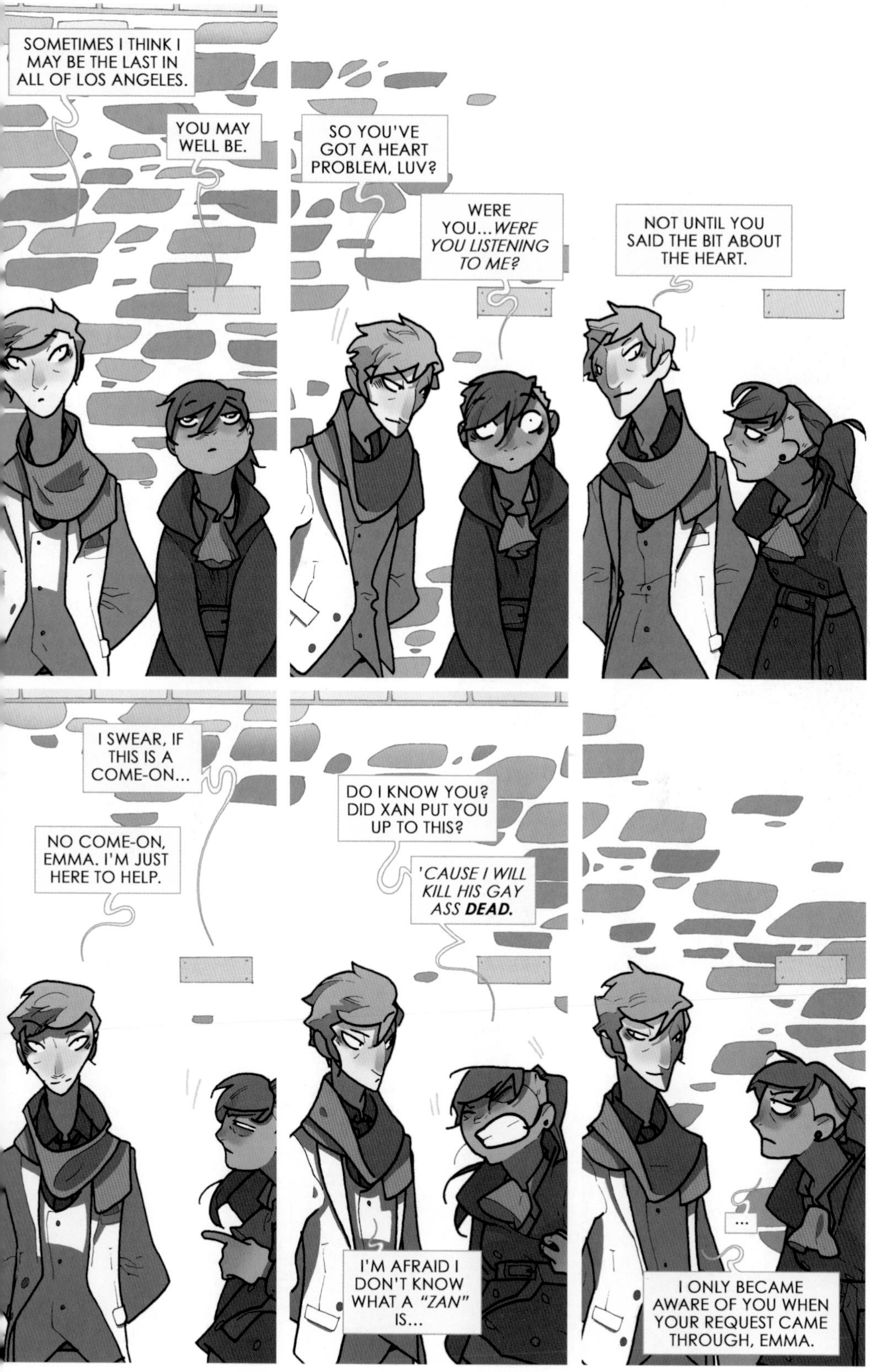
SOMETIMES I THINK I MAY BE THE LAST IN ALL OF LOS ANGELES.
YOU MAY WELL BE.
SO YOU'VE GOT A HEART PROBLEM, LUV?
WERE YOU...*WERE YOU LISTENING TO ME?*
NOT UNTIL YOU SAID THE BIT ABOUT THE HEART.
I SWEAR, IF THIS IS A COME-ON...
NO COME-ON, EMMA. I'M JUST HERE TO HELP.
DO I KNOW YOU? DID XAN PUT YOU UP TO THIS?
'CAUSE I WILL KILL HIS GAY ASS ***DEAD.***
I'M AFRAID I DON'T KNOW WHAT A *"ZAN"* IS...
...
I ONLY BECAME AWARE OF YOU WHEN YOUR REQUEST CAME THROUGH, EMMA.

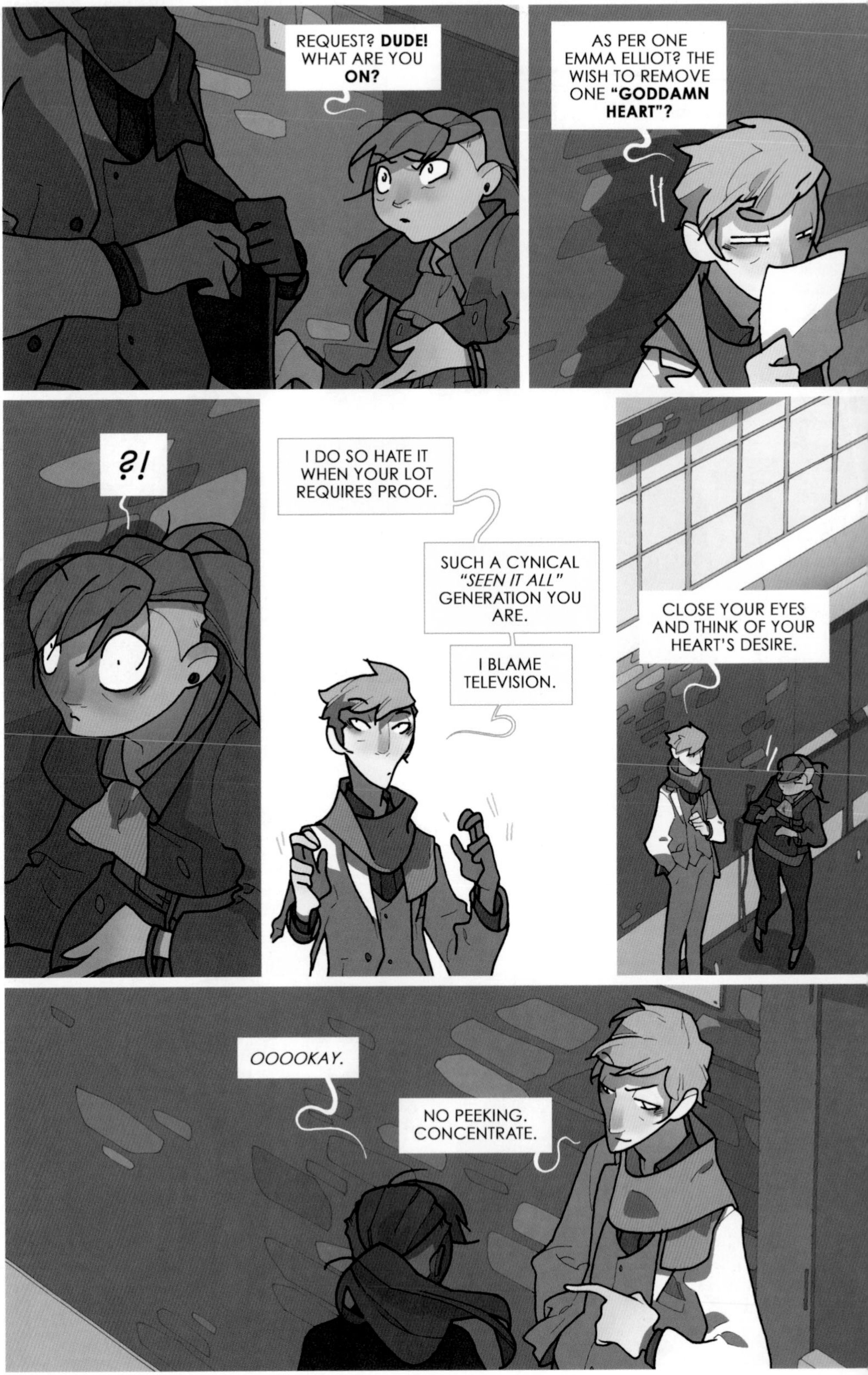

REQUEST? **DUDE!** WHAT ARE YOU **ON?**
AS PER ONE EMMA ELLIOT? THE WISH TO REMOVE ONE **"GODDAMN HEART"?**
?!
I DO SO HATE IT WHEN YOUR LOT REQUIRES PROOF.
SUCH A CYNICAL *"SEEN IT ALL"* GENERATION YOU ARE.
I BLAME TELEVISION.
CLOSE YOUR EYES AND THINK OF YOUR HEART'S DESIRE.
OOOOKAY.
NO PEEKING. CONCENTRATE.

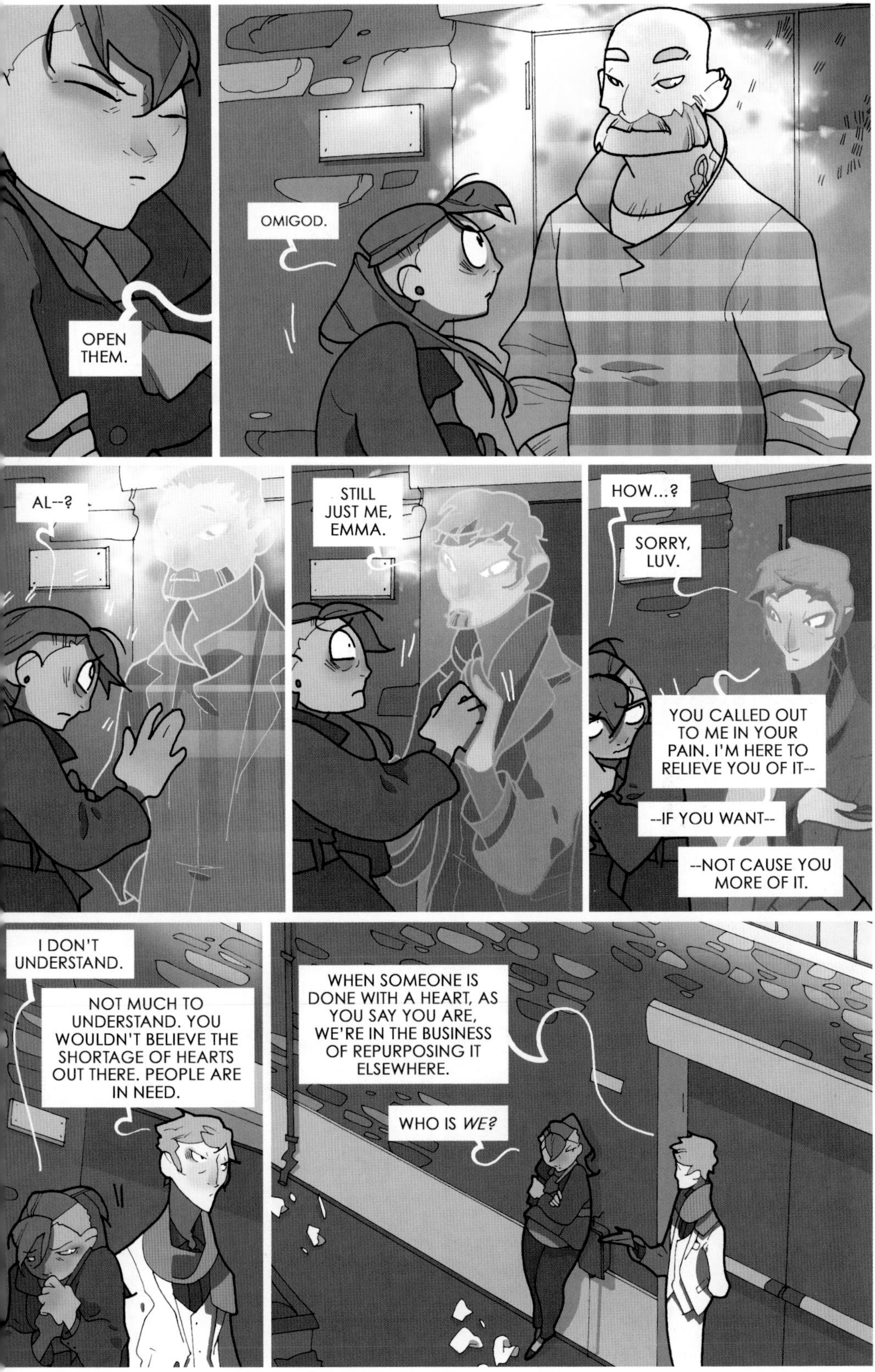
OPEN THEM.
OMIGOD.
AL--?
STILL JUST ME, EMMA.
HOW...?
SORRY, LUV.
YOU CALLED OUT TO ME IN YOUR PAIN. I'M HERE TO RELIEVE YOU OF IT--
--IF YOU WANT--
--NOT CAUSE YOU MORE OF IT.
I DON'T UNDERSTAND.
NOT MUCH TO UNDERSTAND. YOU WOULDN'T BELIEVE THE SHORTAGE OF HEARTS OUT THERE. PEOPLE ARE IN NEED.
WHEN SOMEONE IS DONE WITH A HEART, AS YOU SAY YOU ARE, WE'RE IN THE BUSINESS OF REPURPOSING IT ELSEWHERE.
WHO IS *WE?*

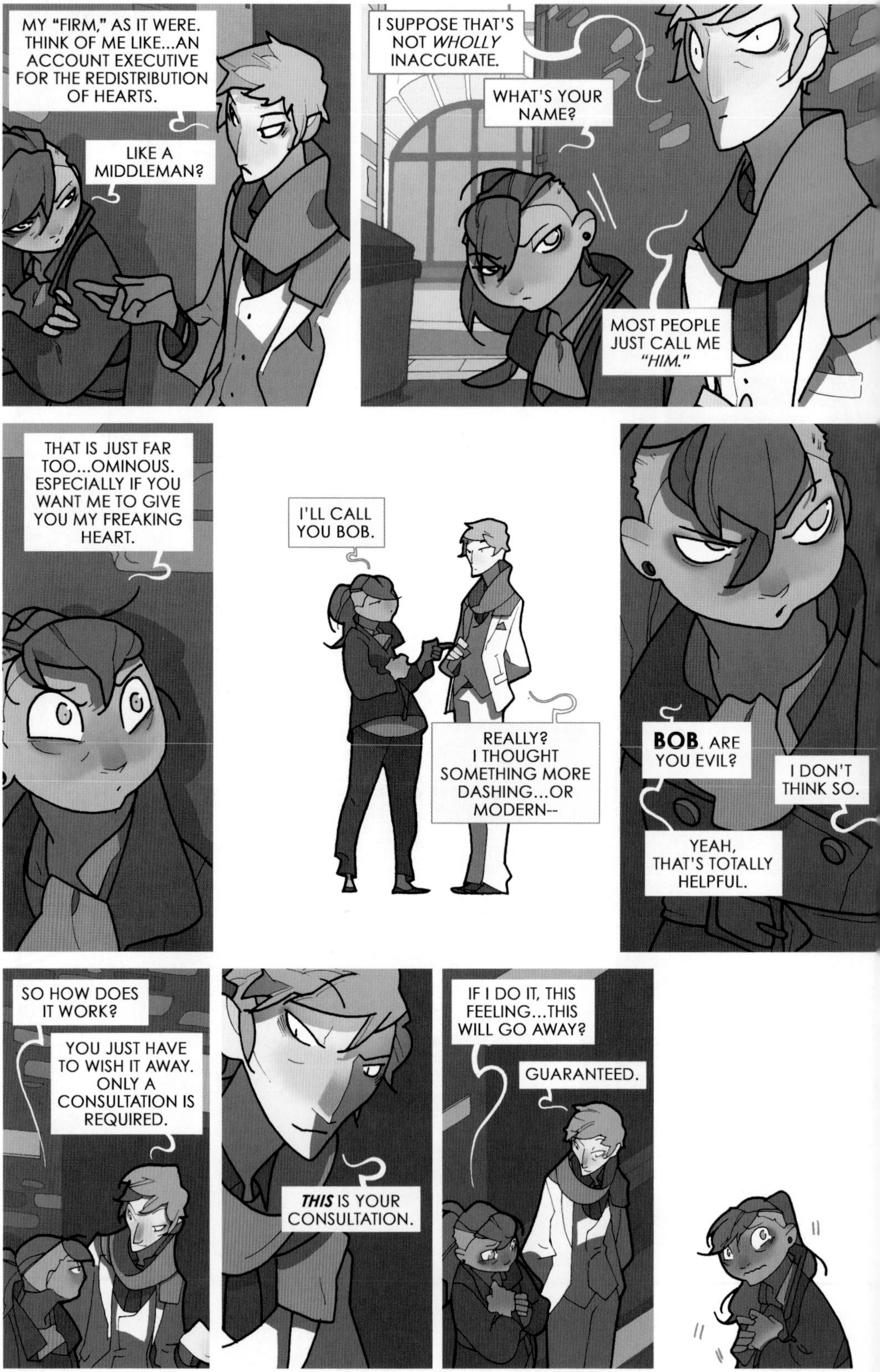
MY "FIRM," AS IT WERE. THINK OF ME LIKE...AN ACCOUNT EXECUTIVE FOR THE REDISTRIBUTION OF HEARTS.
LIKE A MIDDLEMAN?
I SUPPOSE THAT'S NOT *WHOLLY* INACCURATE.
WHAT'S YOUR NAME?
MOST PEOPLE JUST CALL ME *"HIM."*
THAT IS JUST FAR TOO...OMINOUS. ESPECIALLY IF YOU WANT ME TO GIVE YOU MY FREAKING HEART.
I'LL CALL YOU BOB.
REALLY? I THOUGHT SOMETHING MORE DASHING...OR MODERN--
BOB. ARE YOU EVIL?
I DON'T THINK SO.
YEAH, THAT'S TOTALLY HELPFUL.
SO HOW DOES IT WORK?
YOU JUST HAVE TO WISH IT AWAY. ONLY A CONSULTATION IS REQUIRED.
THIS IS YOUR CONSULTATION.
IF I DO IT, THIS FEELING...THIS WILL GO AWAY?
GUARANTEED.

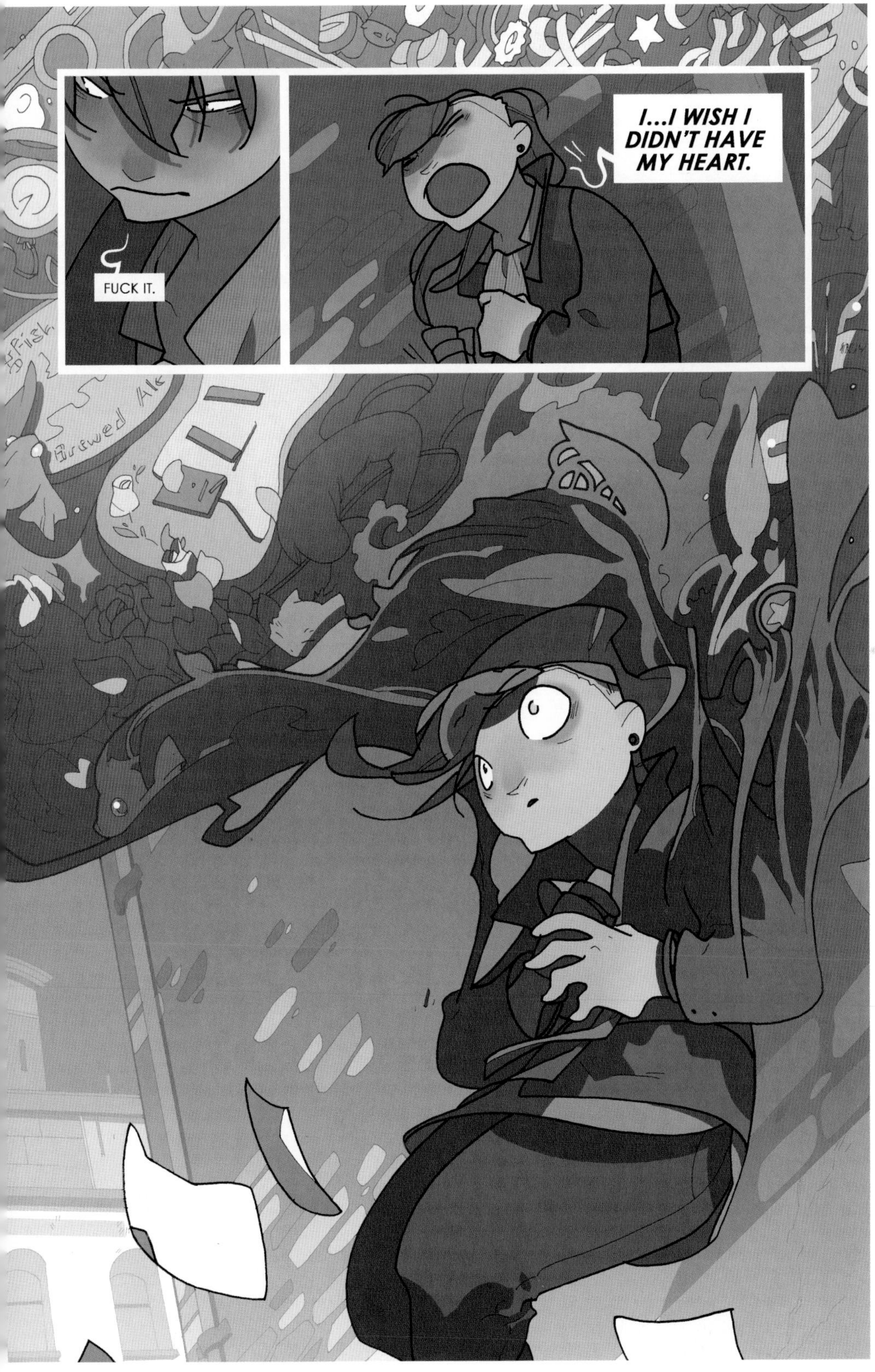
FUCK IT.
I...I WISH I DIDN'T HAVE MY HEART.

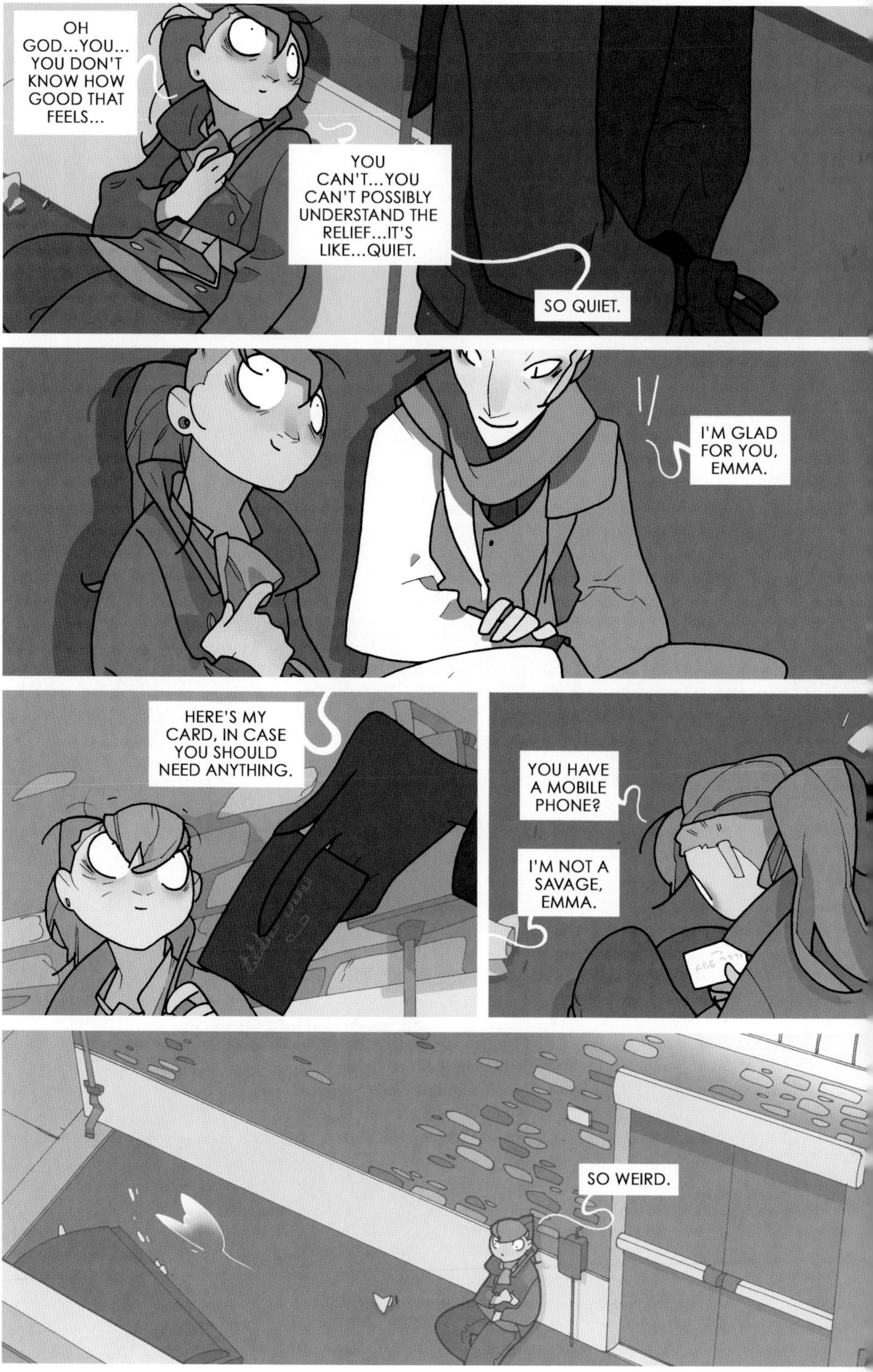
OH GOD...YOU... YOU DON'T KNOW HOW GOOD THAT FEELS...
YOU CAN'T...YOU CAN'T POSSIBLY UNDERSTAND THE RELIEF...IT'S LIKE...QUIET.
SO QUIET.
I'M GLAD FOR YOU, EMMA.
HERE'S MY CARD, IN CASE YOU SHOULD NEED ANYTHING.
YOU HAVE A MOBILE PHONE?
I'M NOT A SAVAGE, EMMA.
SO WEIRD.

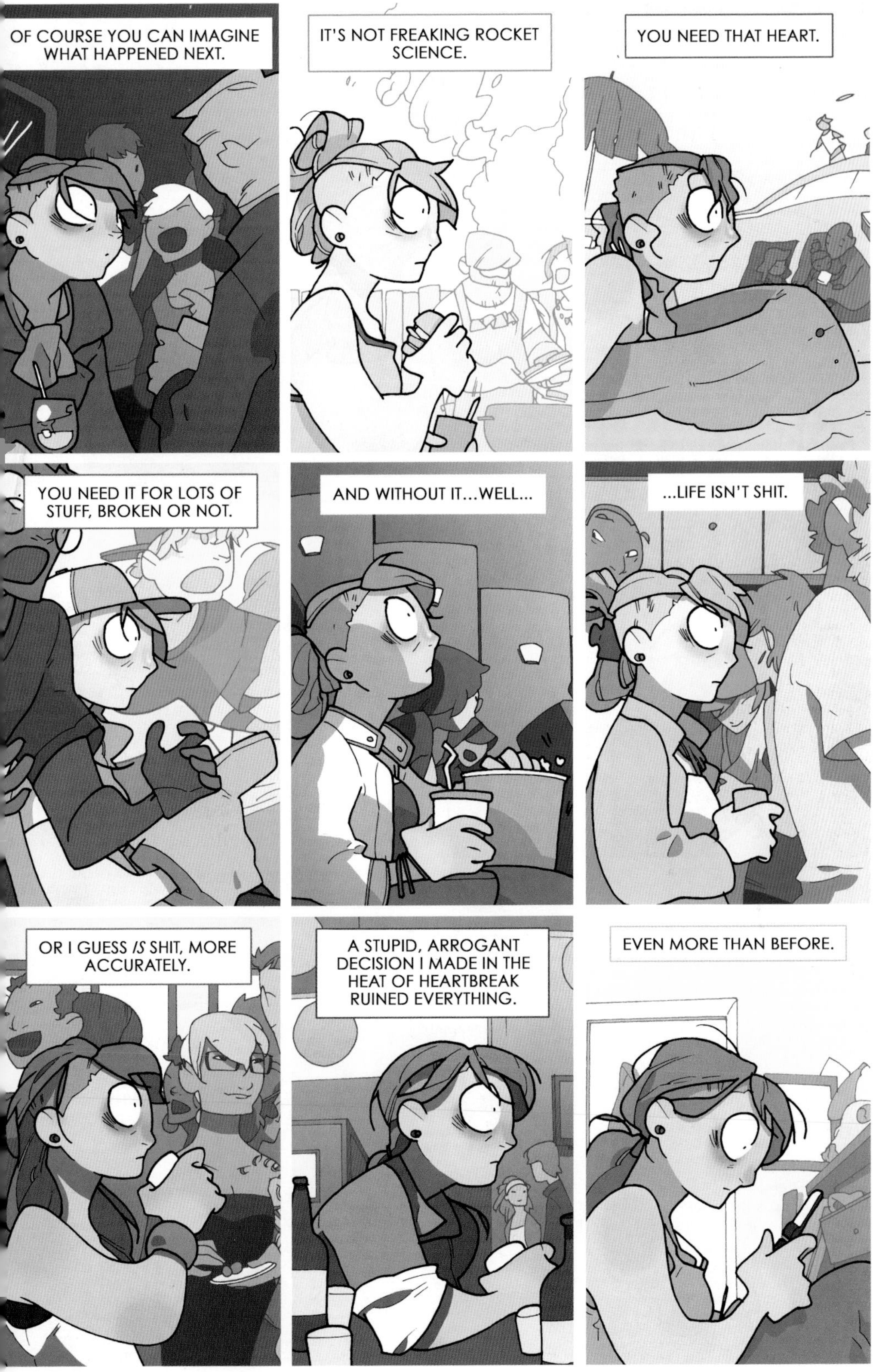
OF COURSE YOU CAN IMAGINE WHAT HAPPENED NEXT.
IT'S NOT FREAKING ROCKET SCIENCE.
YOU NEED THAT HEART.
YOU NEED IT FOR LOTS OF STUFF, BROKEN OR NOT.
AND WITHOUT IT...WELL...
...LIFE ISN'T SHIT.
OR I GUESS *IS* SHIT, MORE ACCURATELY.
A STUPID, ARROGANT DECISION I MADE IN THE HEAT OF HEARTBREAK RUINED EVERYTHING.
EVEN MORE THAN BEFORE.

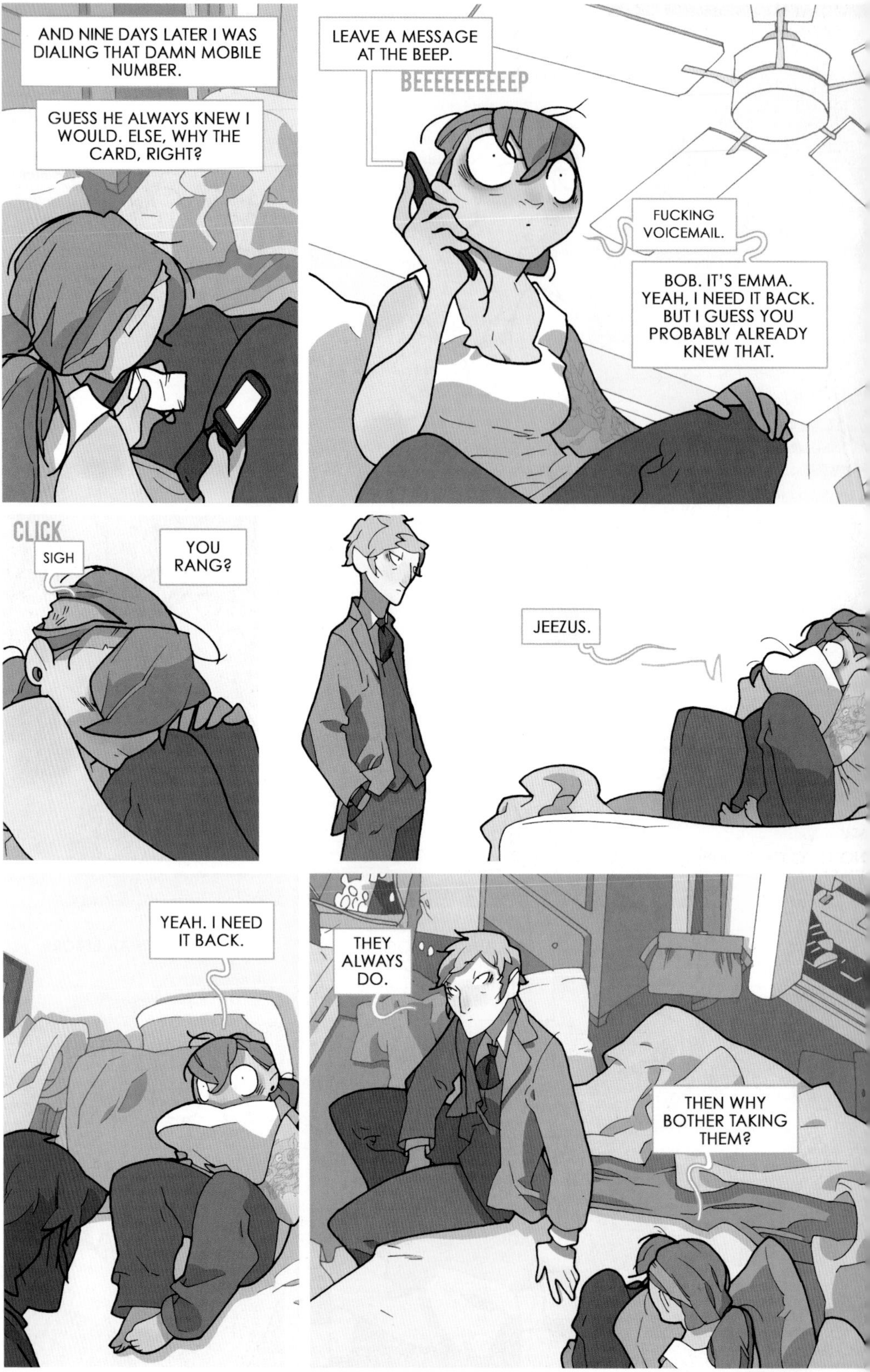
AND NINE DAYS LATER I WAS DIALING THAT DAMN MOBILE NUMBER.
GUESS HE ALWAYS KNEW I WOULD. ELSE, WHY THE CARD, RIGHT?
LEAVE A MESSAGE AT THE BEEP.
BEEEEEEEEEEP
FUCKING VOICEMAIL.
BOB. IT'S EMMA. YEAH, I NEED IT BACK. BUT I GUESS YOU PROBABLY ALREADY KNEW THAT.
CLICK
SIGH
YOU RANG?
JEEZUS.
YEAH. I NEED IT BACK.
THEY ALWAYS DO.
THEN WHY BOTHER TAKING THEM?

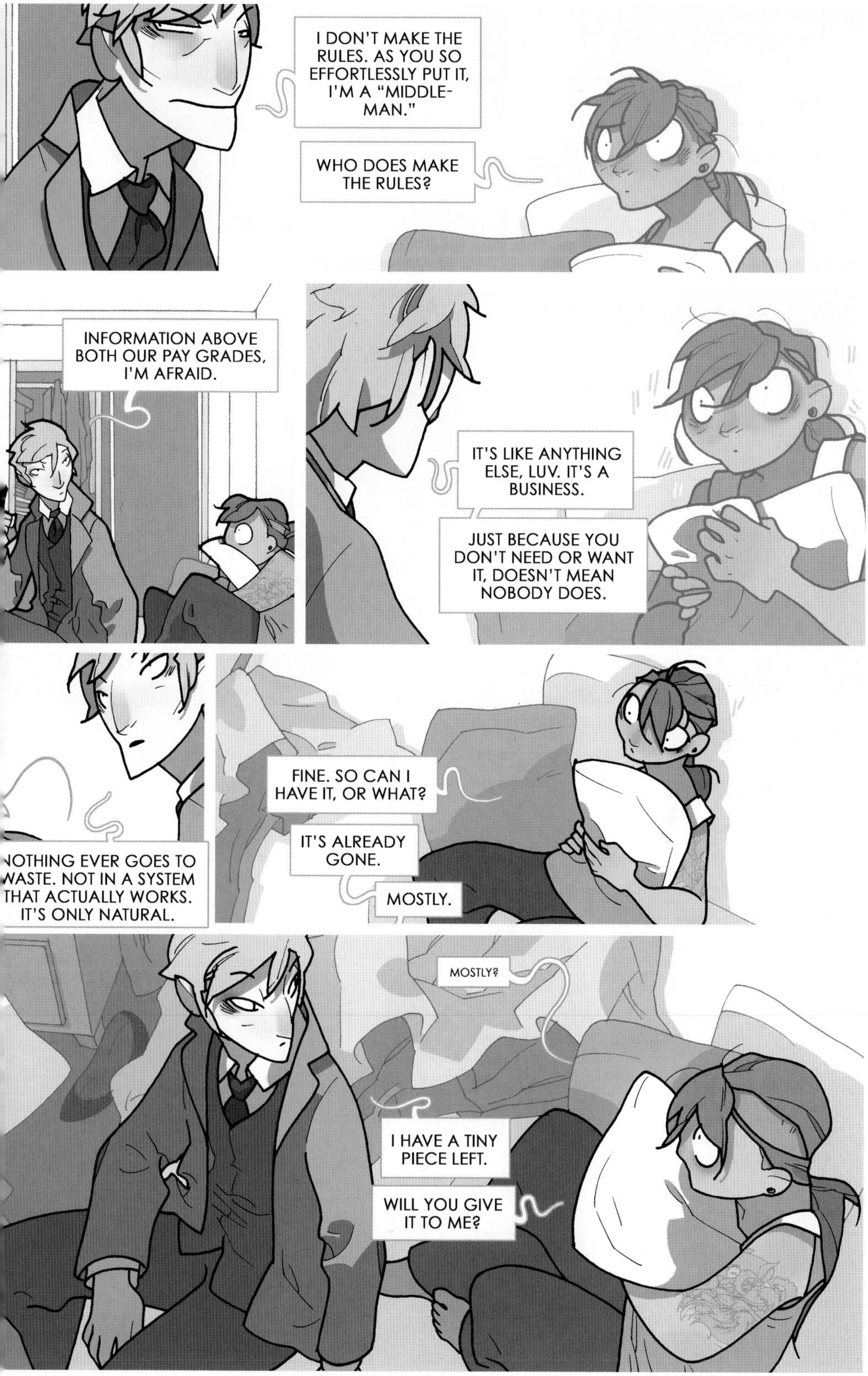
I DON'T MAKE THE RULES. AS YOU SO EFFORTLESSLY PUT IT, I'M A "MIDDLE-MAN."
WHO DOES MAKE THE RULES?
INFORMATION ABOVE BOTH OUR PAY GRADES, I'M AFRAID.
IT'S LIKE ANYTHING ELSE, LUV. IT'S A BUSINESS.
JUST BECAUSE YOU DON'T NEED OR WANT IT, DOESN'T MEAN NOBODY DOES.
NOTHING EVER GOES TO WASTE. NOT IN A SYSTEM THAT ACTUALLY WORKS. IT'S ONLY NATURAL.
FINE. SO CAN I HAVE IT, OR WHAT?
IT'S ALREADY GONE.
MOSTLY.
MOSTLY?
I HAVE A TINY PIECE LEFT.
WILL YOU GIVE IT TO ME?

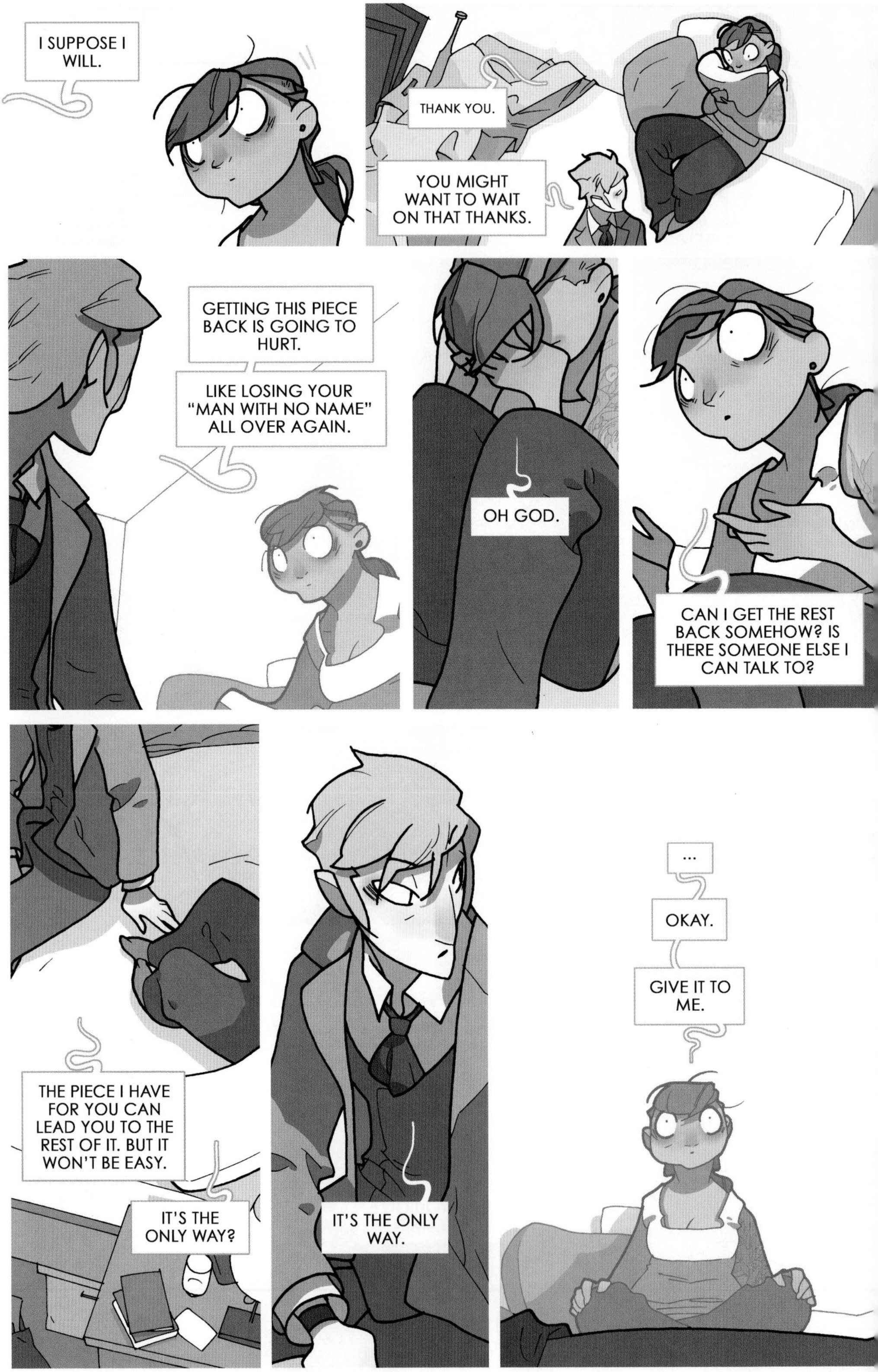
I SUPPOSE I WILL.
THANK YOU.
YOU MIGHT WANT TO WAIT ON THAT THANKS.
GETTING THIS PIECE BACK IS GOING TO HURT.
LIKE LOSING YOUR "MAN WITH NO NAME" ALL OVER AGAIN.
OH GOD.
CAN I GET THE REST BACK SOMEHOW? IS THERE SOMEONE ELSE I CAN TALK TO?
THE PIECE I HAVE FOR YOU CAN LEAD YOU TO THE REST OF IT. BUT IT WON'T BE EASY.
IT'S THE ONLY WAY?
IT'S THE ONLY WAY.
...
OKAY.
GIVE IT TO ME.

PIECE no. 1

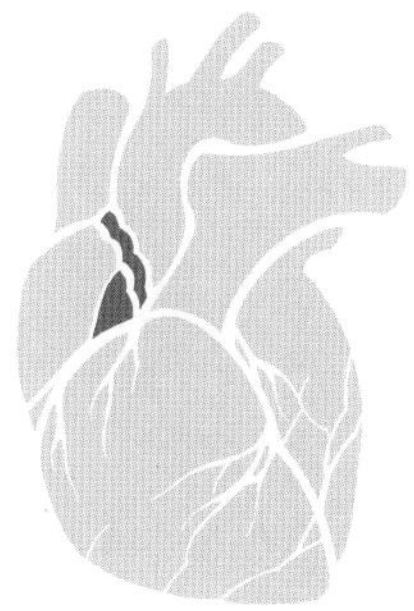

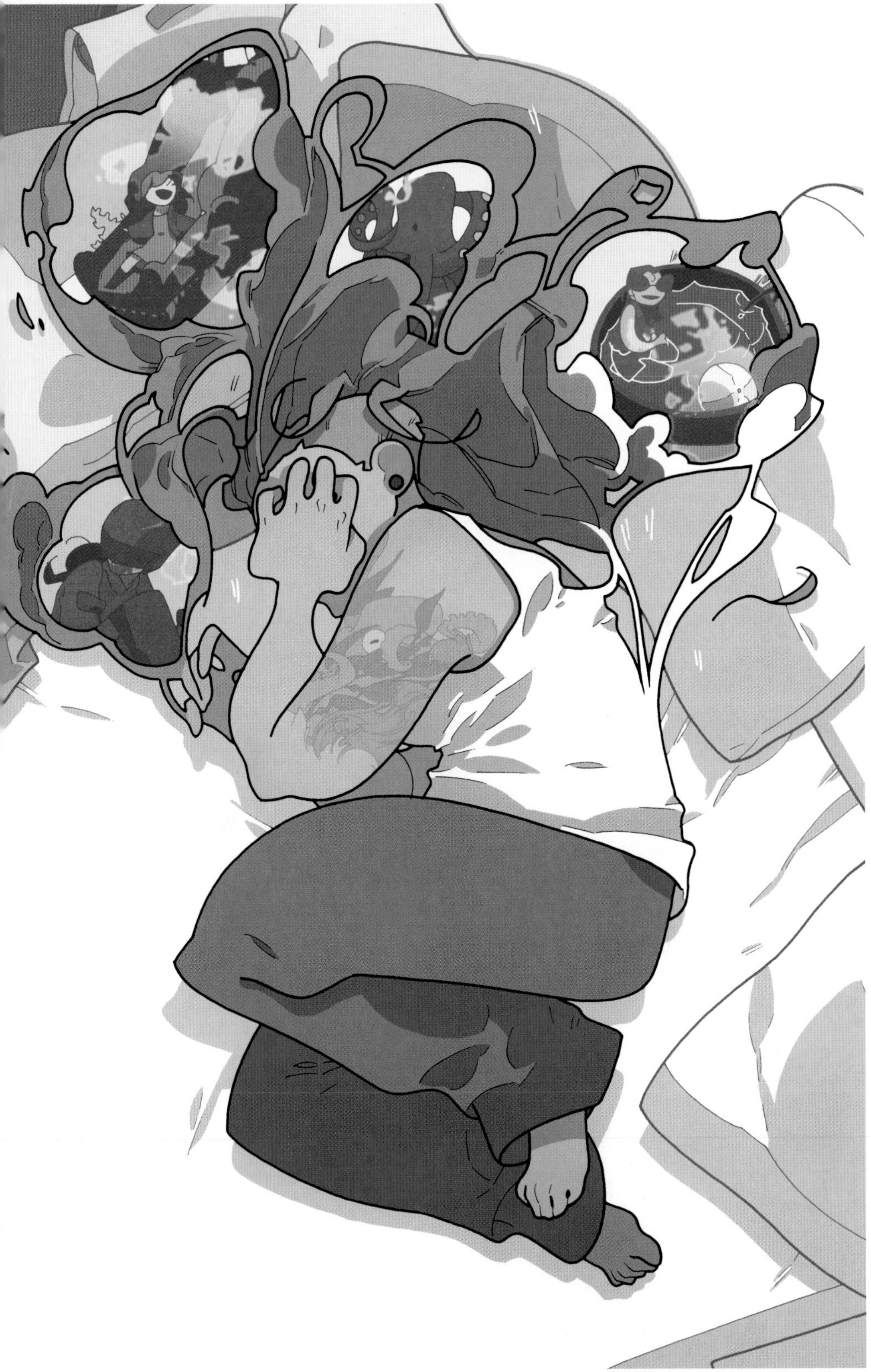

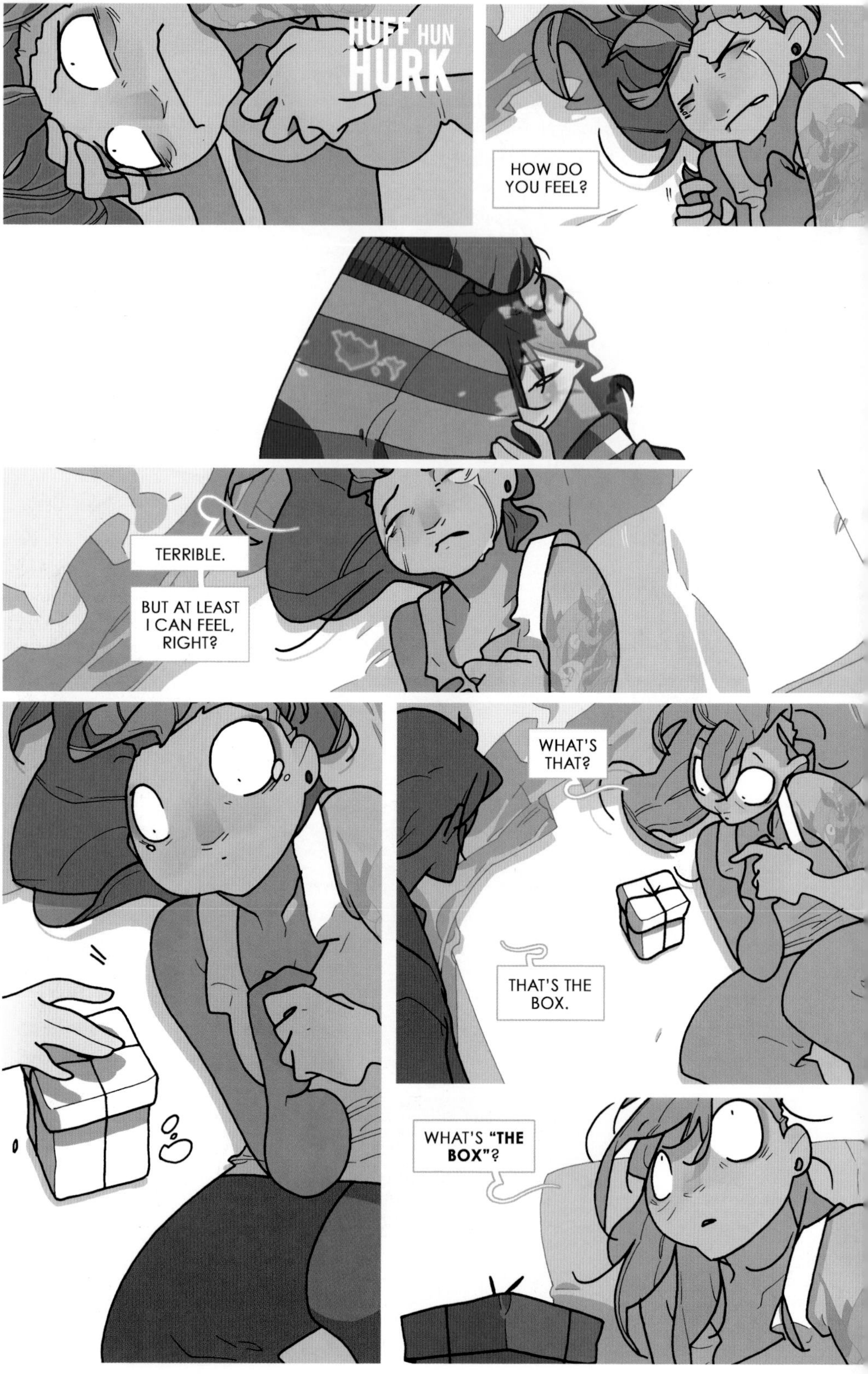
HUFF HUN
HURK
HOW DO YOU FEEL?
TERRIBLE.
BUT AT LEAST I CAN FEEL, RIGHT?
WHAT'S THAT?
THAT'S THE BOX.
WHAT'S **"THE BOX"**?

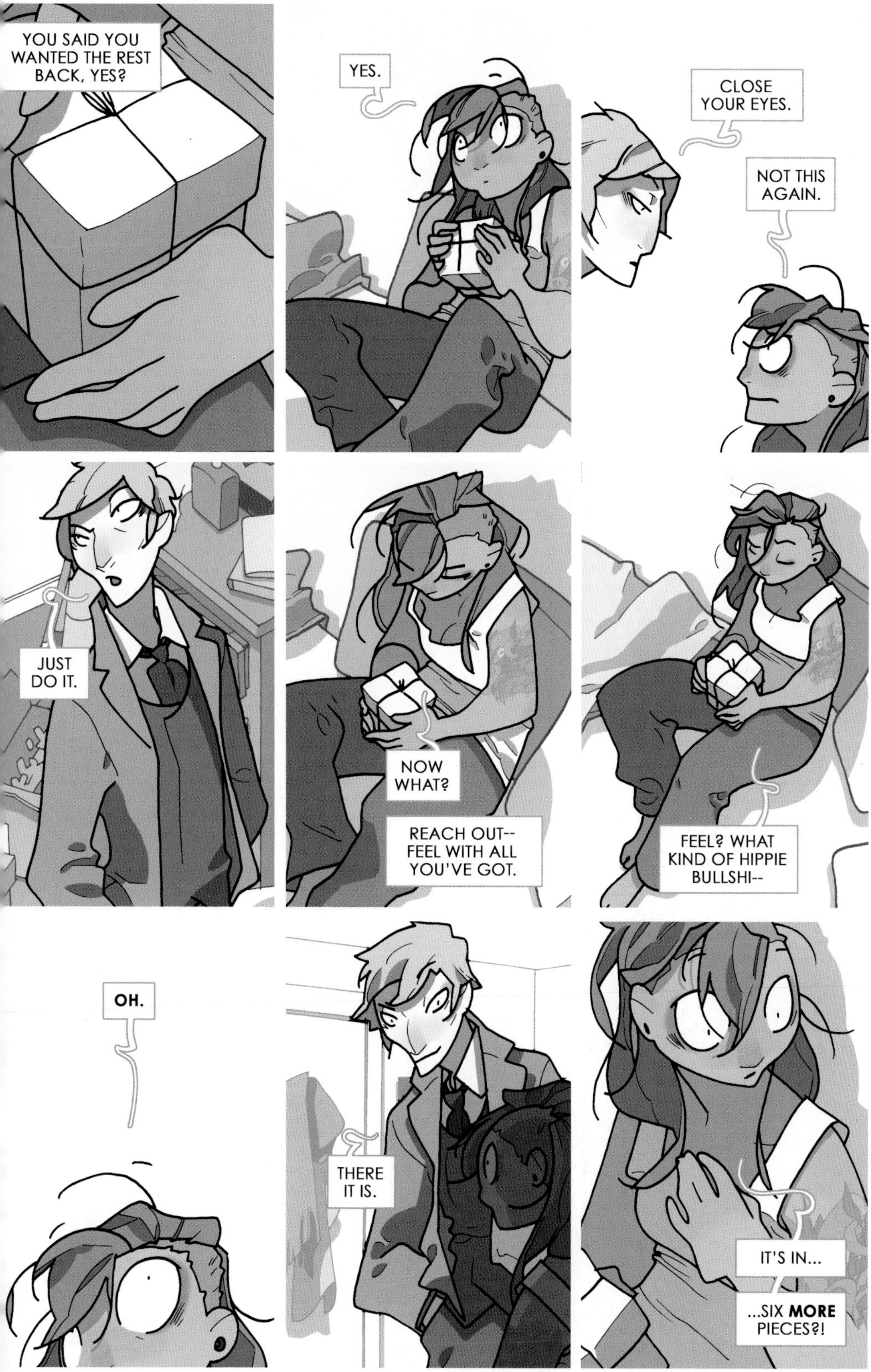
YOU SAID YOU WANTED THE REST BACK, YES?
YES.
CLOSE YOUR EYES.
NOT THIS AGAIN.
JUST DO IT.
NOW WHAT?
REACH OUT-- FEEL WITH ALL YOU'VE GOT.
FEEL? WHAT KIND OF HIPPIE BULLSHI--
OH.
THERE IT IS.
IT'S IN...
...SIX **MORE** PIECES?!

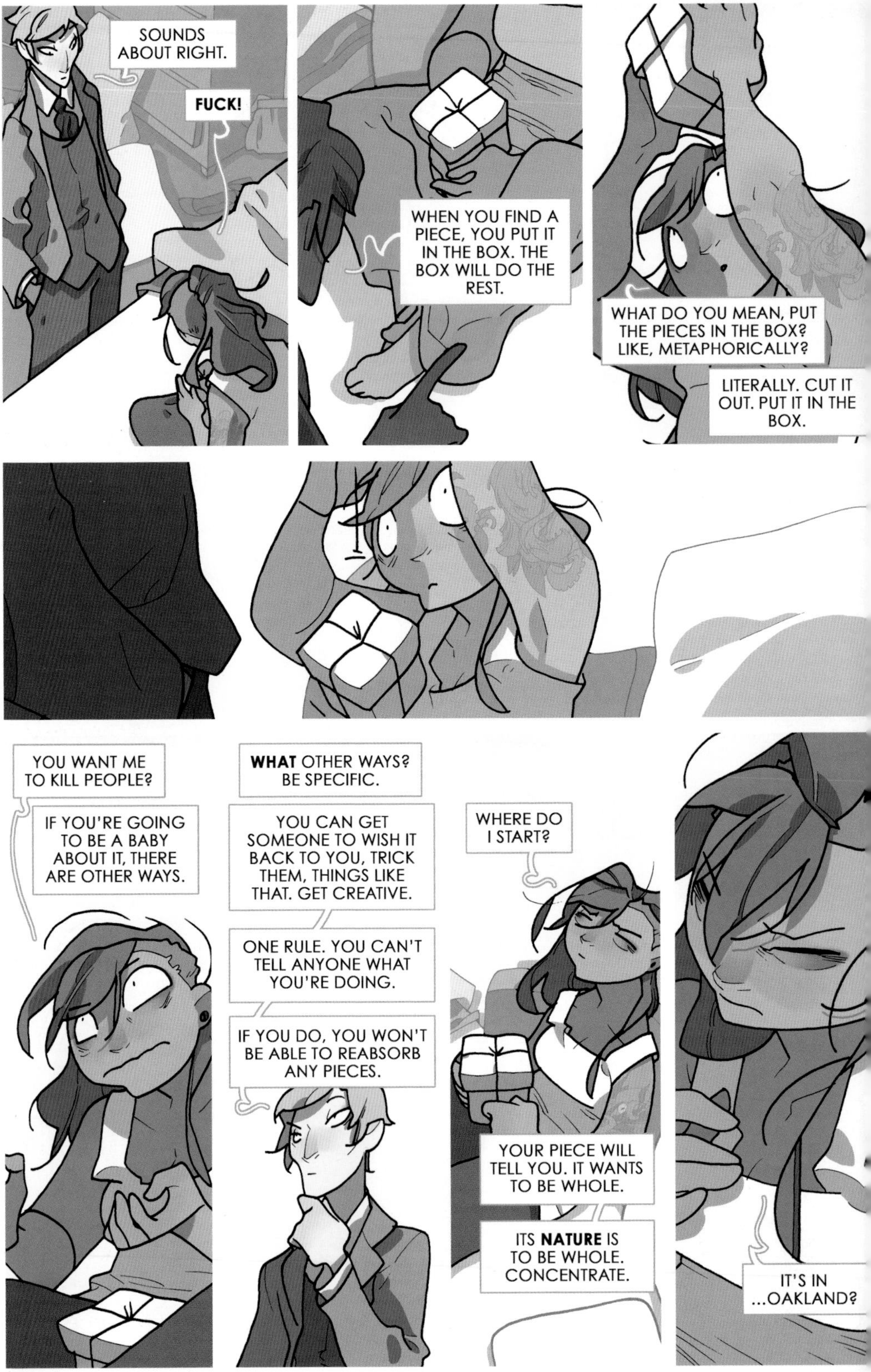
SOUNDS ABOUT RIGHT.
FUCK!
WHEN YOU FIND A PIECE, YOU PUT IT IN THE BOX. THE BOX WILL DO THE REST.
WHAT DO YOU MEAN, PUT THE PIECES IN THE BOX? LIKE, METAPHORICALLY?
LITERALLY. CUT IT OUT. PUT IT IN THE BOX.
YOU WANT ME TO KILL PEOPLE?
IF YOU'RE GOING TO BE A BABY ABOUT IT, THERE ARE OTHER WAYS.
WHAT OTHER WAYS? BE SPECIFIC.
YOU CAN GET SOMEONE TO WISH IT BACK TO YOU, TRICK THEM, THINGS LIKE THAT. GET CREATIVE.
ONE RULE. YOU CAN'T TELL ANYONE WHAT YOU'RE DOING.
IF YOU DO, YOU WON'T BE ABLE TO REABSORB ANY PIECES.
WHERE DO I START?
YOUR PIECE WILL TELL YOU. IT WANTS TO BE WHOLE.
ITS NATURE IS TO BE WHOLE. CONCENTRATE.
IT'S IN ...OAKLAND?

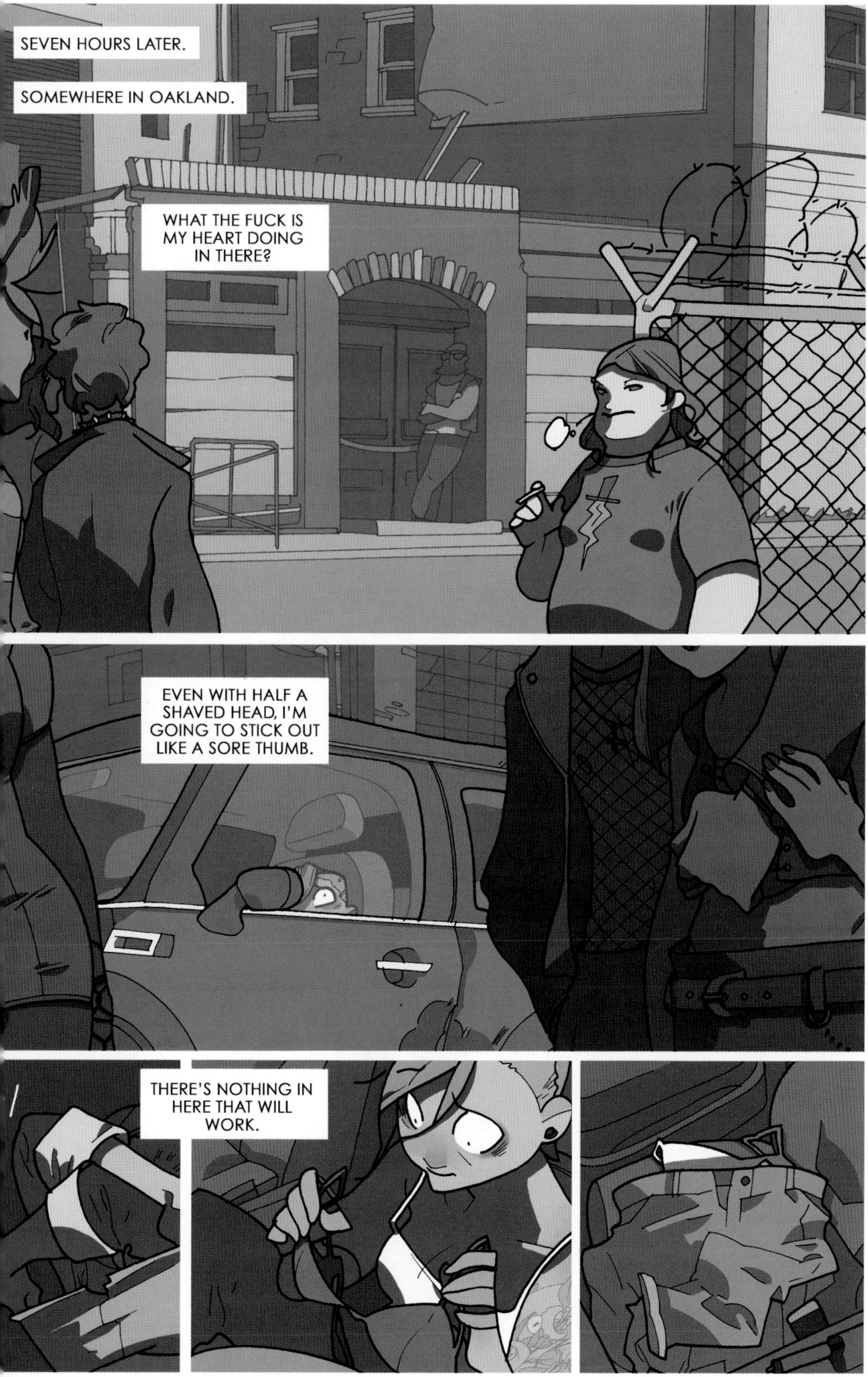
SEVEN HOURS LATER.
SOMEWHERE IN OAKLAND.
WHAT THE FUCK IS MY HEART DOING IN THERE?
EVEN WITH HALF A SHAVED HEAD, I'M GOING TO STICK OUT LIKE A SORE THUMB.
THERE'S NOTHING IN HERE THAT WILL WORK.

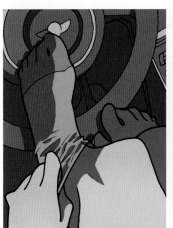

HERE GOES EVERYTHING.

WELCOME TO THE STYX, SWEETHEART.

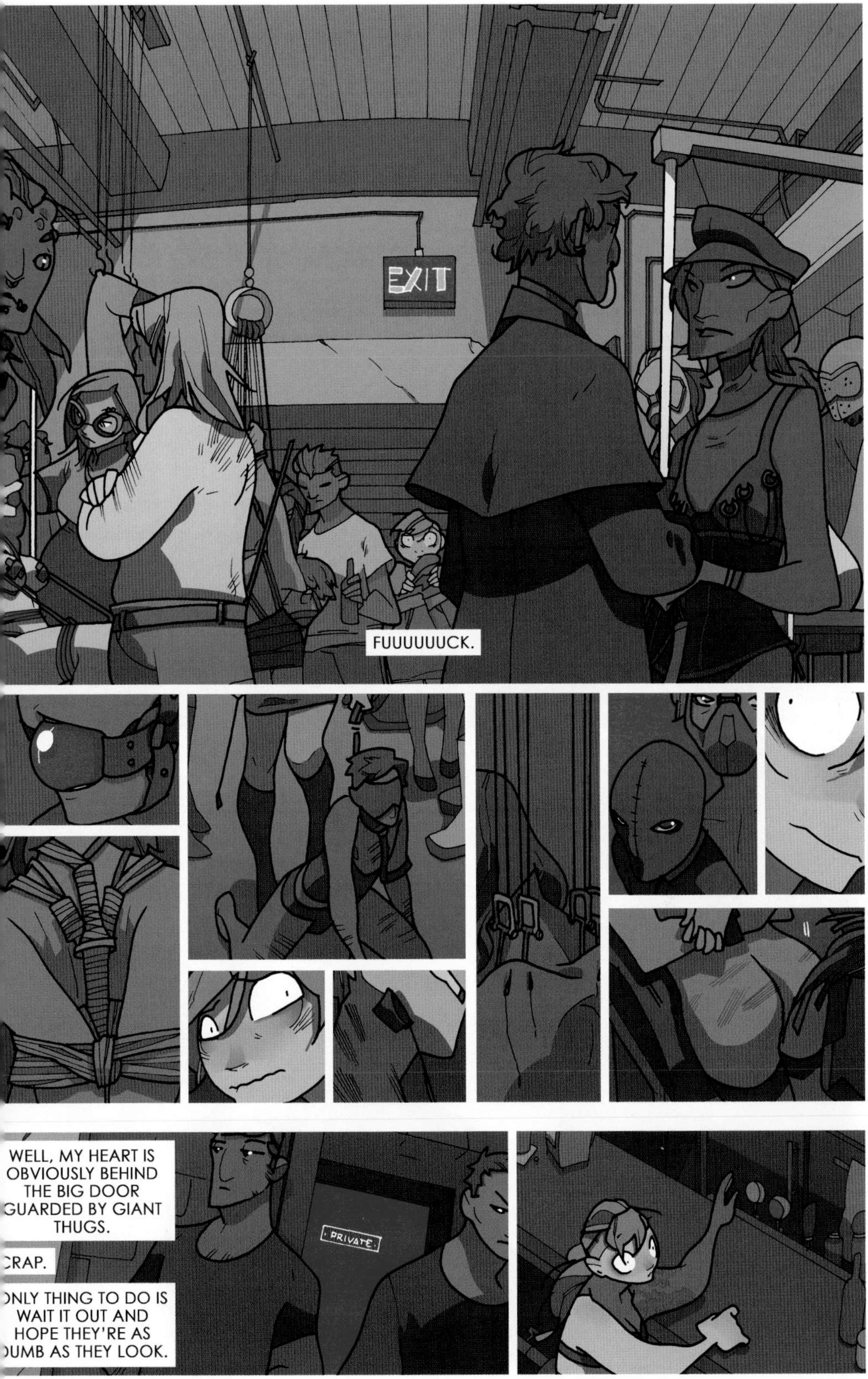
FUUUUUUCK.
EXIT
WELL, MY HEART IS OBVIOUSLY BEHIND THE BIG DOOR GUARDED BY GIANT THUGS.
PRIVATE
CRAP.
ONLY THING TO DO IS WAIT IT OUT AND HOPE THEY'RE AS DUMB AS THEY LOOK.

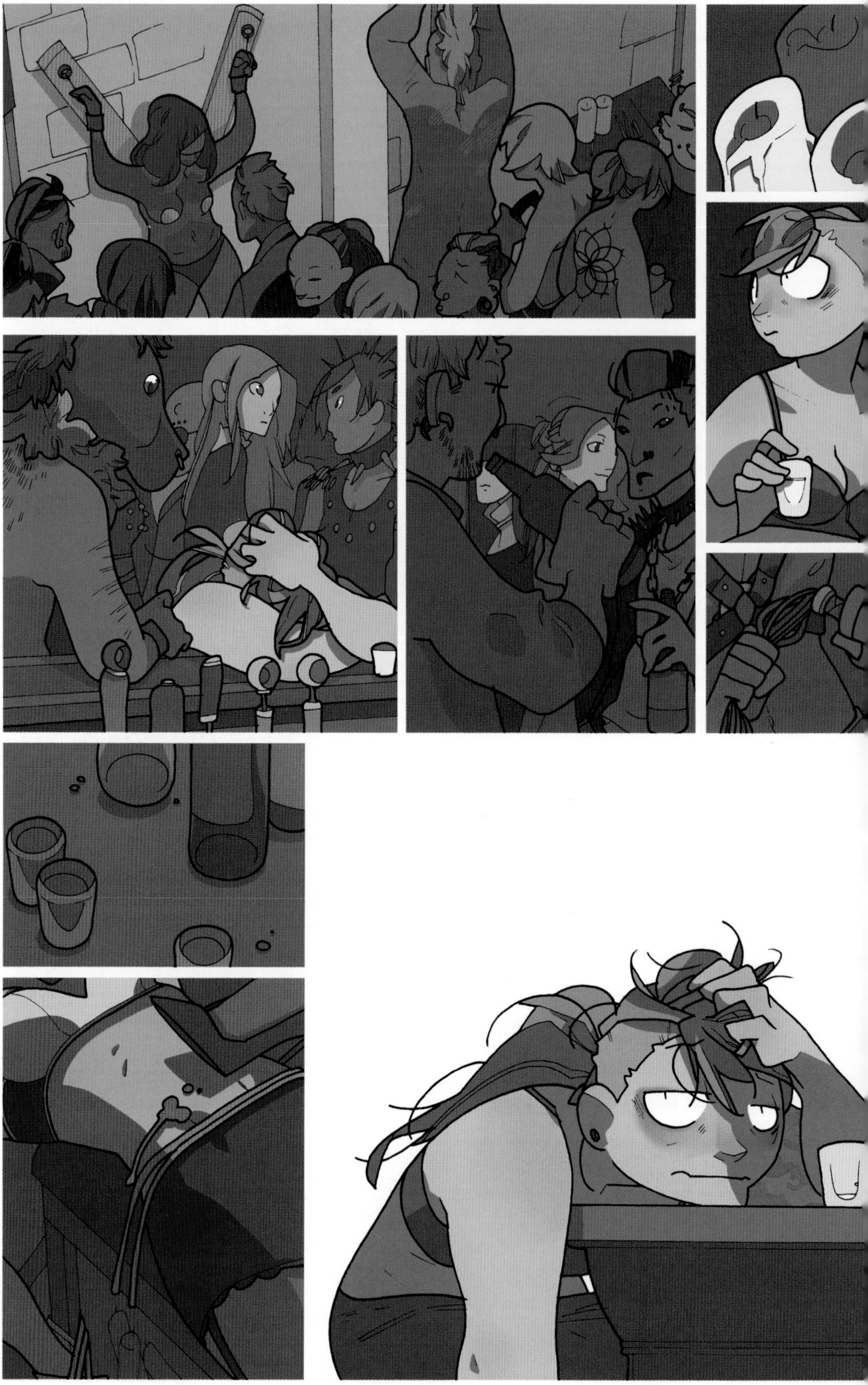

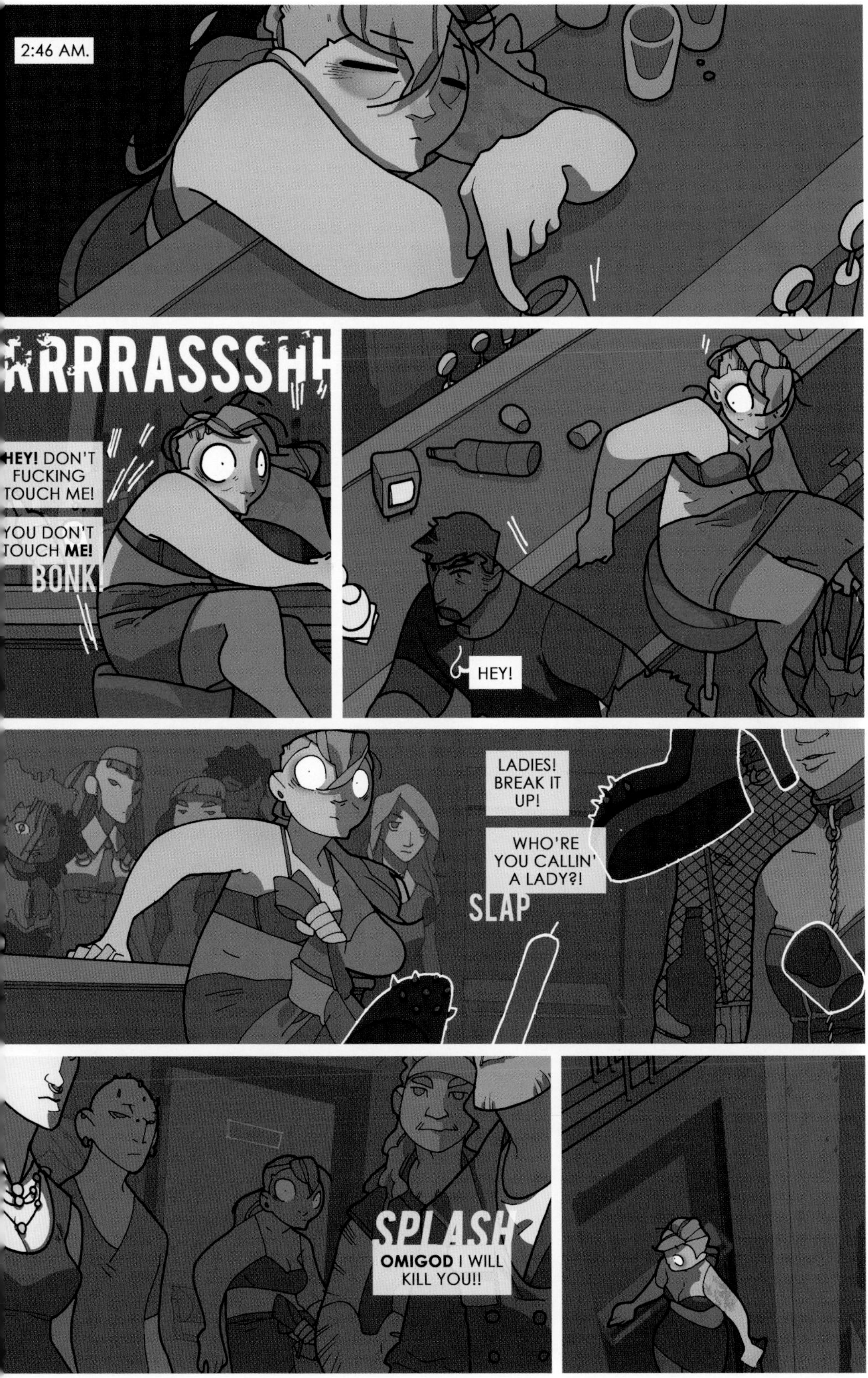

2:46 AM.
RRRRASSSHH
HEY! DON'T FUCKING TOUCH ME!
YOU DON'T TOUCH ME!
BONK!
HEY!
LADIES! BREAK IT UP!
WHO'RE YOU CALLIN' A LADY?!
SLAP
SPLASH
OMIGOD I WILL KILL YOU!!

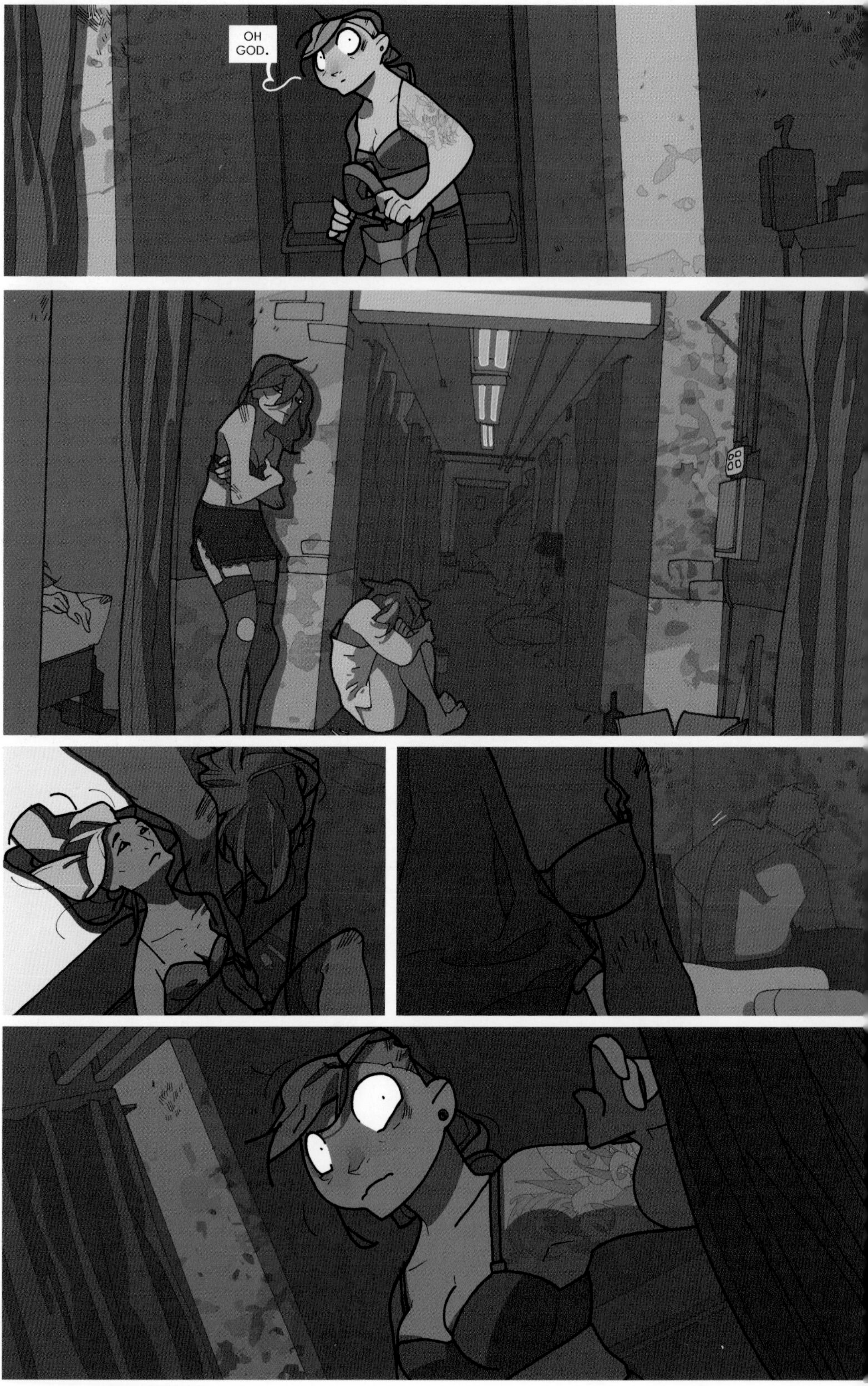
OH GOD.

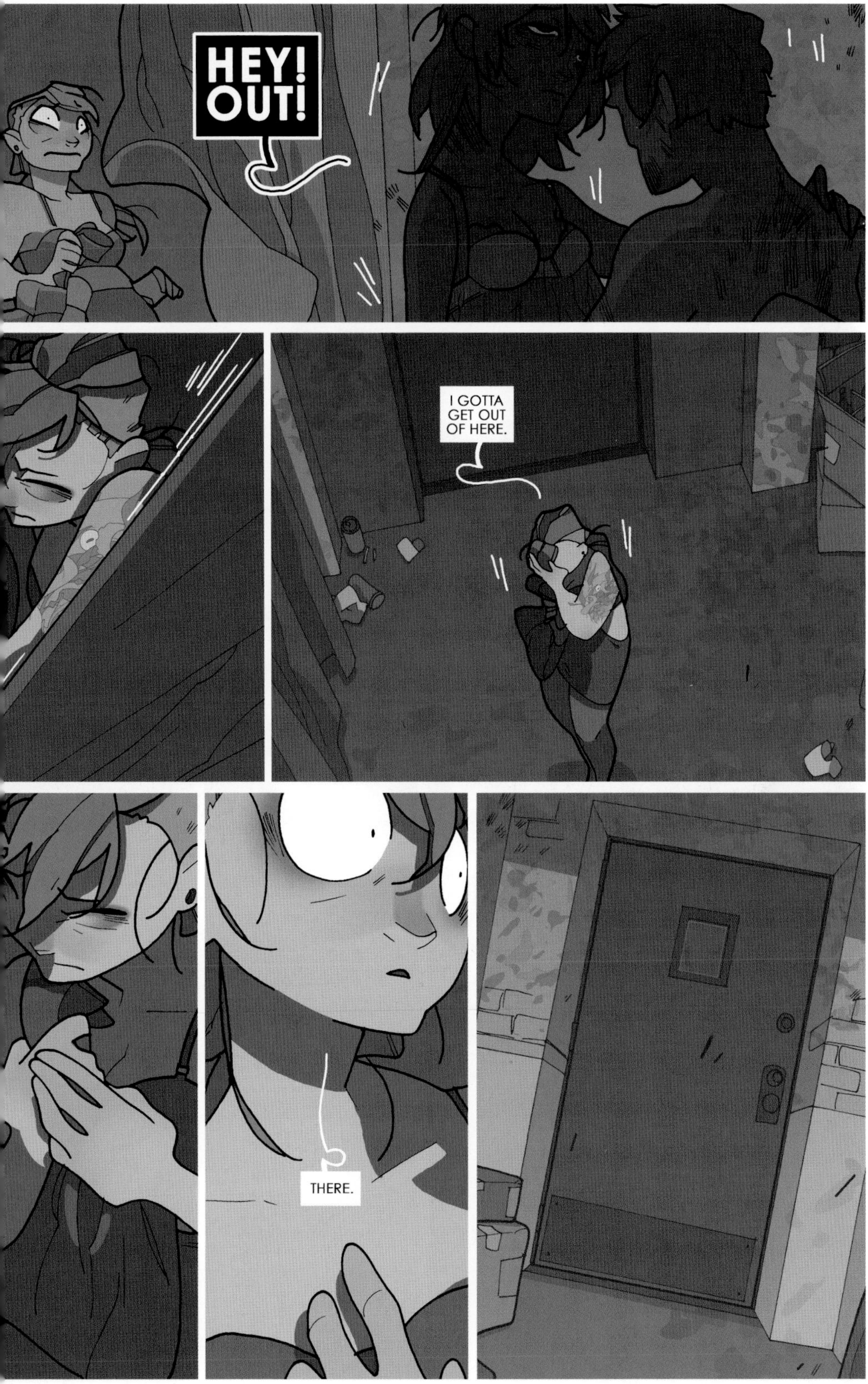
HEY! OUT!
I GOTTA GET OUT OF HERE.
THERE.

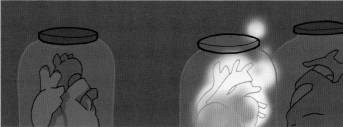

WHAT HAVE WE GOT HERE? YOU ESCAPE FROM A ROOM, OR JUST A GIRL LOST ON HER WAY TO THE BATHROOM?

SHIT.

SO WHICH IS IT? A BIT ON THE... FRESH SIDE TO BE FROM THE ROOMS, I THINK.

I...I'M HERE FOR THIS HEART.

SURE, HONEY. IF THE PRICE IS RIGHT.

HOW MUCH?

I DON'T TAKE MONEY. JUST TRADE.

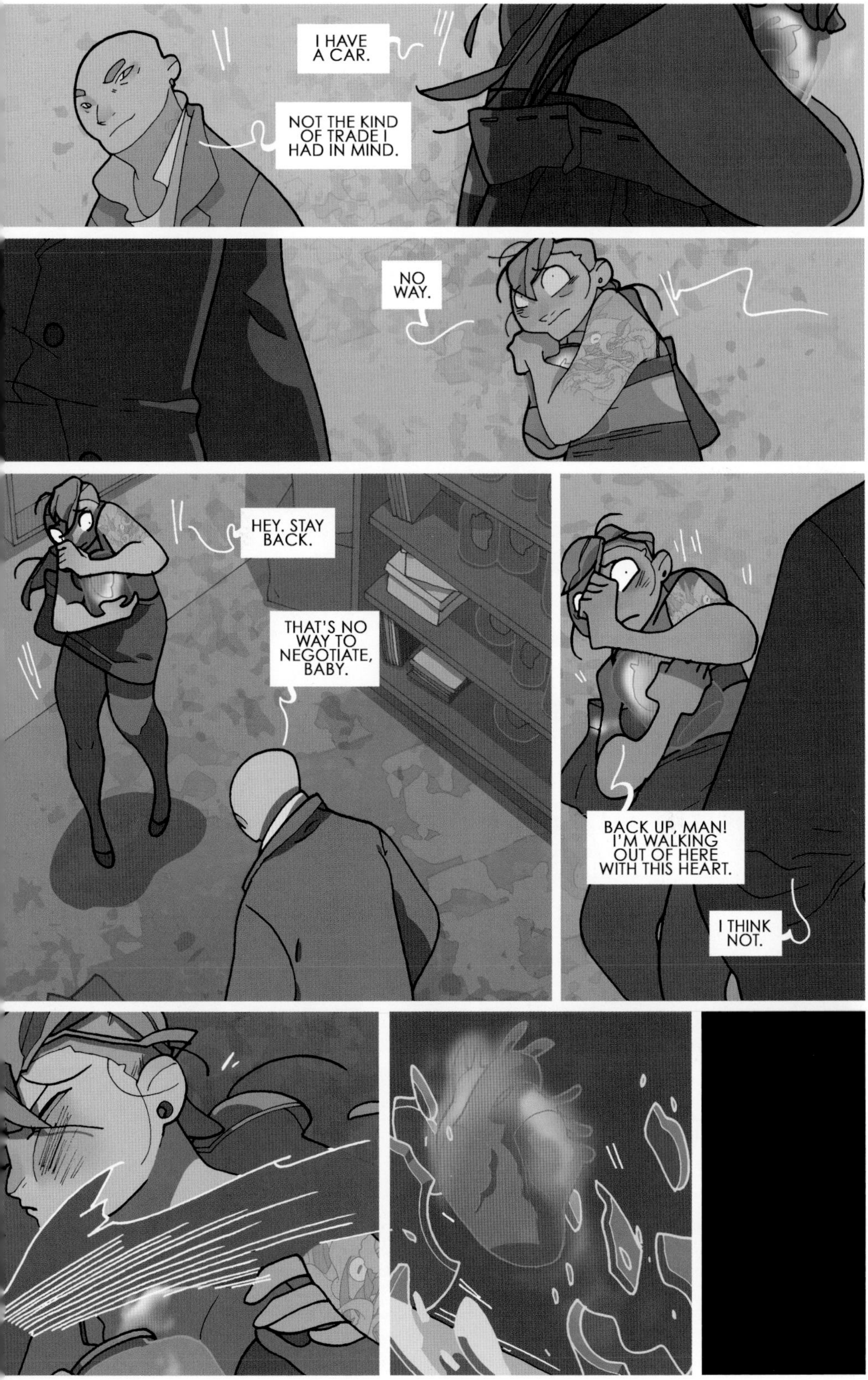

I HAVE A CAR.
NOT THE KIND OF TRADE I HAD IN MIND.
NO WAY.
HEY. STAY BACK.
THAT'S NO WAY TO NEGOTIATE, BABY.
BACK UP, MAN! I'M WALKING OUT OF HERE WITH THIS HEART.
I THINK NOT.

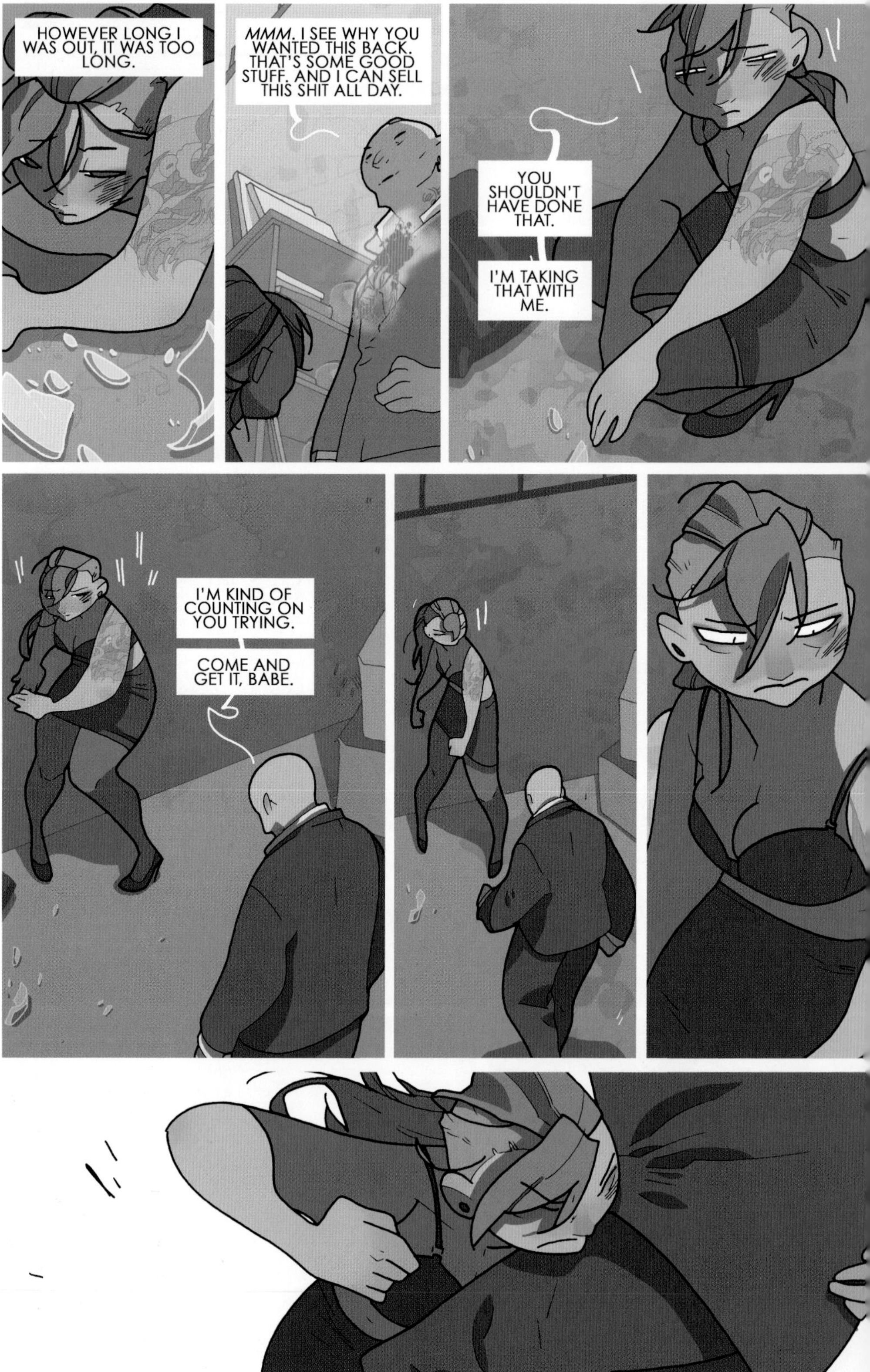
HOWEVER LONG I WAS OUT, IT WAS TOO LONG.
MMM. I SEE WHY YOU WANTED THIS BACK. THAT'S SOME GOOD STUFF. AND I CAN SELL THIS SHIT ALL DAY.
YOU SHOULDN'T HAVE DONE THAT.
I'M TAKING THAT WITH ME.
I'M KIND OF COUNTING ON YOU TRYING.
COME AND GET IT, BABE.

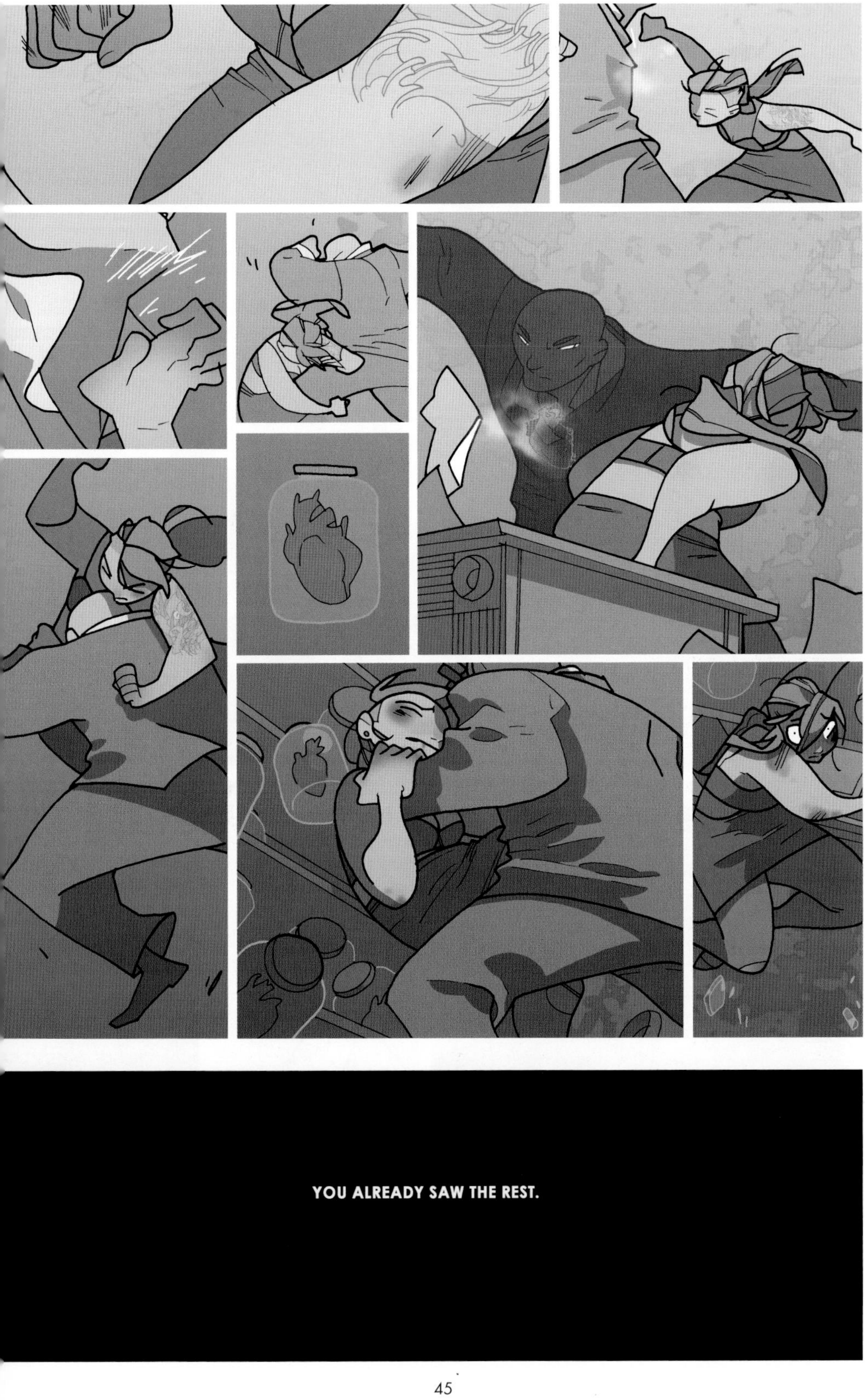

YOU ALREADY SAW THE REST.

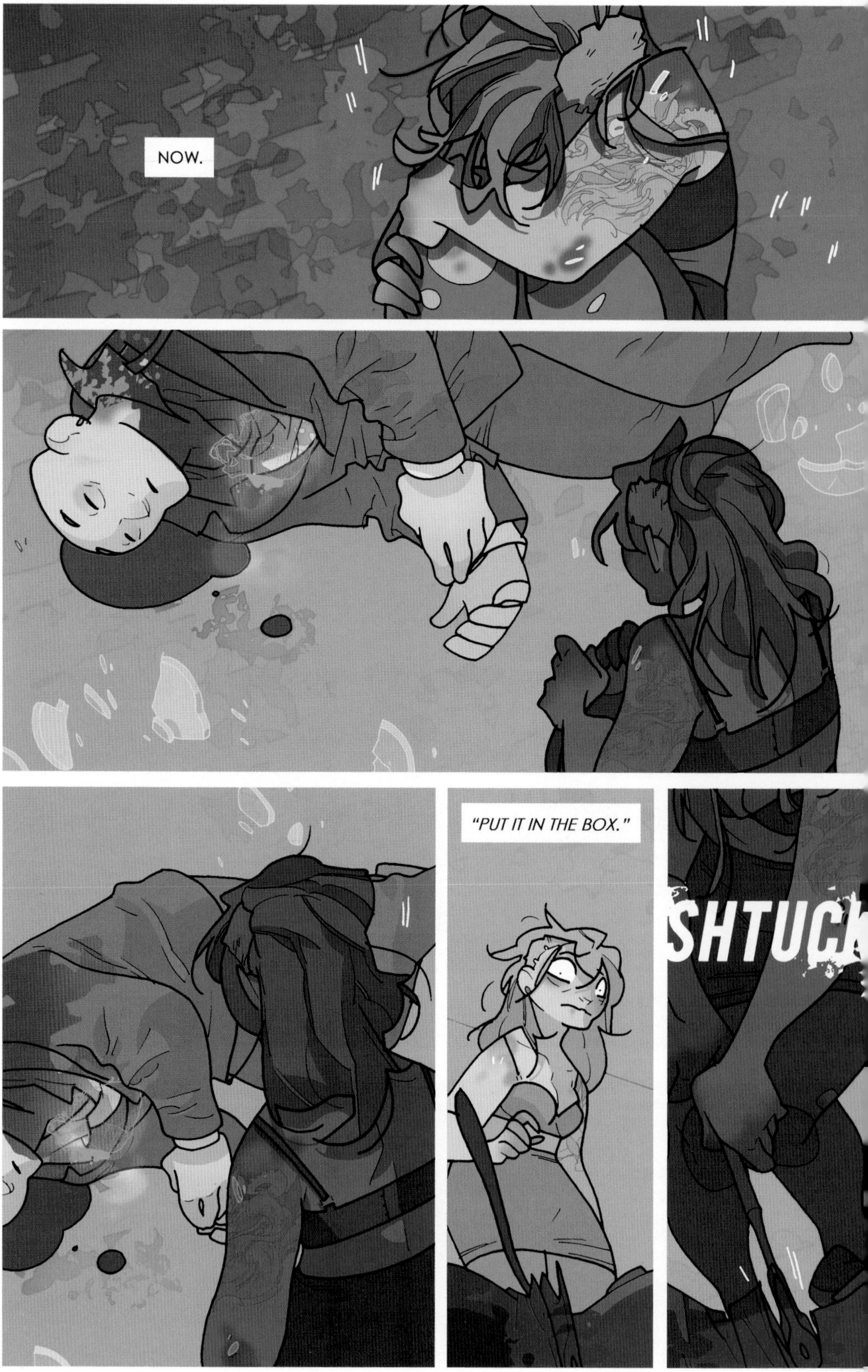
NOW.
"PUT IT IN THE BOX."
SHTUCK

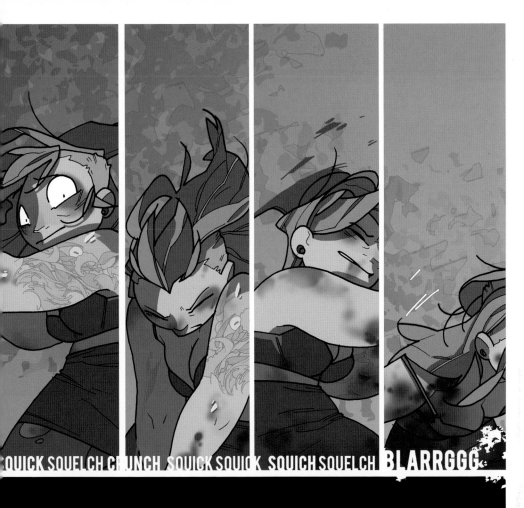

QUICK SQUELCH CRUNCH SQUICK SQUICK SQUICH SQUELCH **BLARRGGG**

CHOKE CHOKE **COUGH.**

PIECE no. 2

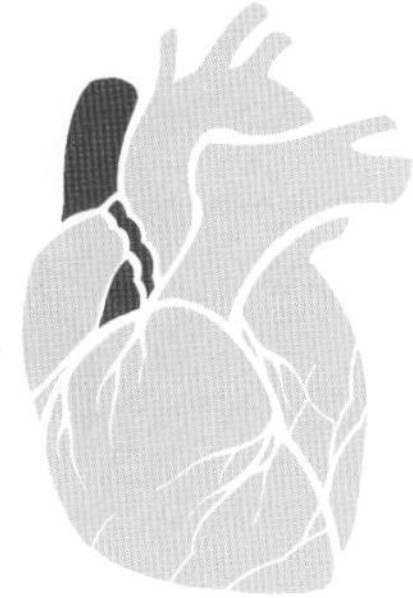

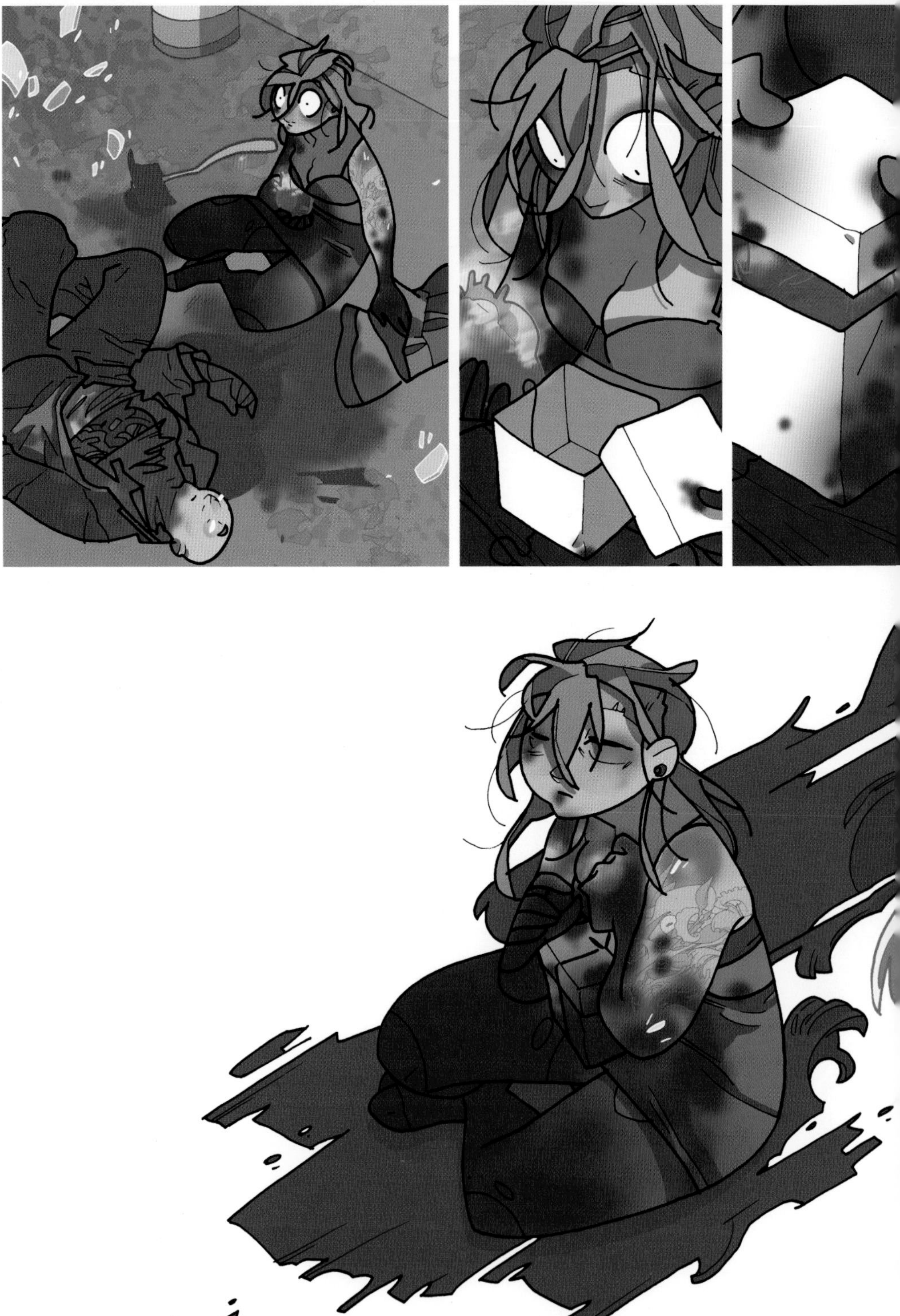

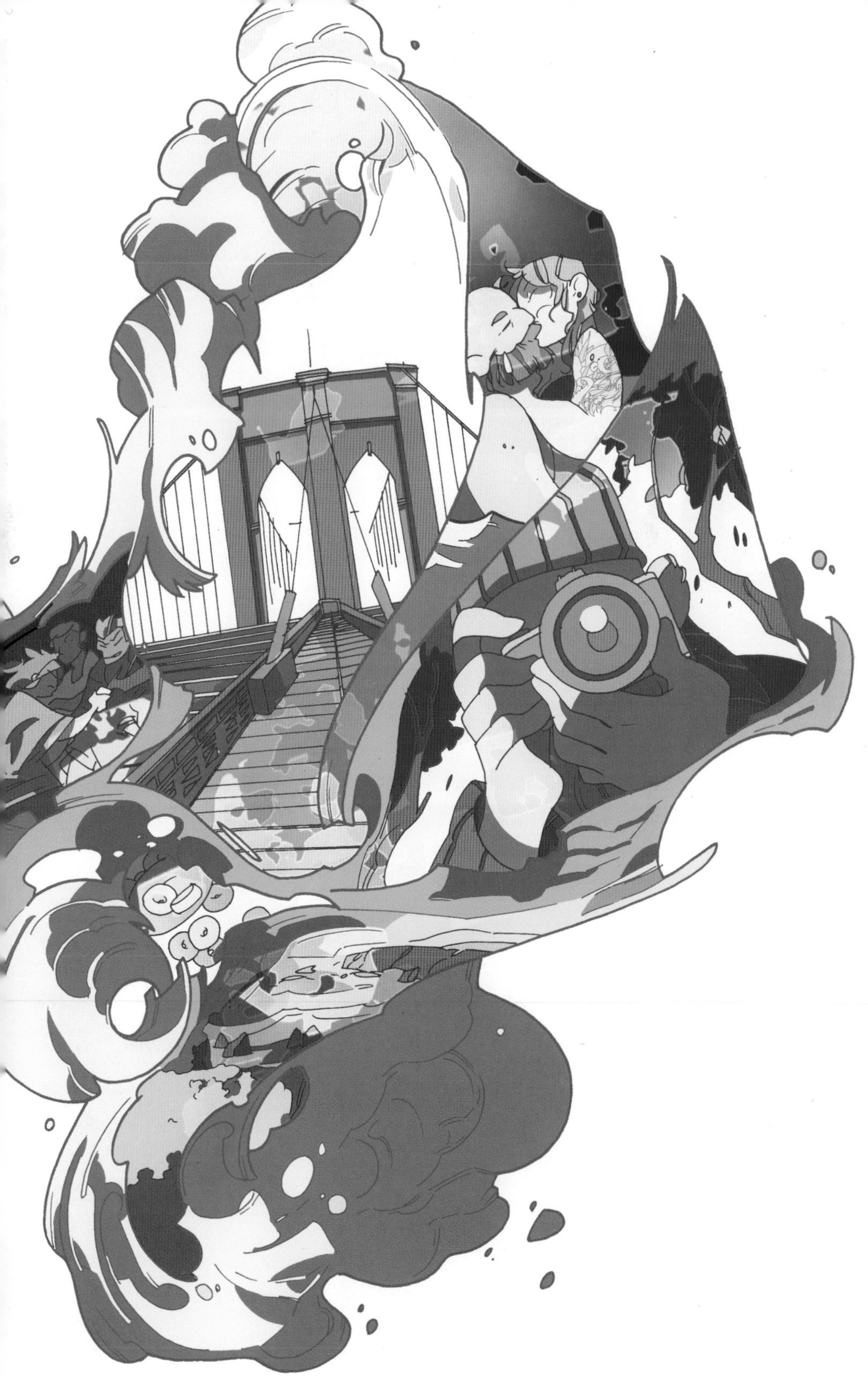

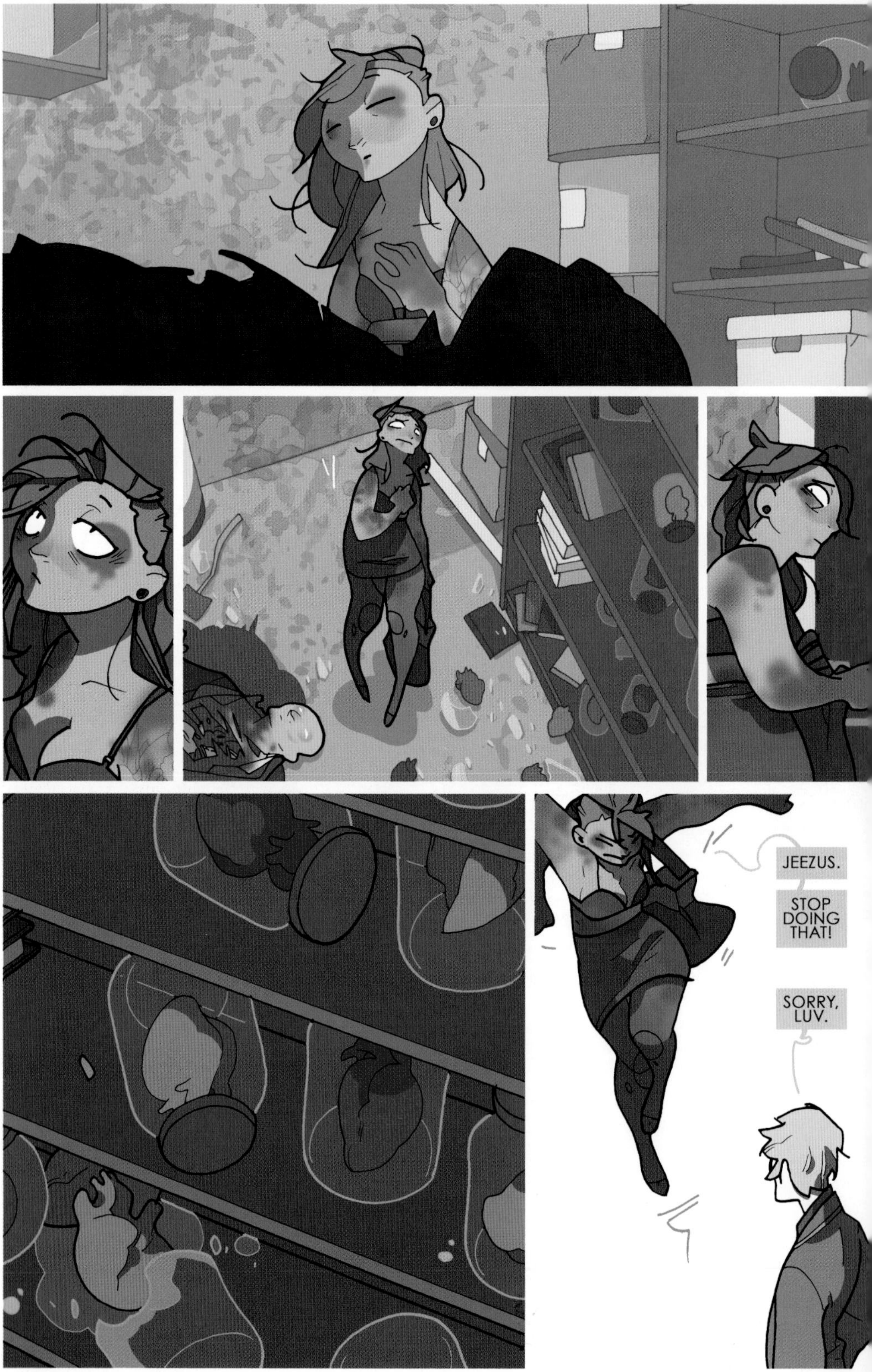
JEEZUS.
STOP DOING THAT!
SORRY, LUV.

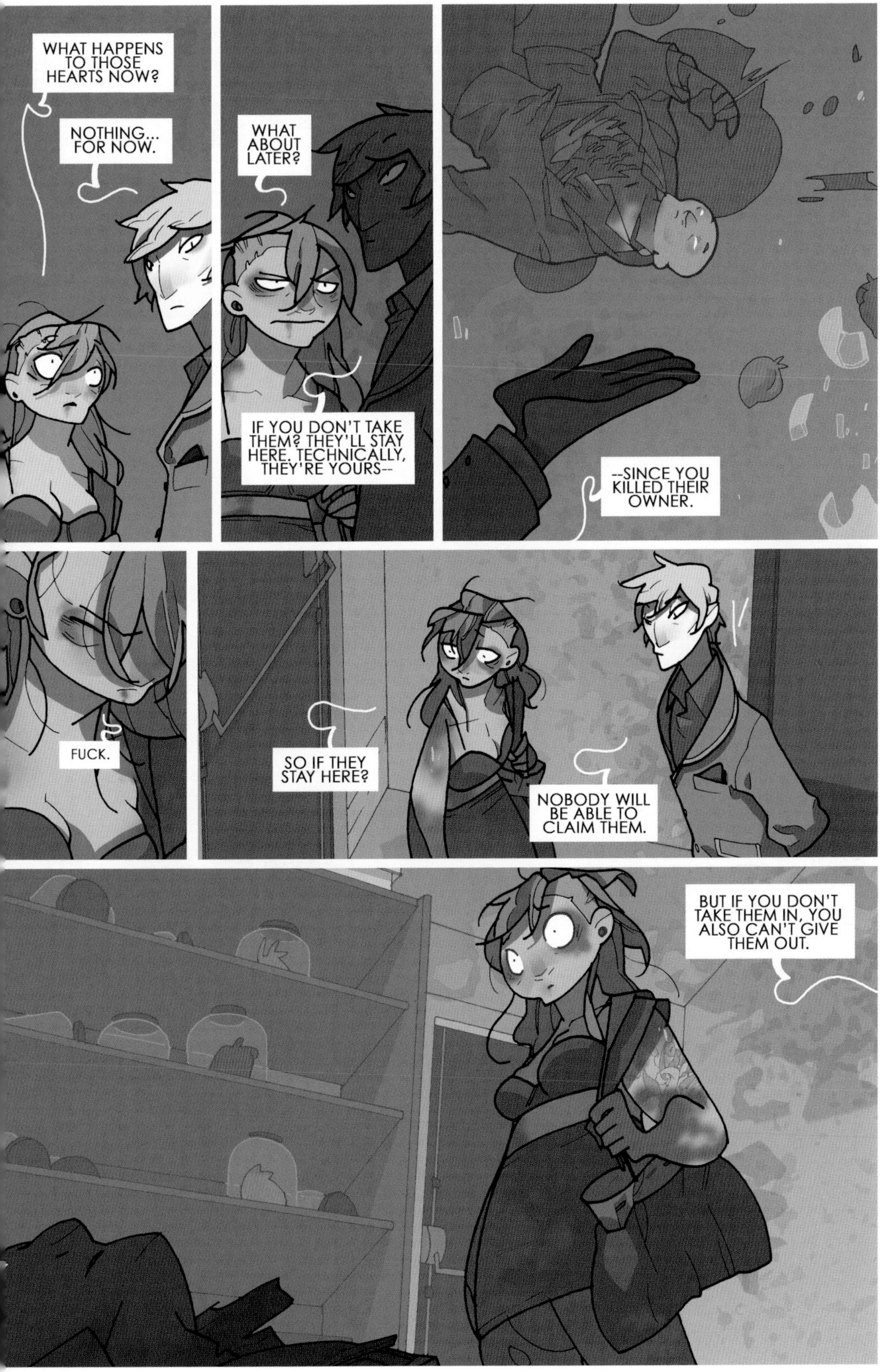
WHAT HAPPENS TO THOSE HEARTS NOW?
NOTHING... FOR NOW.
WHAT ABOUT LATER?
IF YOU DON'T TAKE THEM? THEY'LL STAY HERE. TECHNICALLY, THEY'RE YOURS--
--SINCE YOU KILLED THEIR OWNER.
FUCK.
SO IF THEY STAY HERE?
NOBODY WILL BE ABLE TO CLAIM THEM.
BUT IF YOU DON'T TAKE THEM IN, YOU ALSO CAN'T GIVE THEM OUT.

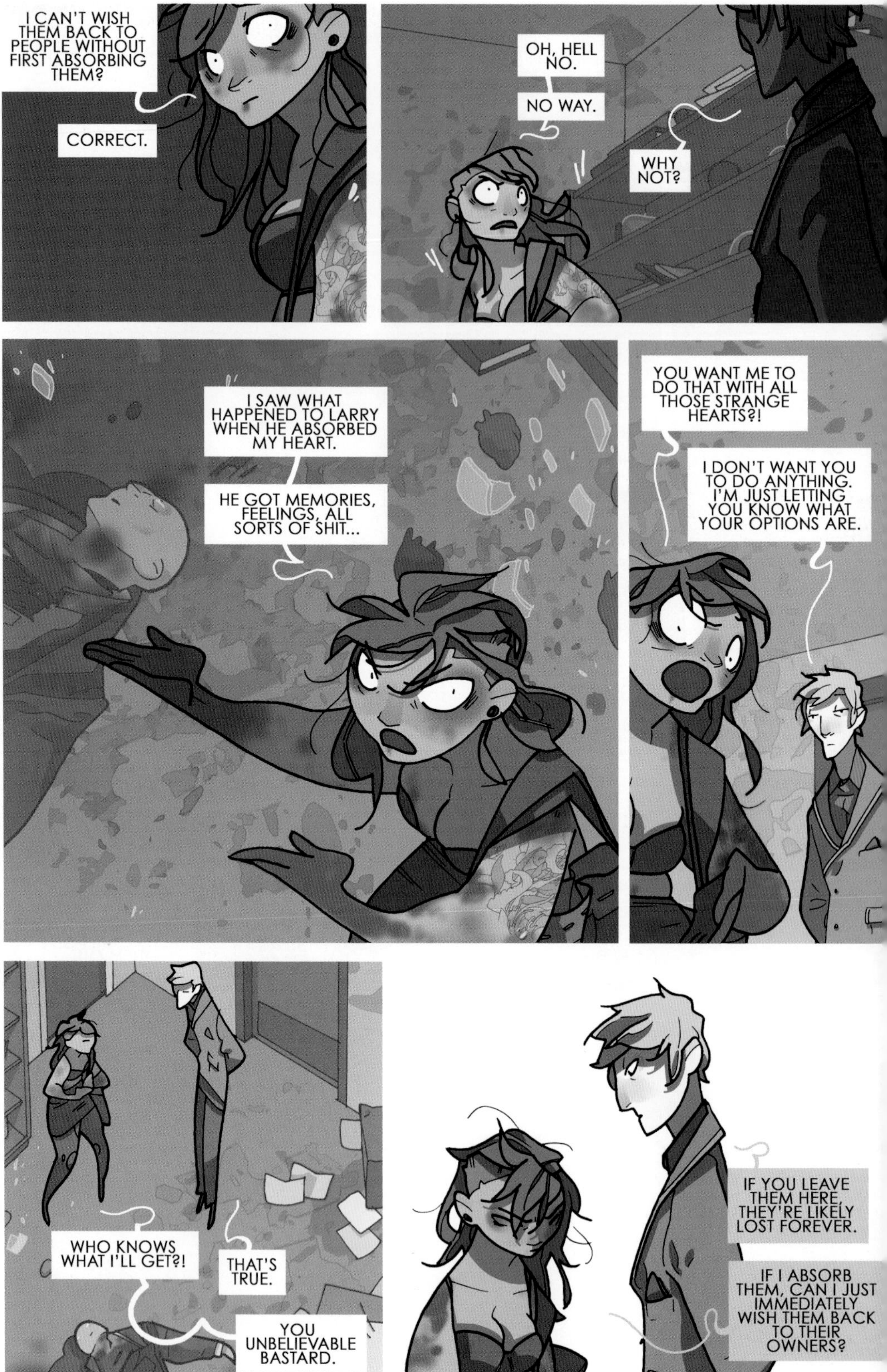

I CAN'T WISH THEM BACK TO PEOPLE WITHOUT FIRST ABSORBING THEM?
CORRECT.
OH, HELL NO.
NO WAY.
WHY NOT?
I SAW WHAT HAPPENED TO LARRY WHEN HE ABSORBED MY HEART.
HE GOT MEMORIES, FEELINGS, ALL SORTS OF SHIT...
YOU WANT ME TO DO THAT WITH ALL THOSE STRANGE HEARTS?!
I DON'T WANT YOU TO DO ANYTHING. I'M JUST LETTING YOU KNOW WHAT YOUR OPTIONS ARE.
WHO KNOWS WHAT I'LL GET?!
THAT'S TRUE.
YOU UNBELIEVABLE BASTARD.
IF YOU LEAVE THEM HERE, THEY'RE LIKELY LOST FOREVER.
IF I ABSORB THEM, CAN I JUST IMMEDIATELY WISH THEM BACK TO THEIR OWNERS?

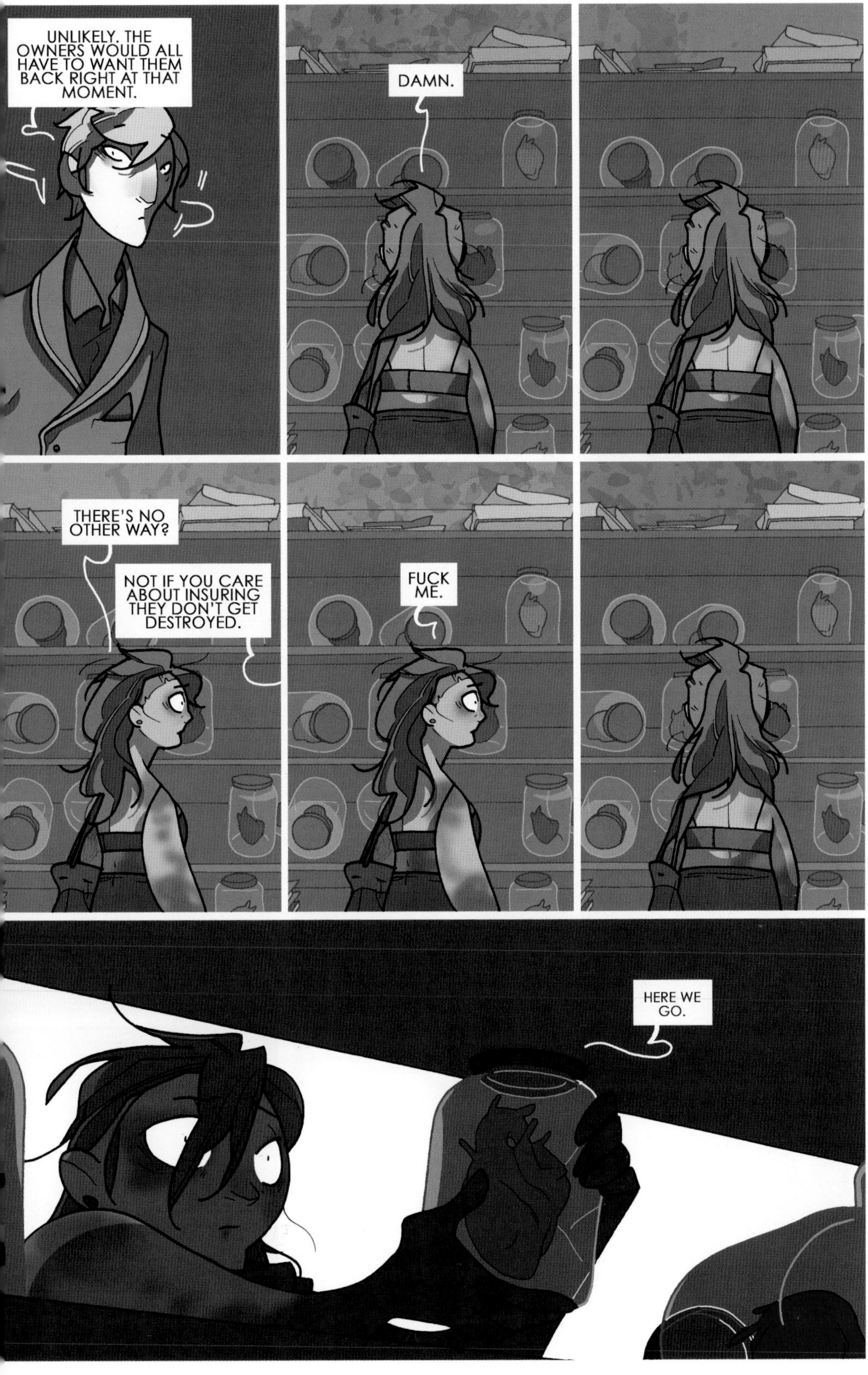
UNLIKELY. THE OWNERS WOULD ALL HAVE TO WANT THEM BACK RIGHT AT THAT MOMENT.
DAMN.
THERE'S NO OTHER WAY?
NOT IF YOU CARE ABOUT INSURING THEY DON'T GET DESTROYED.
FUCK ME.
HERE WE GO.

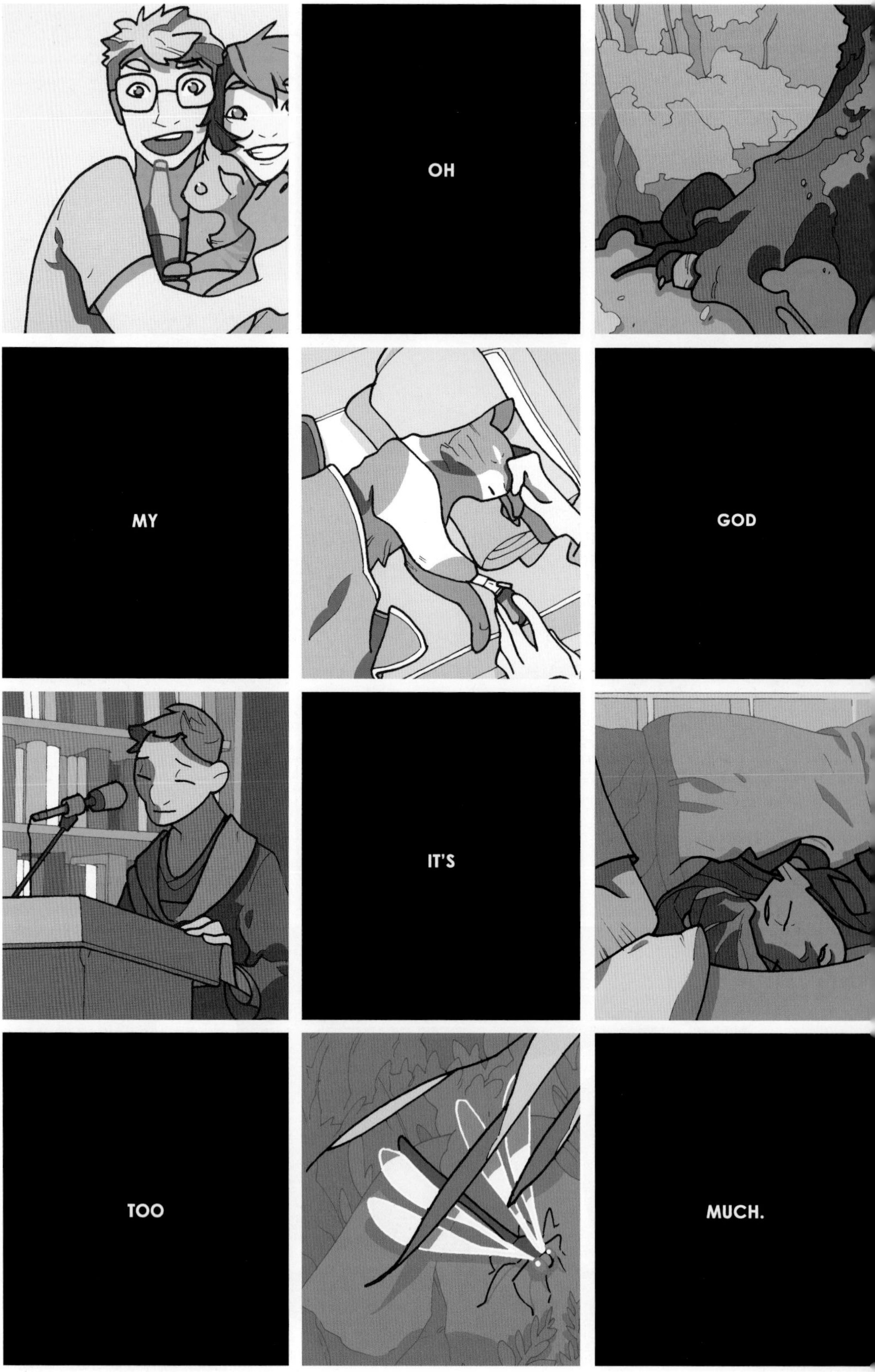
OH
MY
GOD
IT'S
TOO
MUCH.

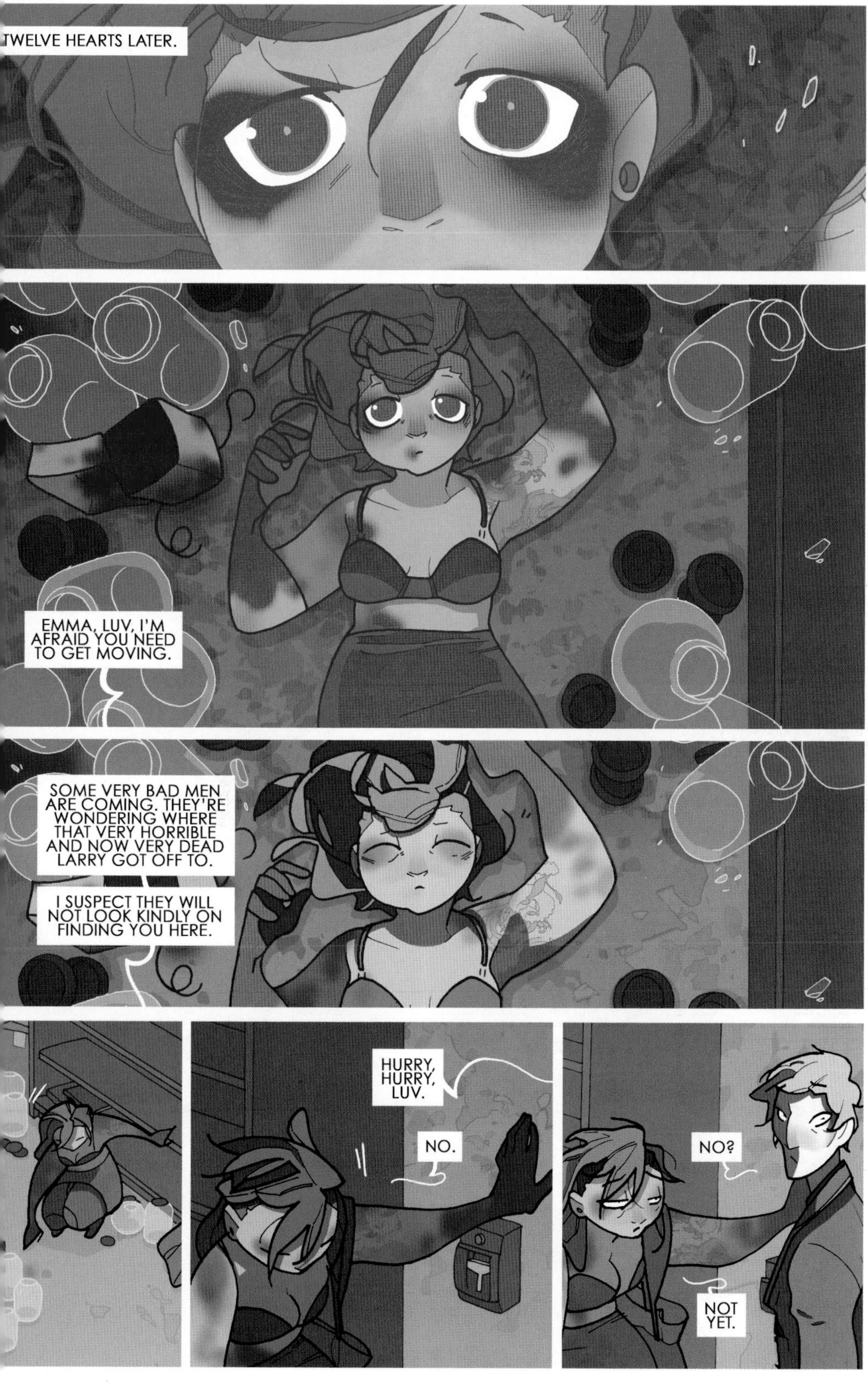
TWELVE HEARTS LATER.
EMMA, LUV, I'M AFRAID YOU NEED TO GET MOVING.
SOME VERY BAD MEN ARE COMING. THEY'RE WONDERING WHERE THAT VERY HORRIBLE AND NOW VERY DEAD LARRY GOT OFF TO.
I SUSPECT THEY WILL NOT LOOK KINDLY ON FINDING YOU HERE.
HURRY, HURRY, LUV.
NO.
NO?
NOT YET.

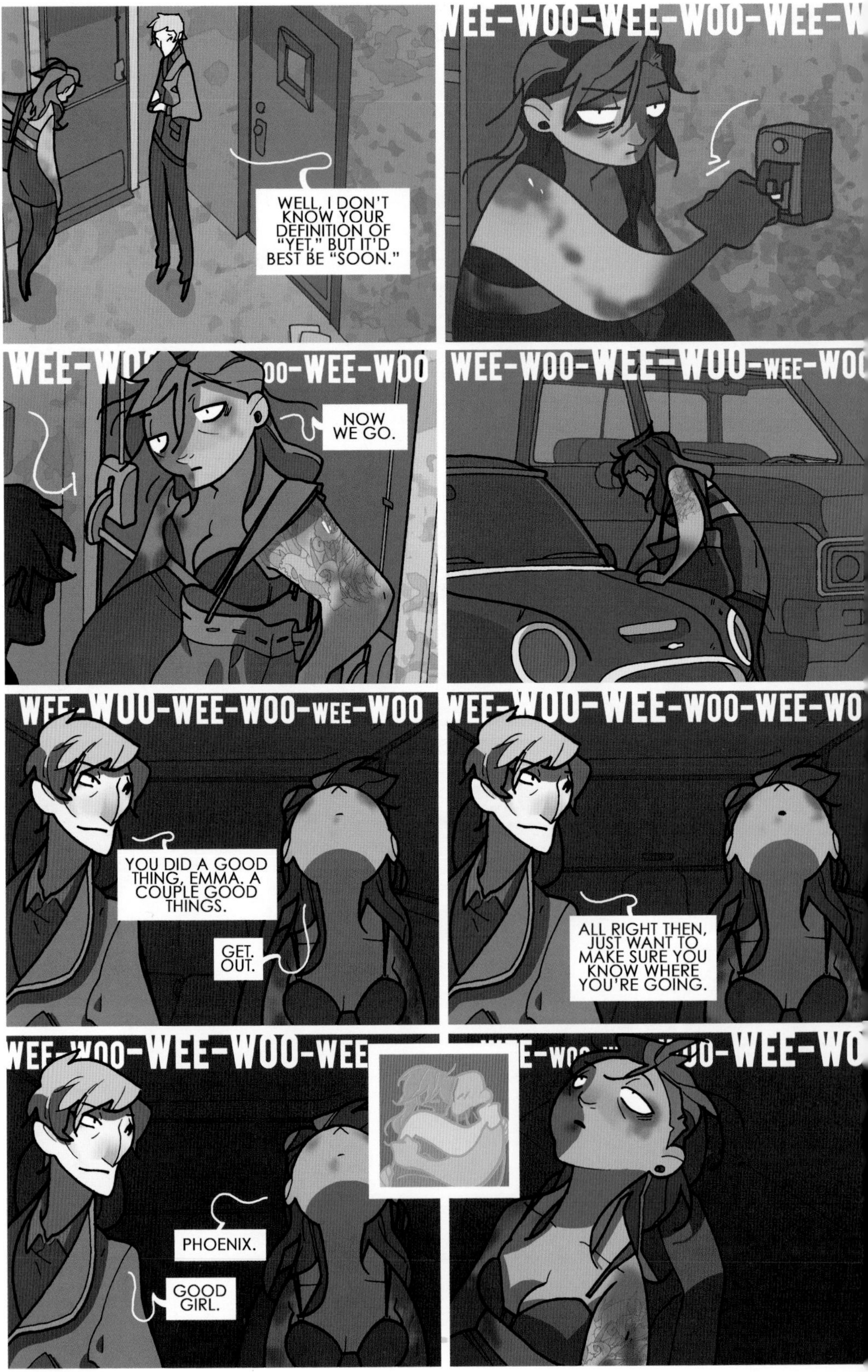
WELL, I DON'T KNOW YOUR DEFINITION OF "YET," BUT IT'D BEST BE "SOON."
WEE-WOO-WEE-WOO-WEE-W
WEE-WO
OO-WEE-WOO
NOW WE GO.
WEE-WOO-WEE-WOO-WEE-WOO
WEE-WOO-WEE-WOO-WEE-WOO
YOU DID A GOOD THING, EMMA. A COUPLE GOOD THINGS.
GET. OUT.
WEE-WOO-WEE-WOO-WEE-WO
ALL RIGHT THEN, JUST WANT TO MAKE SURE YOU KNOW WHERE YOU'RE GOING.
WEE-WOO-WEE-WOO-WEE
PHOENIX.
GOOD GIRL.
OO-WEE-WO

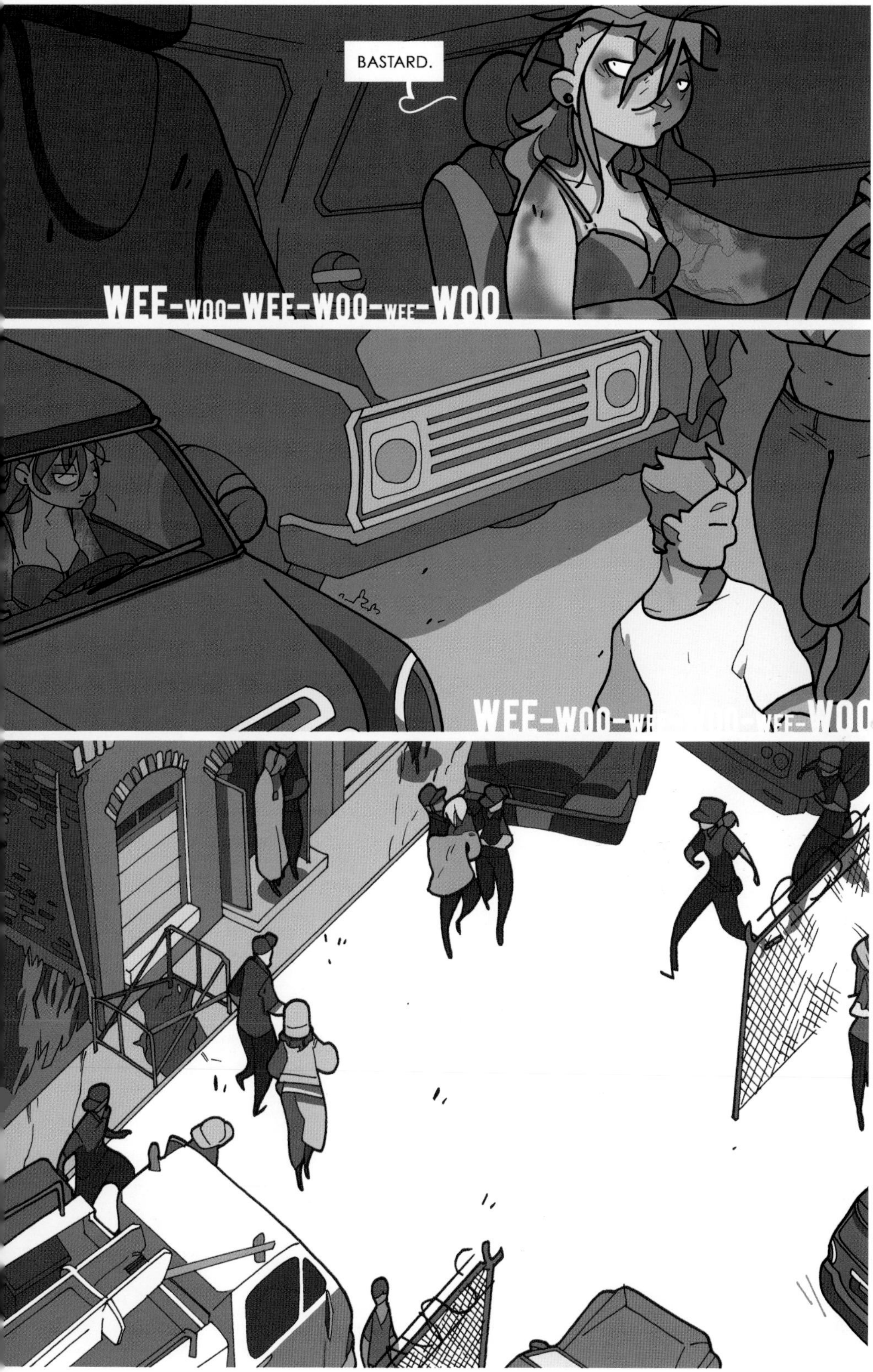
BASTARD.
WEE-woo-WEE-WOO-wee-WOO

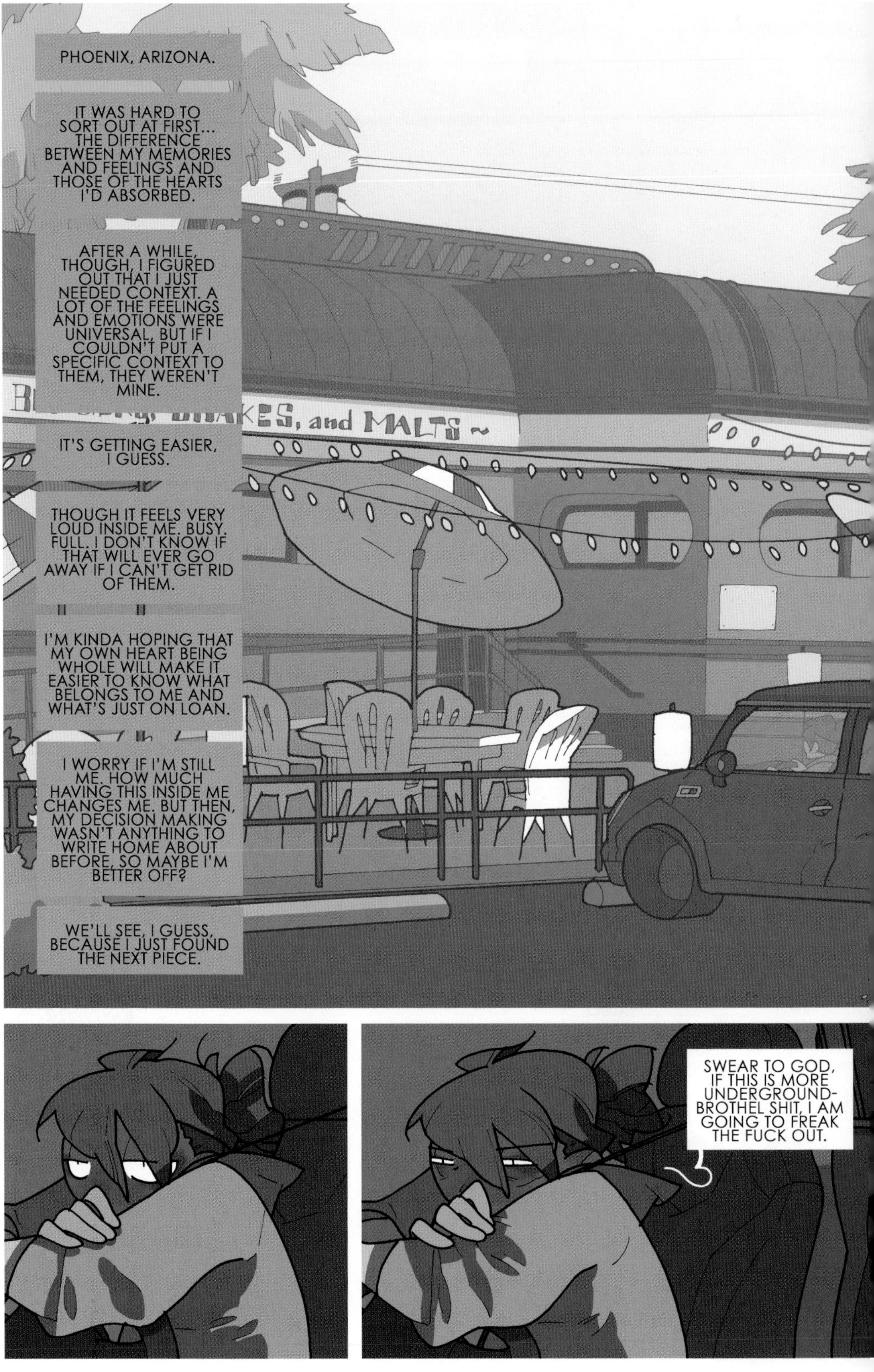
PHOENIX, ARIZONA.
IT WAS HARD TO SORT OUT AT FIRST... THE DIFFERENCE BETWEEN MY MEMORIES AND FEELINGS AND THOSE OF THE HEARTS I'D ABSORBED.
DINER
AFTER A WHILE, THOUGH, I FIGURED OUT THAT I JUST NEEDED CONTEXT. A LOT OF THE FEELINGS AND EMOTIONS WERE UNIVERSAL, BUT IF I COULDN'T PUT A SPECIFIC CONTEXT TO THEM, THEY WEREN'T MINE.
and MALTS ~
IT'S GETTING EASIER, I GUESS.
THOUGH IT FEELS VERY LOUD INSIDE ME. BUSY. FULL. I DON'T KNOW IF THAT WILL EVER GO AWAY IF I CAN'T GET RID OF THEM.
I'M KINDA HOPING THAT MY OWN HEART BEING WHOLE WILL MAKE IT EASIER TO KNOW WHAT BELONGS TO ME AND WHAT'S JUST ON LOAN.
I WORRY IF I'M STILL ME. HOW MUCH HAVING THIS INSIDE ME CHANGES ME. BUT THEN, MY DECISION MAKING WASN'T ANYTHING TO WRITE HOME ABOUT BEFORE, SO MAYBE I'M BETTER OFF?
WE'LL SEE, I GUESS, BECAUSE I JUST FOUND THE NEXT PIECE.
SWEAR TO GOD, IF THIS IS MORE UNDERGROUND-BROTHEL SHIT, I AM GOING TO FREAK THE FUCK OUT.

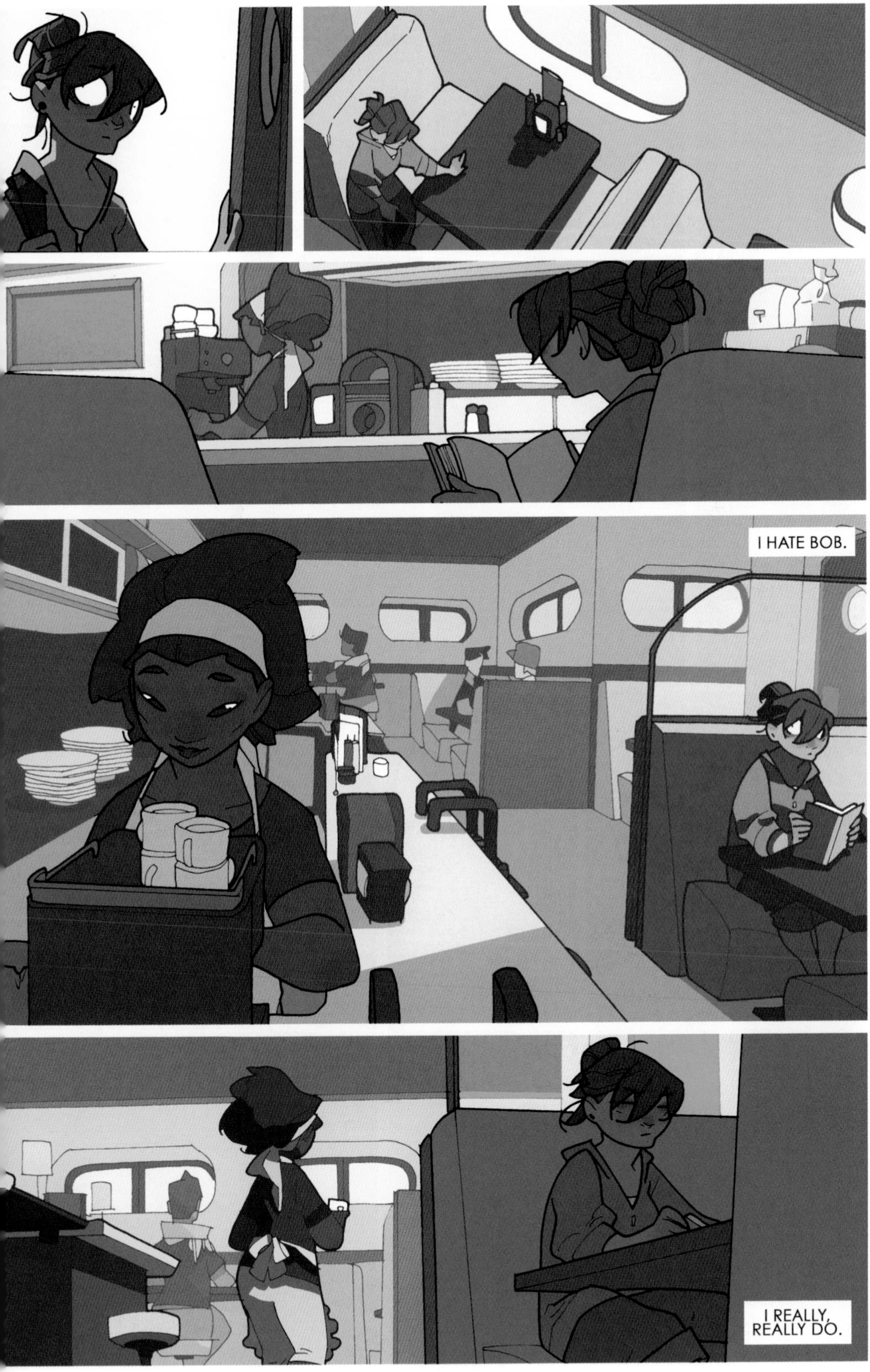
I HATE BOB.
I REALLY, REALLY DO.

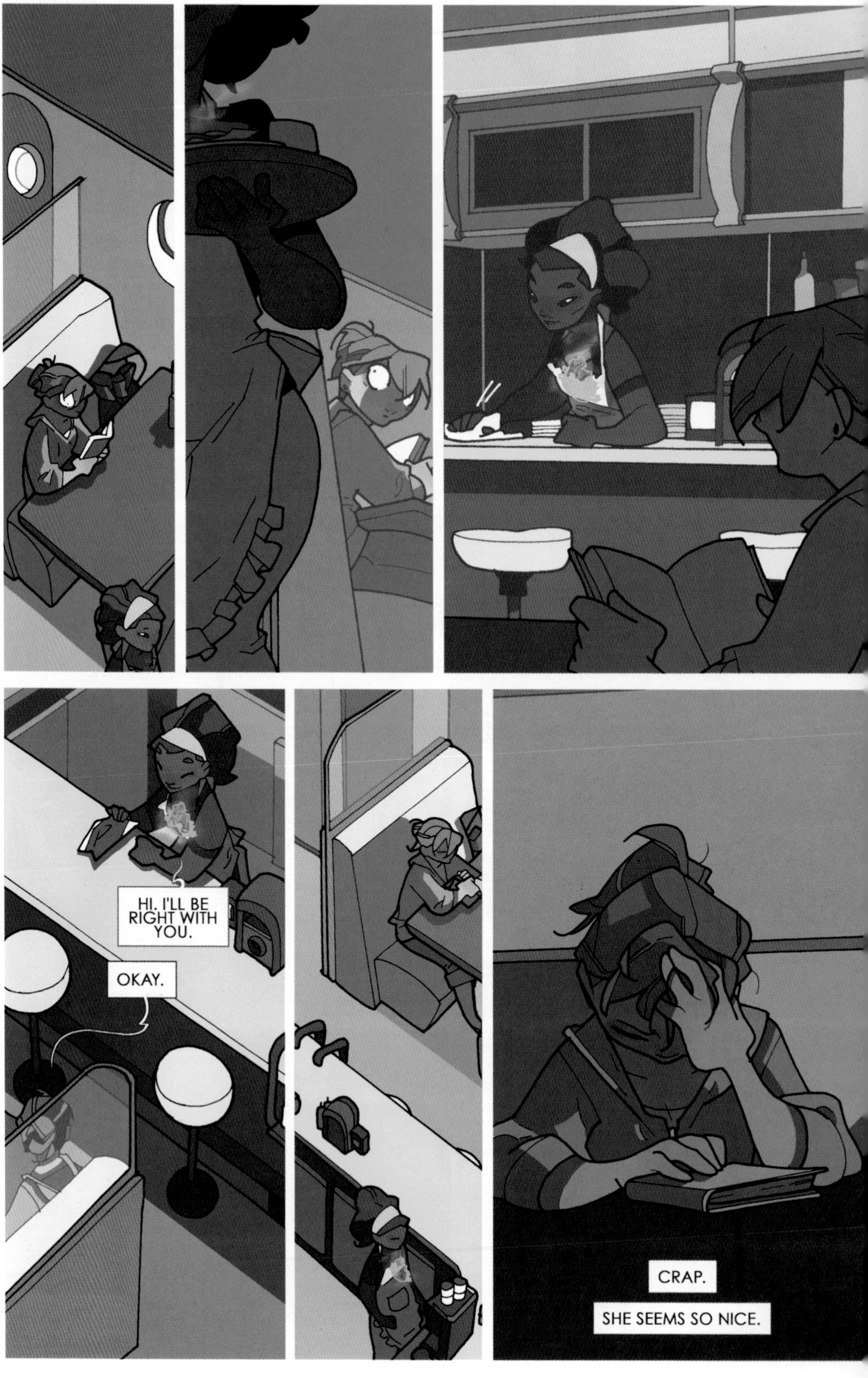
HI. I'LL BE RIGHT WITH YOU.
OKAY.
CRAP.
SHE SEEMS SO NICE.

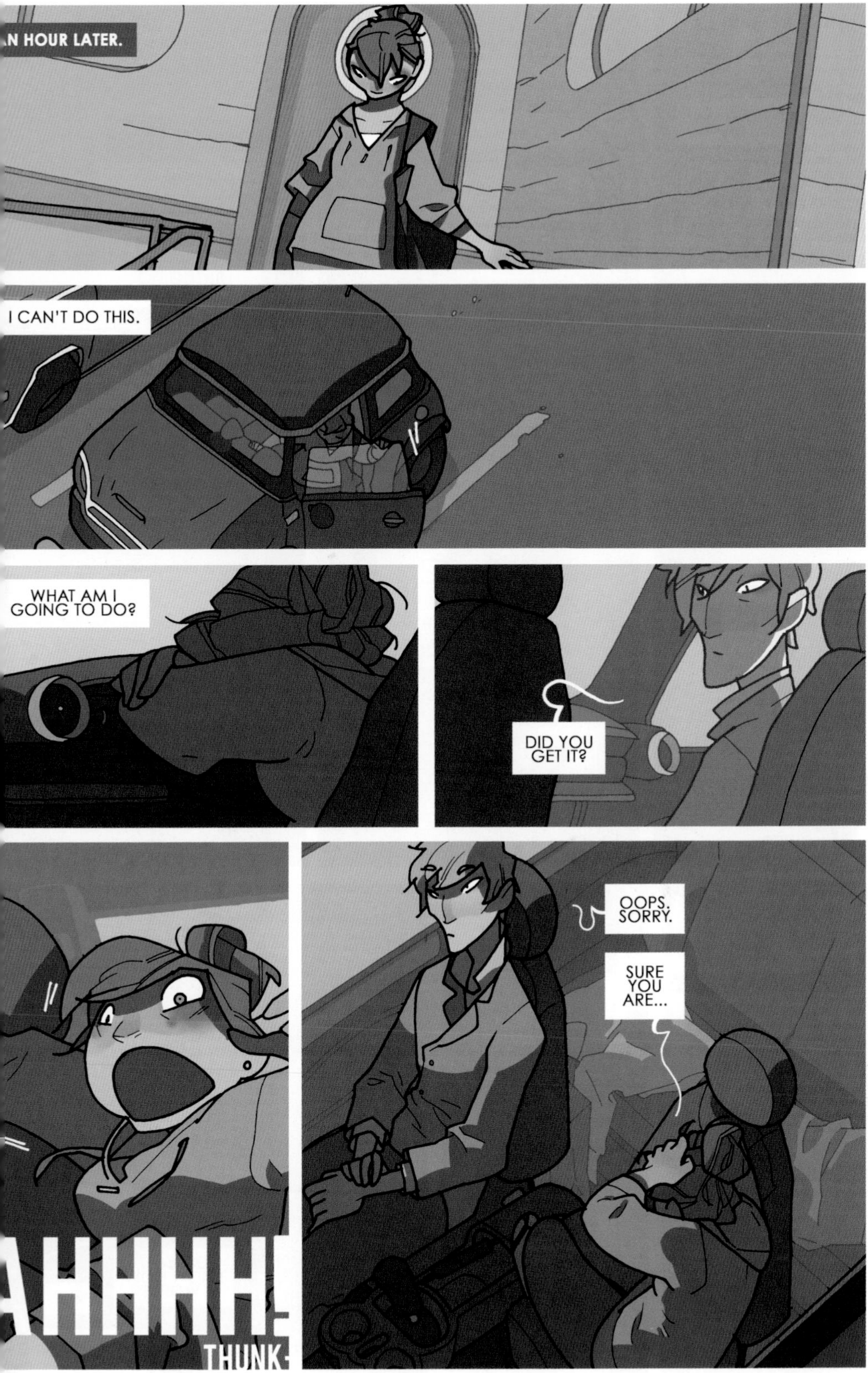
N HOUR LATER.
I CAN'T DO THIS.
WHAT AM I GOING TO DO?
DID YOU GET IT?
AHHHH!
THUNK-
OOPS. SORRY.
SURE YOU ARE...

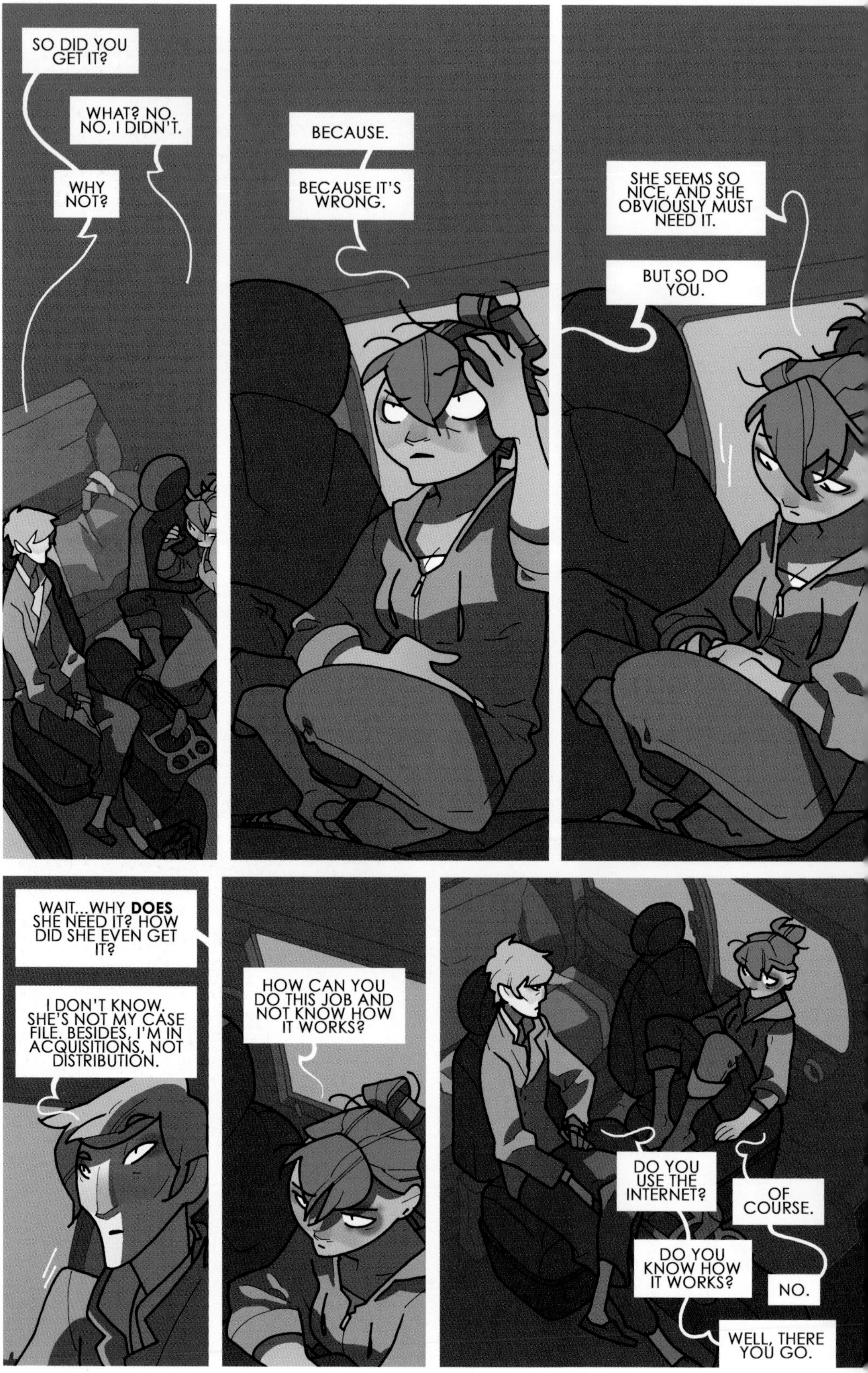
SO DID YOU GET IT?
WHAT? NO. NO, I DIDN'T.
WHY NOT?
BECAUSE.
BECAUSE IT'S WRONG.
SHE SEEMS SO NICE, AND SHE OBVIOUSLY MUST NEED IT.
BUT SO DO YOU.
WAIT...WHY **DOES** SHE NEED IT? HOW DID SHE EVEN GET IT?
I DON'T KNOW. SHE'S NOT MY CASE FILE. BESIDES, I'M IN ACQUISITIONS, NOT DISTRIBUTION.
HOW CAN YOU DO THIS JOB AND NOT KNOW HOW IT WORKS?
DO YOU USE THE INTERNET?
OF COURSE.
DO YOU KNOW HOW IT WORKS?
NO.
WELL, THERE YOU GO.

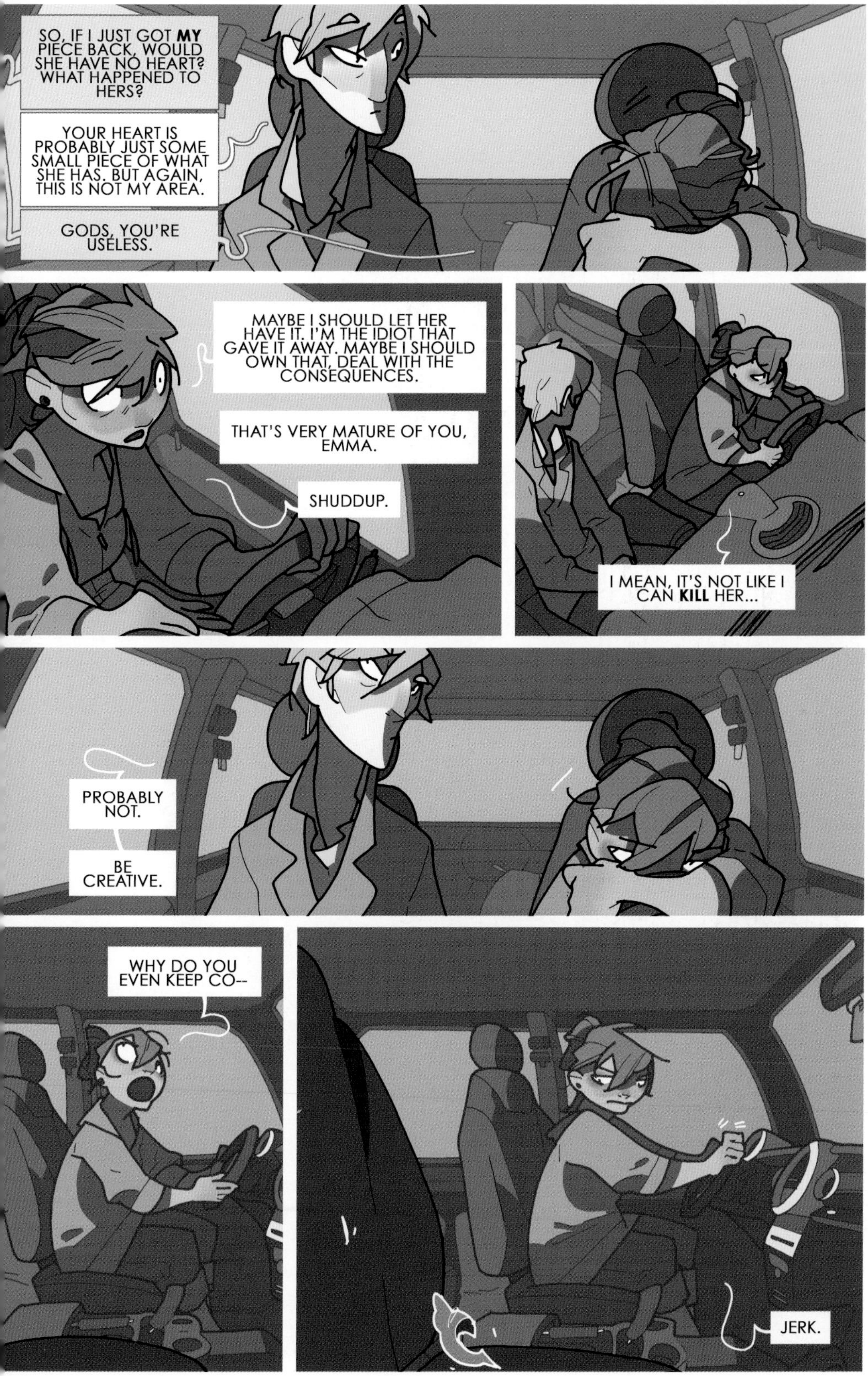
SO, IF I JUST GOT **MY** PIECE BACK, WOULD SHE HAVE NO HEART? WHAT HAPPENED TO HERS?
YOUR HEART IS PROBABLY JUST SOME SMALL PIECE OF WHAT SHE HAS. BUT AGAIN, THIS IS NOT MY AREA.
GODS, YOU'RE USELESS.
MAYBE I SHOULD LET HER HAVE IT. I'M THE IDIOT THAT GAVE IT AWAY. MAYBE I SHOULD OWN THAT, DEAL WITH THE CONSEQUENCES.
THAT'S VERY MATURE OF YOU, EMMA.
SHUDDUP.
I MEAN, IT'S NOT LIKE I CAN **KILL** HER...
PROBABLY NOT.
BE CREATIVE.
WHY DO YOU EVEN KEEP CO--
JERK.

WHAT AM I DOING?

THIS IS A TERRIBLE IDEA.

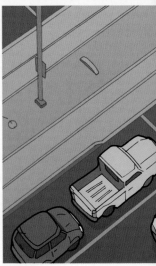

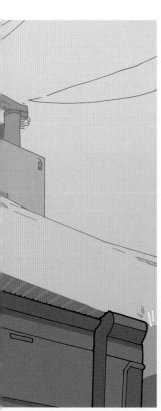

AT LEAST I DON'T HAVE TO TEAR UP MY CLOTHES THIS TIME.

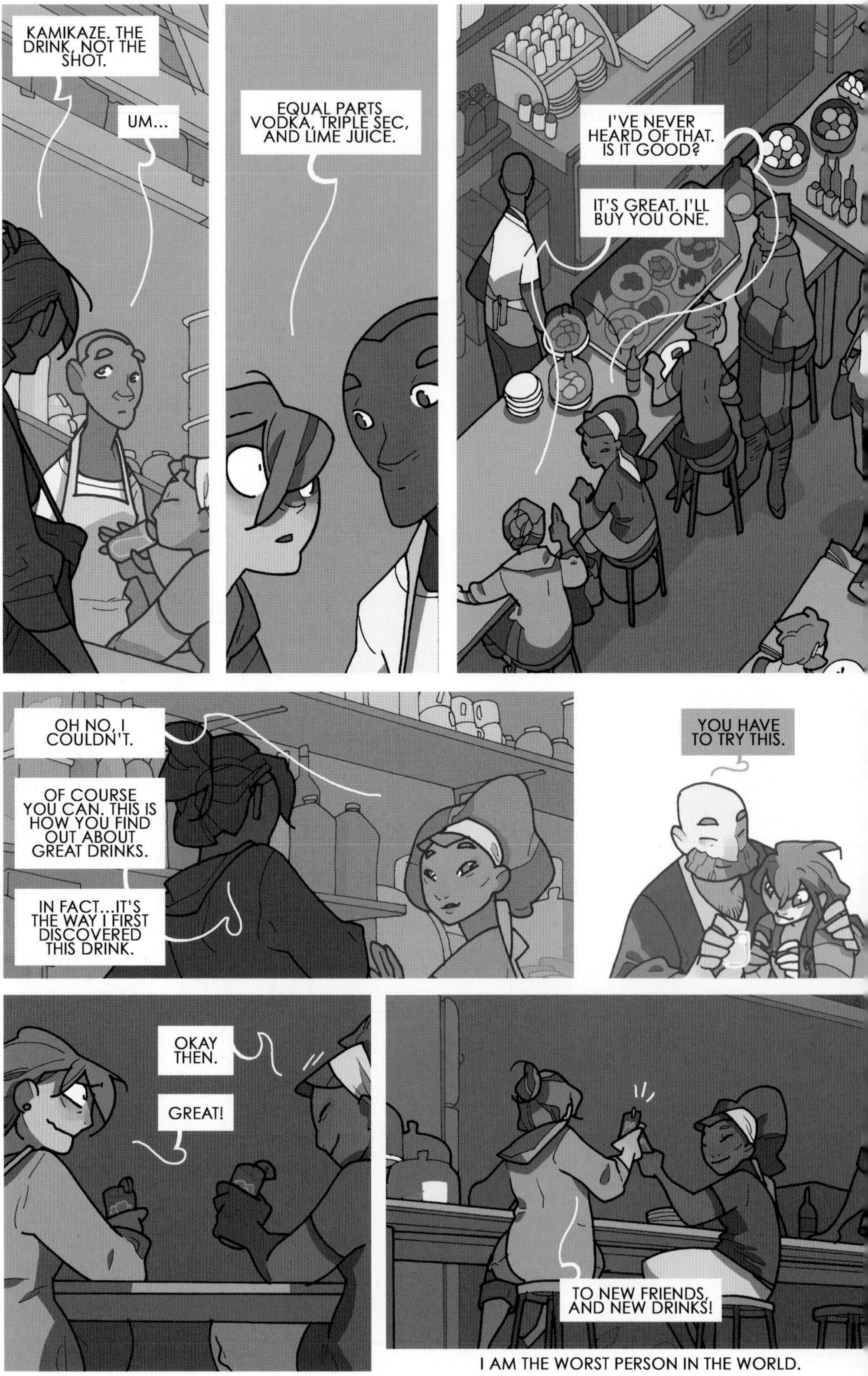
KAMIKAZE. THE DRINK, NOT THE SHOT.
UM...
EQUAL PARTS VODKA, TRIPLE SEC, AND LIME JUICE.
I'VE NEVER HEARD OF THAT. IS IT GOOD?
IT'S GREAT. I'LL BUY YOU ONE.
OH NO, I COULDN'T.
OF COURSE YOU CAN. THIS IS HOW YOU FIND OUT ABOUT GREAT DRINKS.
IN FACT...IT'S THE WAY I FIRST DISCOVERED THIS DRINK.
YOU HAVE TO TRY THIS.
OKAY THEN.
GREAT!
TO NEW FRIENDS, AND NEW DRINKS!
I AM THE WORST PERSON IN THE WORLD.

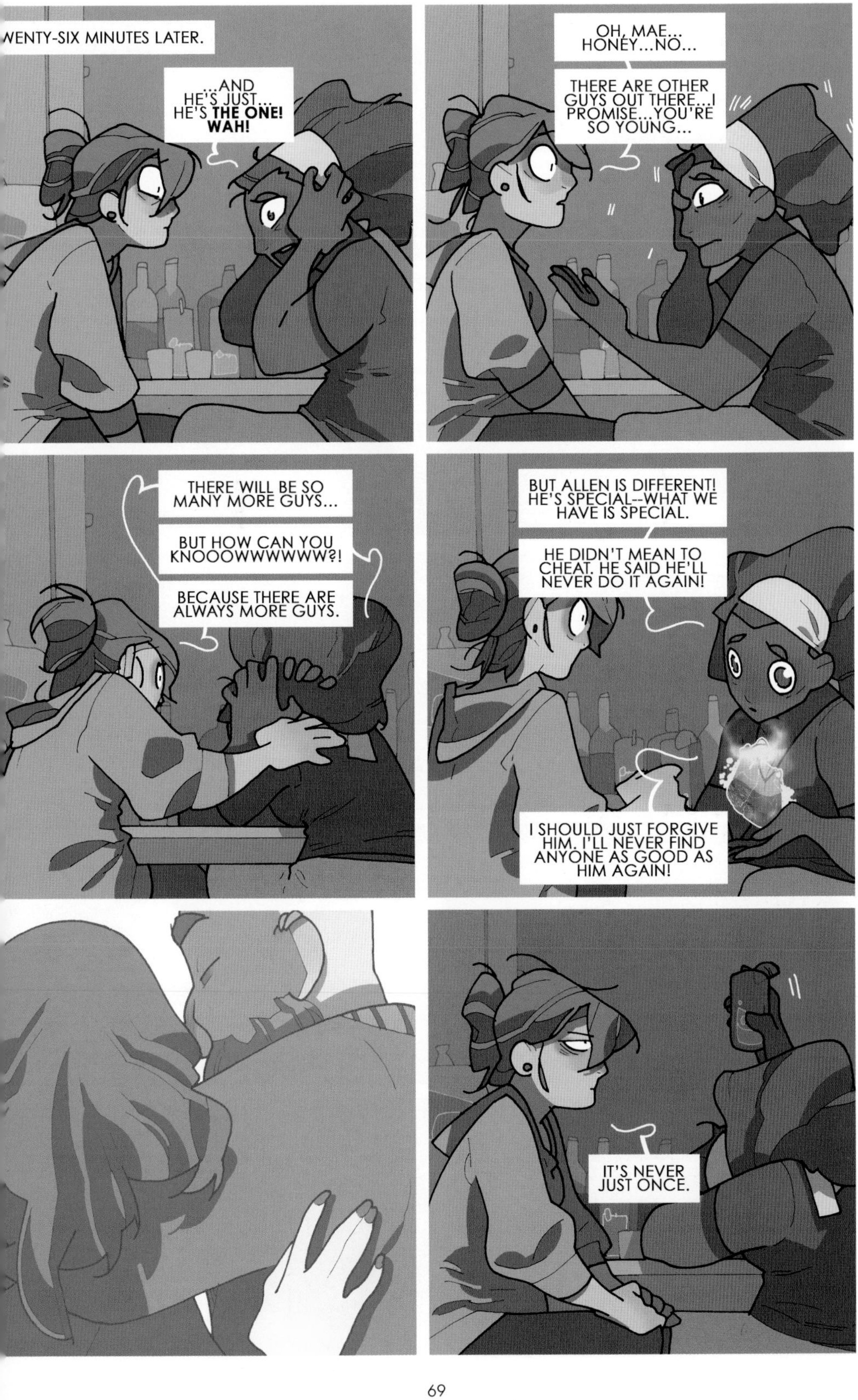
WENTY-SIX MINUTES LATER.
...AND HE'S JUST... HE'S **THE ONE! WAH!**
OH, MAE... HONEY...NO...
THERE ARE OTHER GUYS OUT THERE...I PROMISE...YOU'RE SO YOUNG...
THERE WILL BE SO MANY MORE GUYS...
BUT HOW CAN YOU KNOOOWWWWWW?!
BECAUSE THERE ARE ALWAYS MORE GUYS.
BUT ALLEN IS DIFFERENT! HE'S SPECIAL--WHAT WE HAVE IS SPECIAL.
HE DIDN'T MEAN TO CHEAT. HE SAID HE'LL NEVER DO IT AGAIN!
I SHOULD JUST FORGIVE HIM. I'LL NEVER FIND ANYONE AS GOOD AS HIM AGAIN!
IT'S NEVER JUST ONCE.

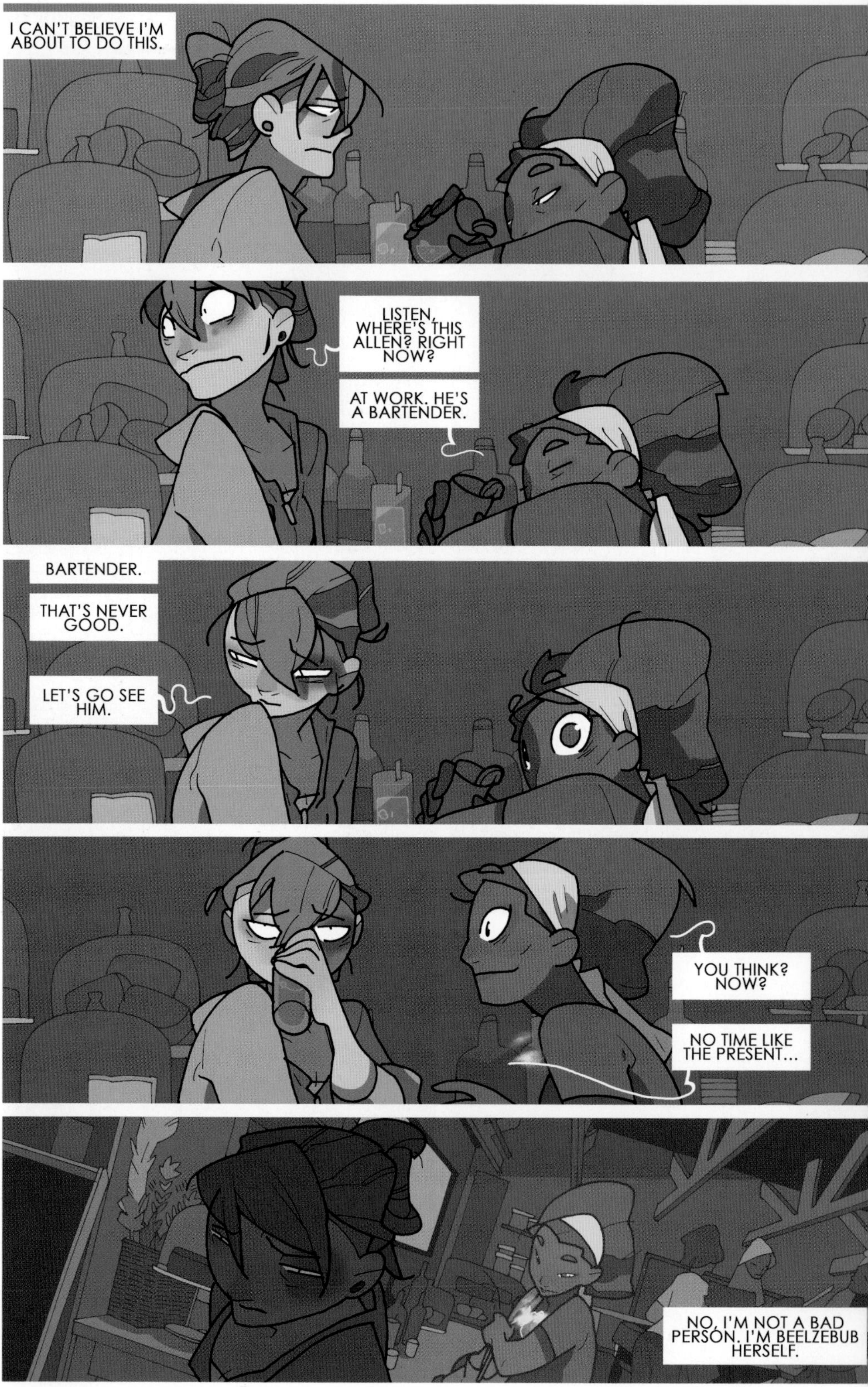
I CAN'T BELIEVE I'M ABOUT TO DO THIS.
LISTEN, WHERE'S THIS ALLEN? RIGHT NOW?
AT WORK. HE'S A BARTENDER.
BARTENDER.
THAT'S NEVER GOOD.
LET'S GO SEE HIM.
YOU THINK? NOW?
NO TIME LIKE THE PRESENT...
NO, I'M NOT A BAD PERSON. I'M BEELZEBUB HERSELF.

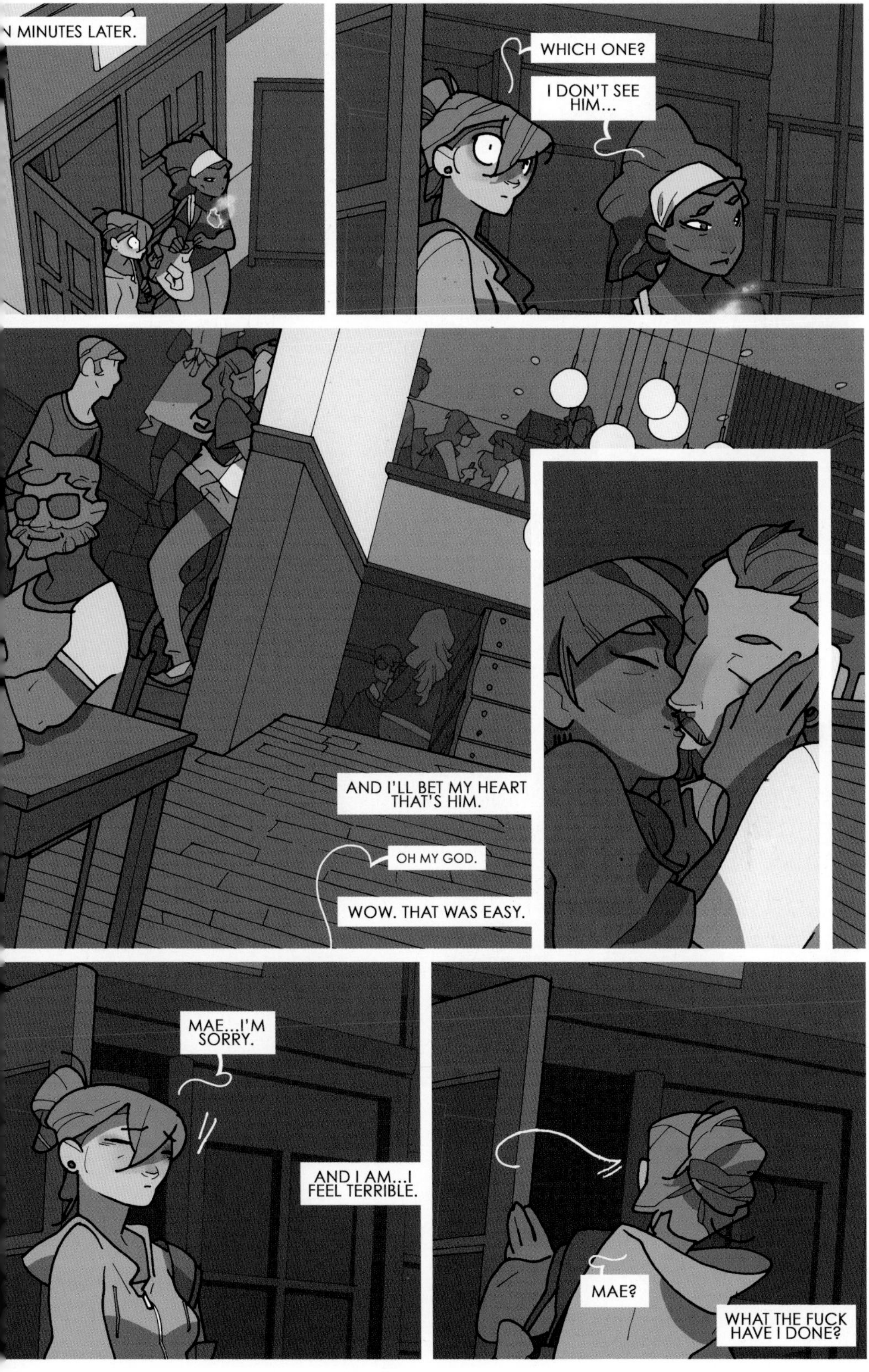
N MINUTES LATER.
WHICH ONE?
I DON'T SEE HIM...
AND I'LL BET MY HEART THAT'S HIM.
OH MY GOD.
WOW. THAT WAS EASY.
MAE...I'M SORRY.
AND I AM...I FEEL TERRIBLE.
MAE?
WHAT THE FUCK HAVE I DONE?

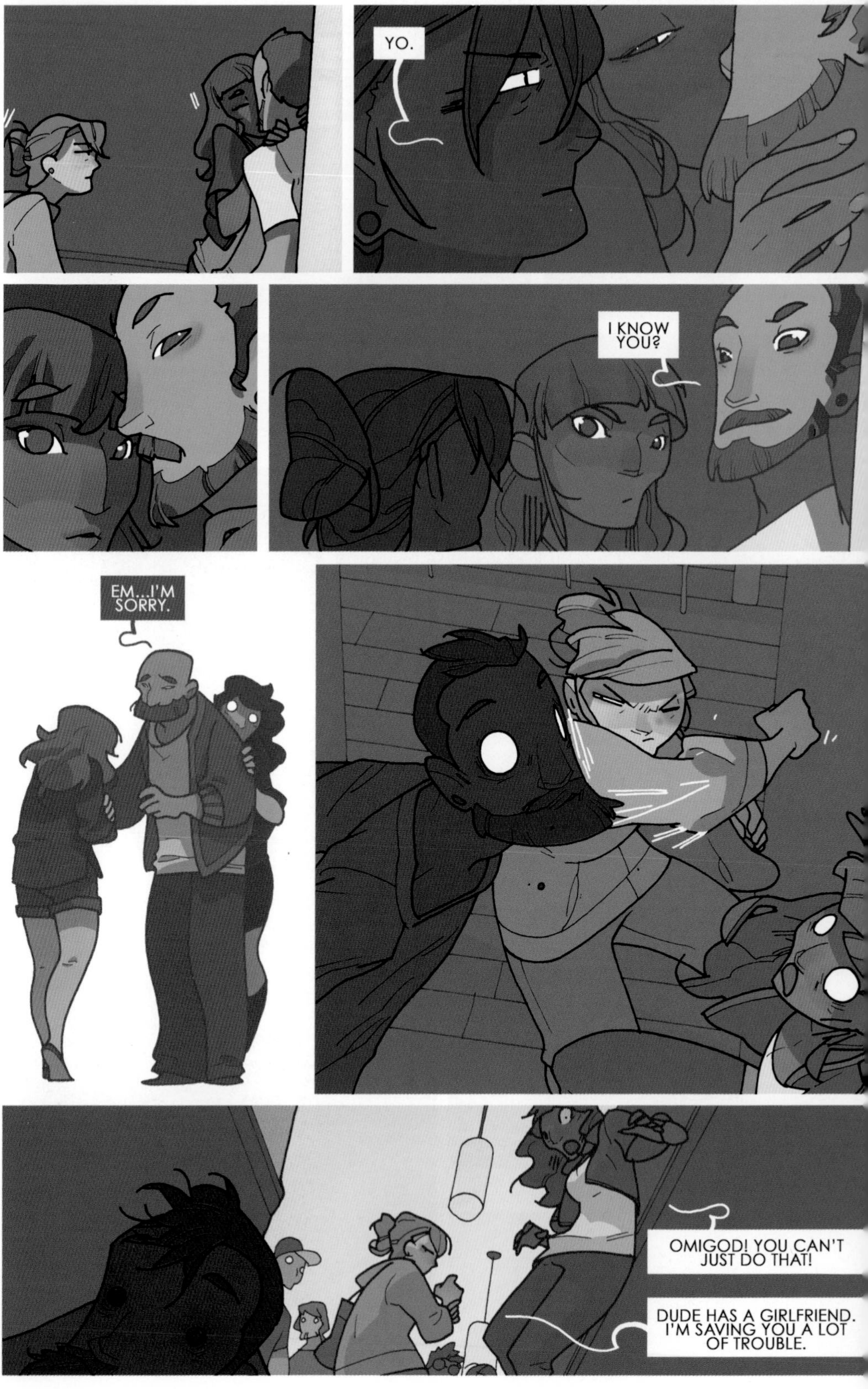
YO.
I KNOW YOU?
EM...I'M SORRY.
OMIGOD! YOU CAN'T JUST DO THAT!
DUDE HAS A GIRLFRIEND. I'M SAVING YOU A LOT OF TROUBLE.

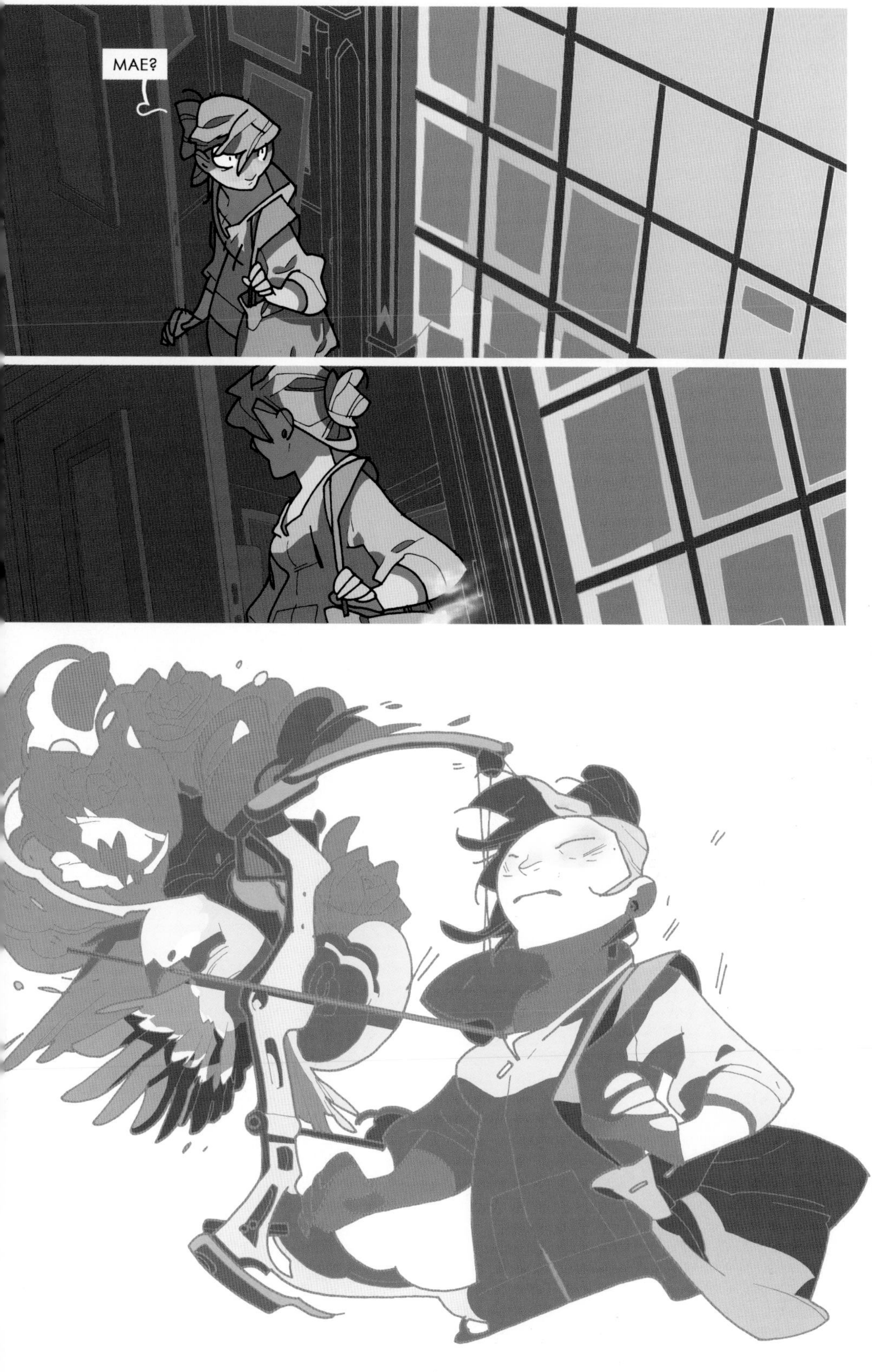
MAE?

PIECE
no.
3

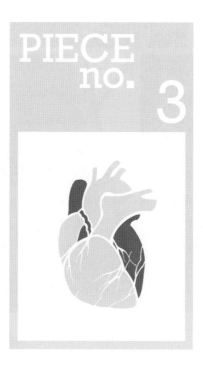

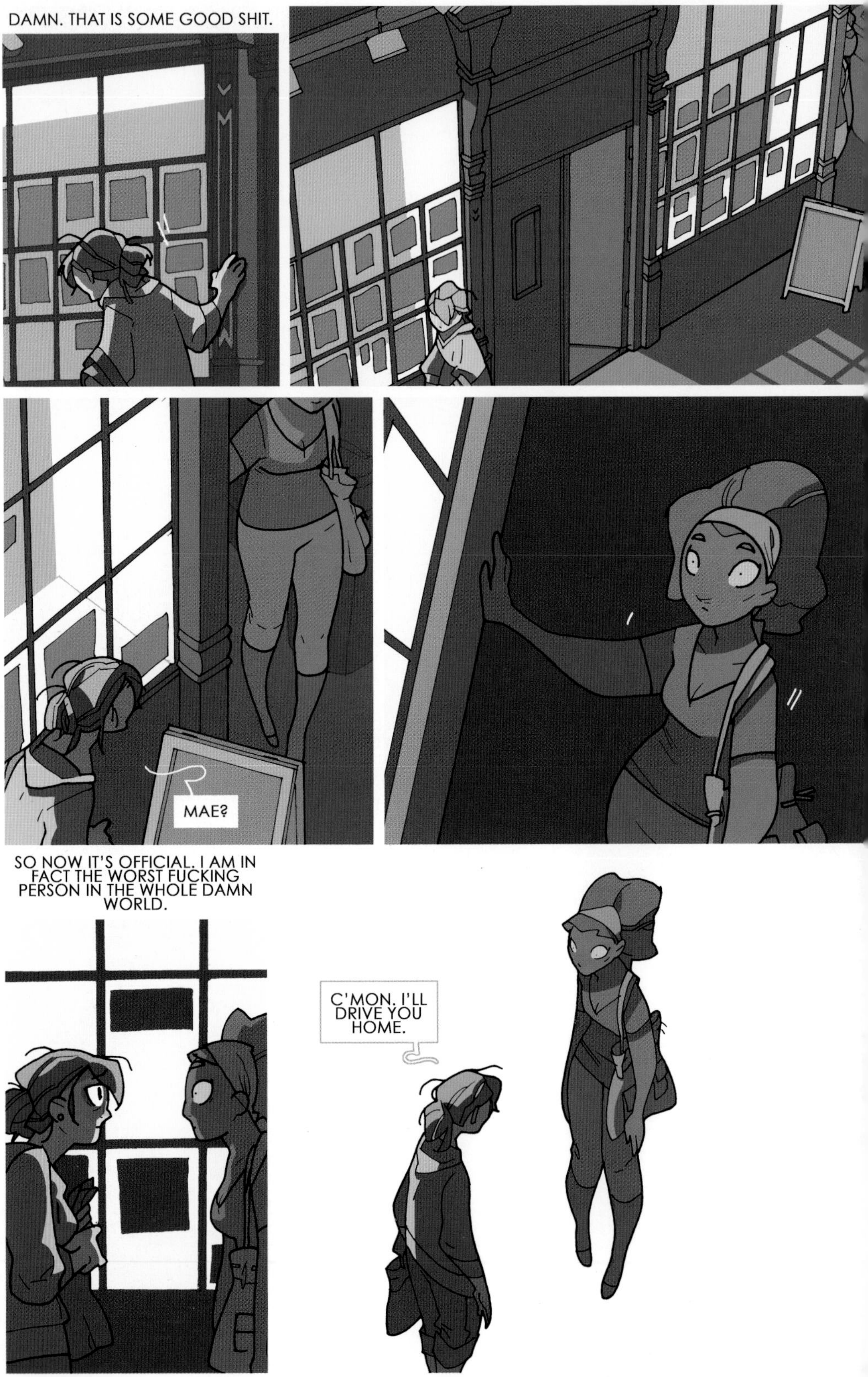
DAMN. THAT IS SOME GOOD SHIT.
MAE?
SO NOW IT'S OFFICIAL. I AM IN FACT THE WORST FUCKING PERSON IN THE WHOLE DAMN WORLD.
C'MON. I'LL DRIVE YOU HOME.

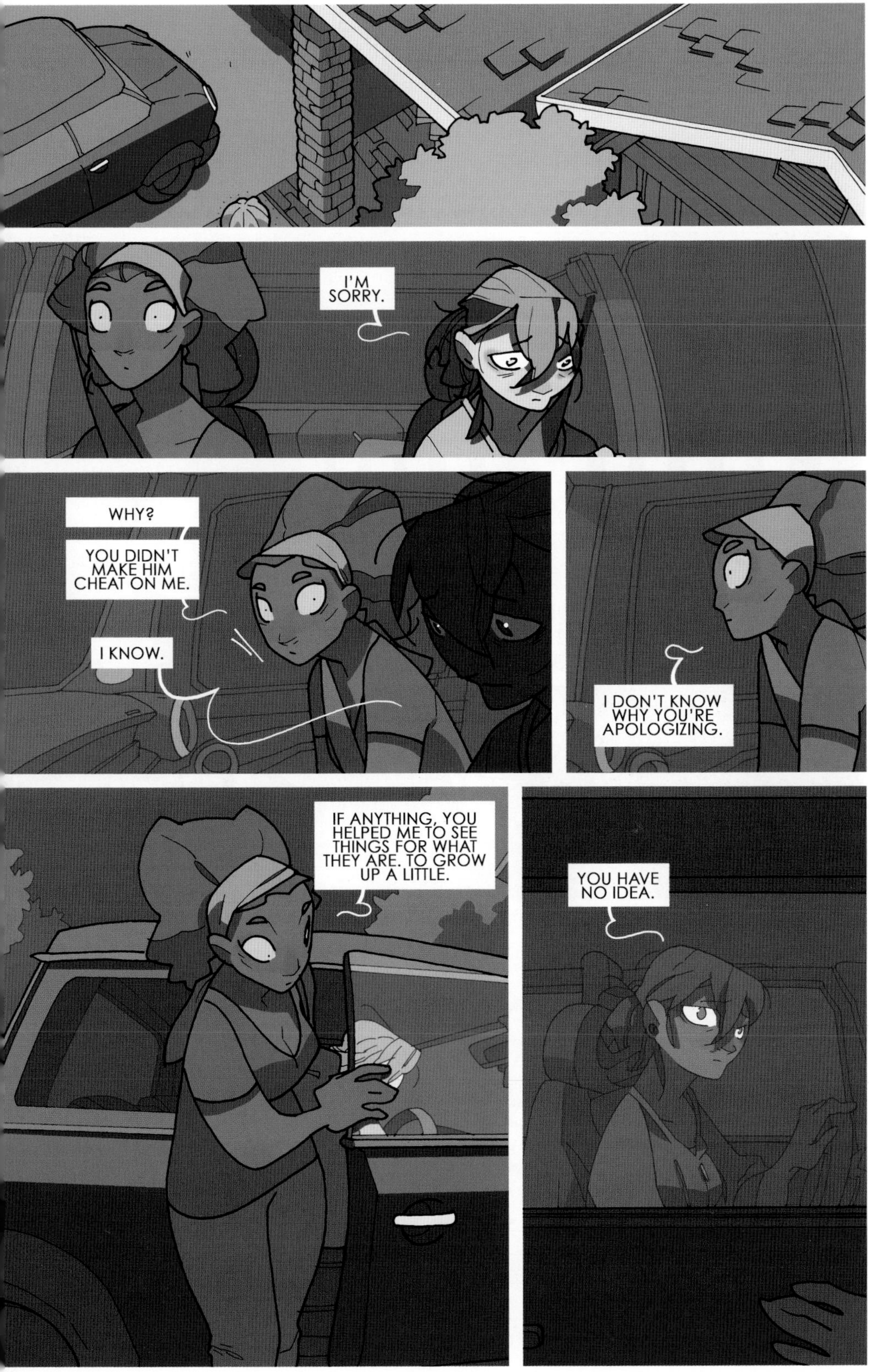
I'M SORRY.
WHY?
YOU DIDN'T MAKE HIM CHEAT ON ME.
I KNOW.
I DON'T KNOW WHY YOU'RE APOLOGIZING.
IF ANYTHING, YOU HELPED ME TO SEE THINGS FOR WHAT THEY ARE. TO GROW UP A LITTLE.
YOU HAVE NO IDEA.

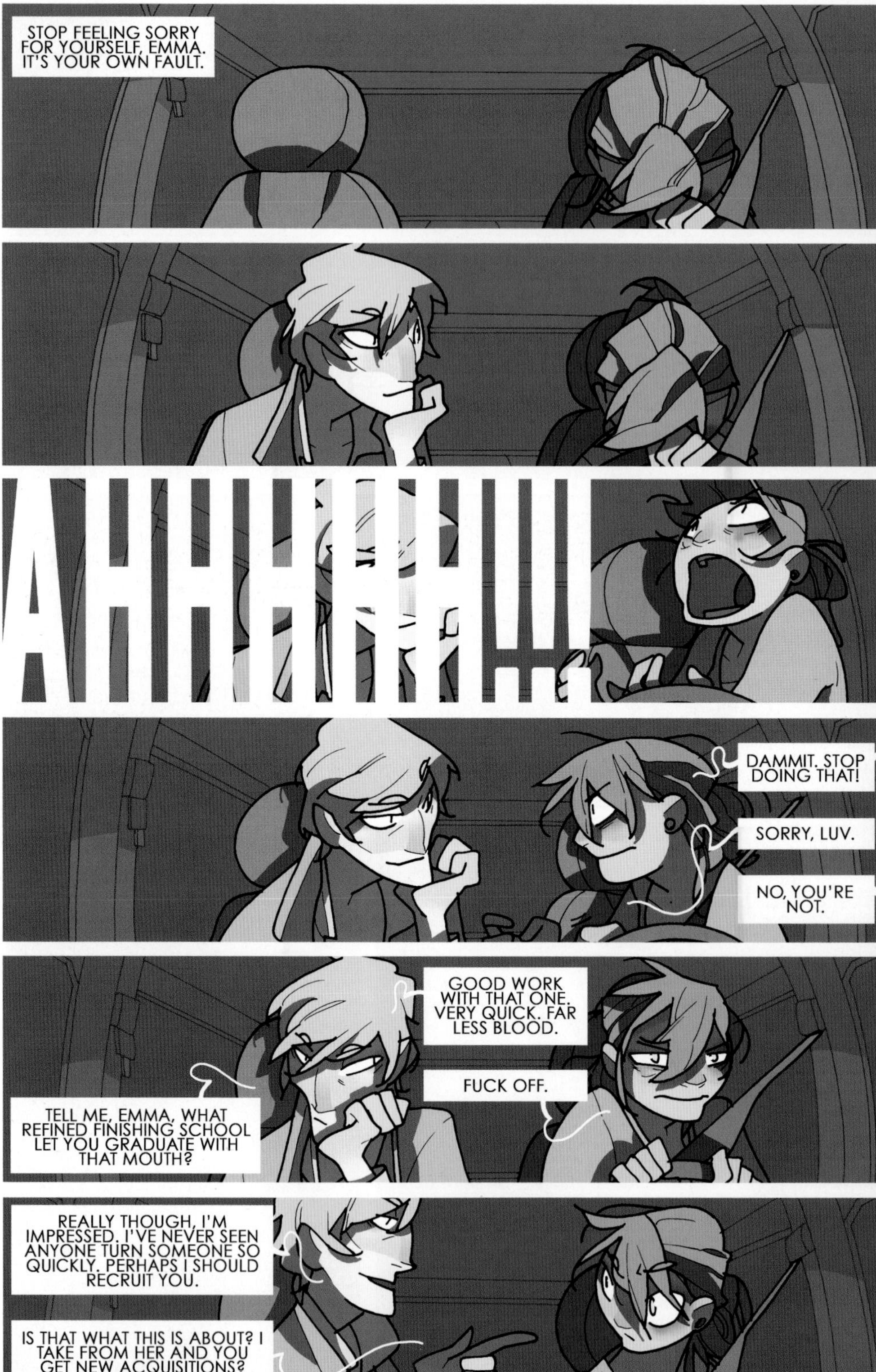

STOP FEELING SORRY FOR YOURSELF, EMMA. IT'S YOUR OWN FAULT.
AHHHHHHH!!!
DAMMIT. STOP DOING THAT!
SORRY, LUV.
NO, YOU'RE NOT.
GOOD WORK WITH THAT ONE. VERY QUICK. FAR LESS BLOOD.
FUCK OFF.
TELL ME, EMMA, WHAT REFINED FINISHING SCHOOL LET YOU GRADUATE WITH THAT MOUTH?
REALLY THOUGH, I'M IMPRESSED. I'VE NEVER SEEN ANYONE TURN SOMEONE SO QUICKLY. PERHAPS I SHOULD RECRUIT YOU.
IS THAT WHAT THIS IS ABOUT? I TAKE FROM HER AND YOU GET NEW ACQUISITIONS?

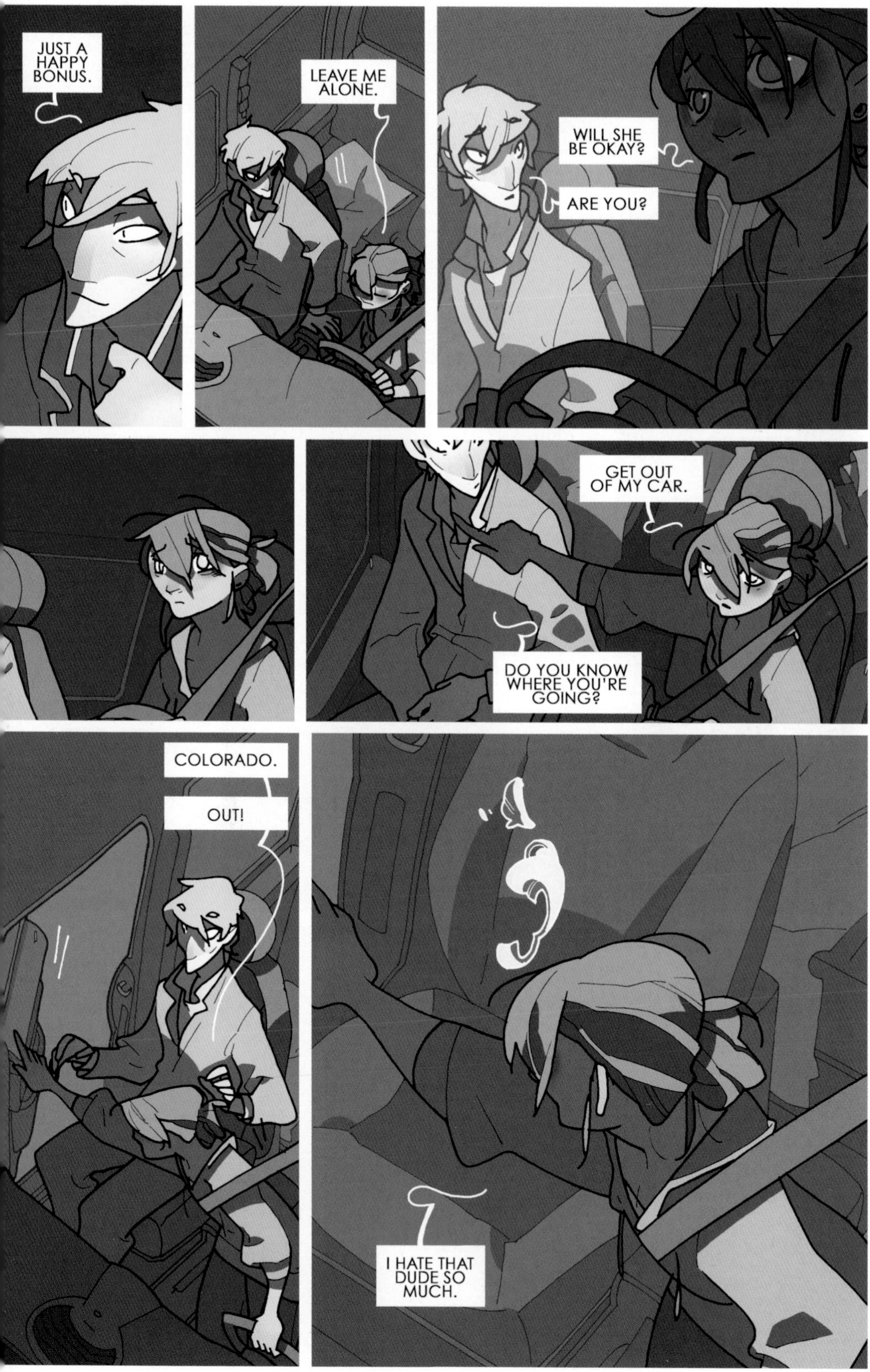
JUST A HAPPY BONUS.
LEAVE ME ALONE.
WILL SHE BE OKAY?
ARE YOU?
GET OUT OF MY CAR.
DO YOU KNOW WHERE YOU'RE GOING?
COLORADO.
OUT!
I HATE THAT DUDE SO MUCH.

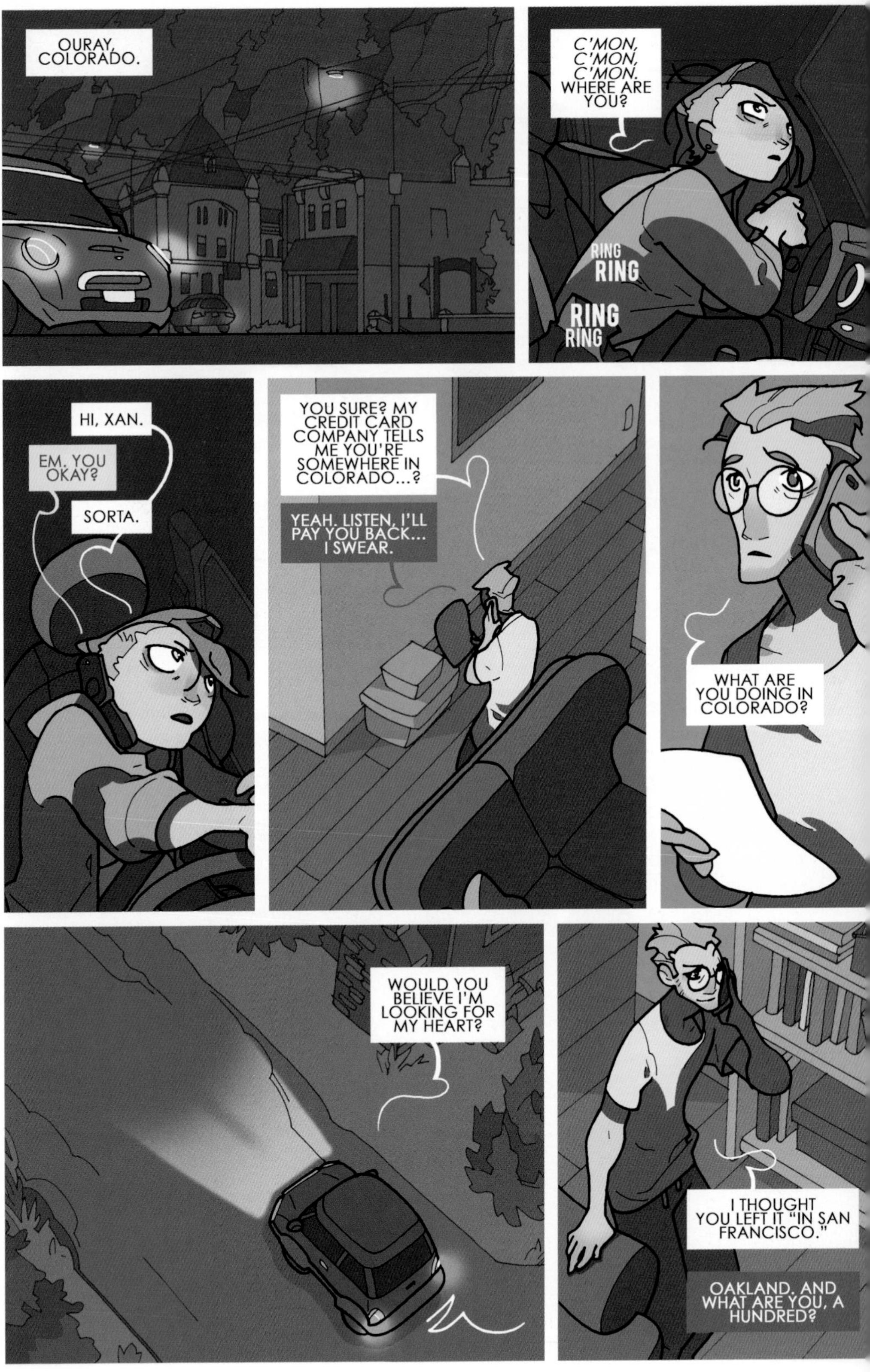
OURAY, COLORADO.
C'MON, C'MON, C'MON. WHERE ARE YOU?
RING RING
RING RING
HI, XAN.
EM. YOU OKAY?
SORTA.
YOU SURE? MY CREDIT CARD COMPANY TELLS ME YOU'RE SOMEWHERE IN COLORADO...?
YEAH. LISTEN, I'LL PAY YOU BACK... I SWEAR.
WHAT ARE YOU DOING IN COLORADO?
WOULD YOU BELIEVE I'M LOOKING FOR MY HEART?
I THOUGHT YOU LEFT IT "IN SAN FRANCISCO."
OAKLAND. AND WHAT ARE YOU, A HUNDRED?

WHAT HAPPENED TO OAKLAND?

I WASN'T THERE LONG.

WHEN ARE YOU COMING BACK?

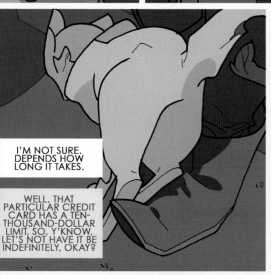

I'M NOT SURE. DEPENDS HOW LONG IT TAKES.

WELL, THAT PARTICULAR CREDIT CARD HAS A TEN-THOUSAND-DOLLAR LIMIT, SO, Y'KNOW, LET'S NOT HAVE IT BE INDEFINITELY, OKAY?

YOU'RE A GOOD FRIEND.

I'M THE BEST.

LET'S NOT GET EXTREME.

WHAT SHOULD I SAY TO YOUR BOSS? HE'S CALLED SIX TIMES.

TELL HIM...

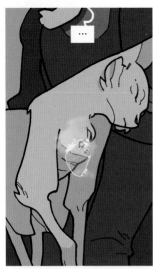

...

EMMA?

XAN, I HAVE TO GO...

IS EVERYTHING OKAY?

NO. I HAVE TO KILL SOMEONE.

RIGHT.

NOW.

THIS IS NOT HAPPENING.

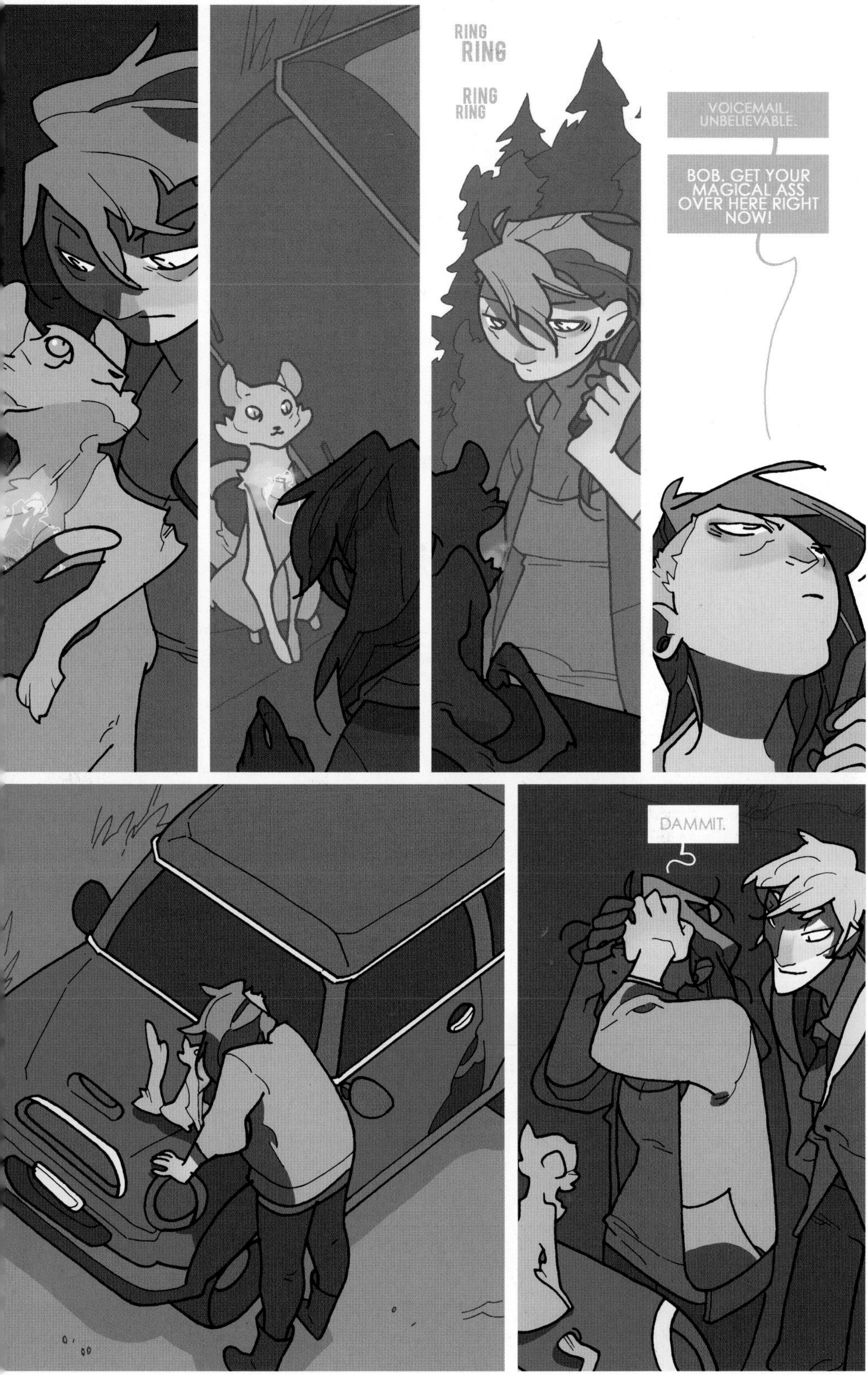
RING RING
RING RING
VOICEMAIL. UNBELIEVABLE.
BOB. GET YOUR MAGICAL ASS OVER HERE RIGHT NOW!
DAMMIT.

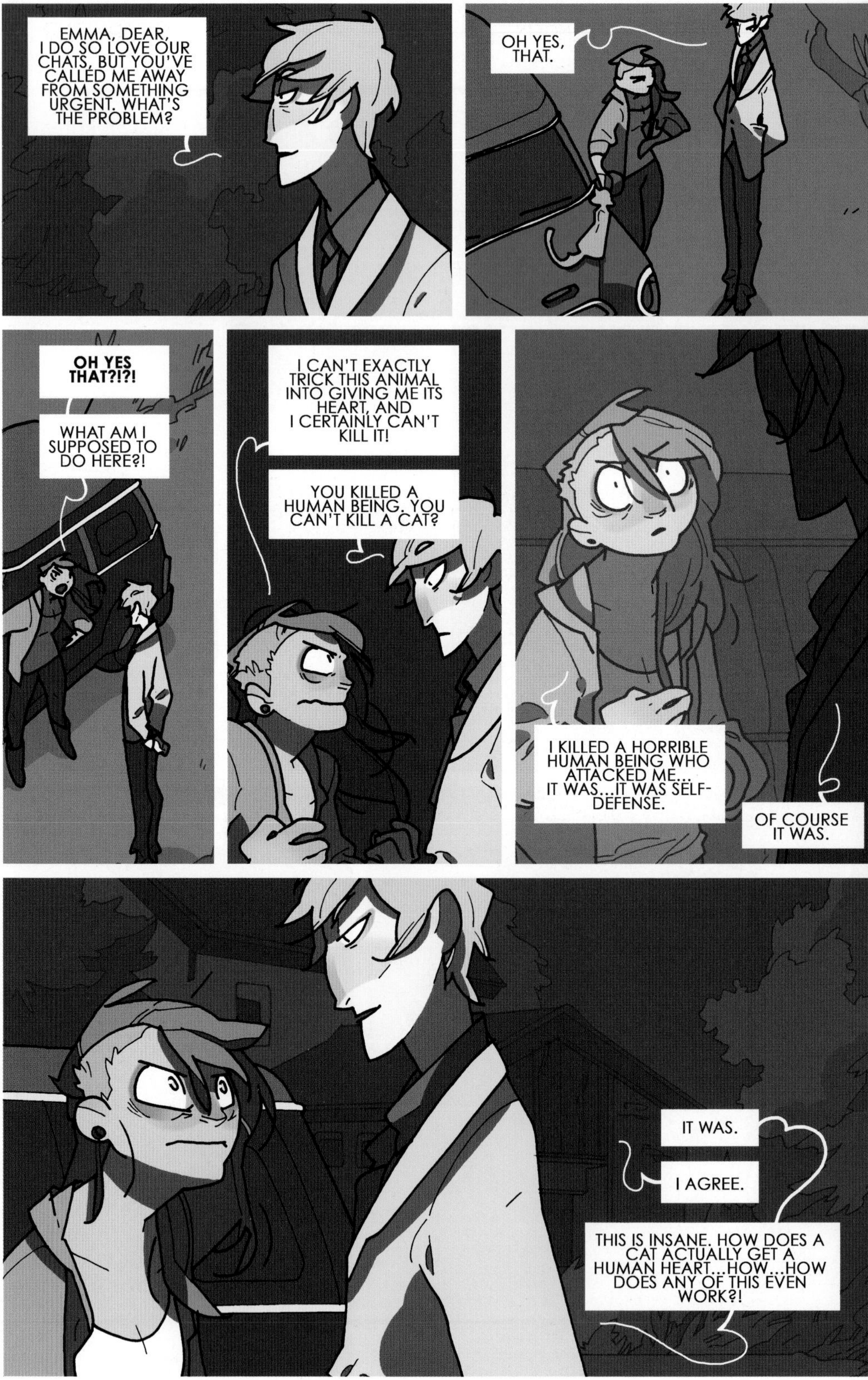
EMMA, DEAR, I DO SO LOVE OUR CHATS, BUT YOU'VE CALLED ME AWAY FROM SOMETHING URGENT. WHAT'S THE PROBLEM?
OH YES, THAT.
OH YES THAT?!?!
WHAT AM I SUPPOSED TO DO HERE?!
I CAN'T EXACTLY TRICK THIS ANIMAL INTO GIVING ME ITS HEART, AND I CERTAINLY CAN'T KILL IT!
YOU KILLED A HUMAN BEING. YOU CAN'T KILL A CAT?
I KILLED A HORRIBLE HUMAN BEING WHO ATTACKED ME... IT WAS...IT WAS SELF-DEFENSE.
OF COURSE IT WAS.
IT WAS.
I AGREE.
THIS IS INSANE. HOW DOES A CAT ACTUALLY GET A HUMAN HEART...HOW...HOW DOES ANY OF THIS EVEN WORK?!

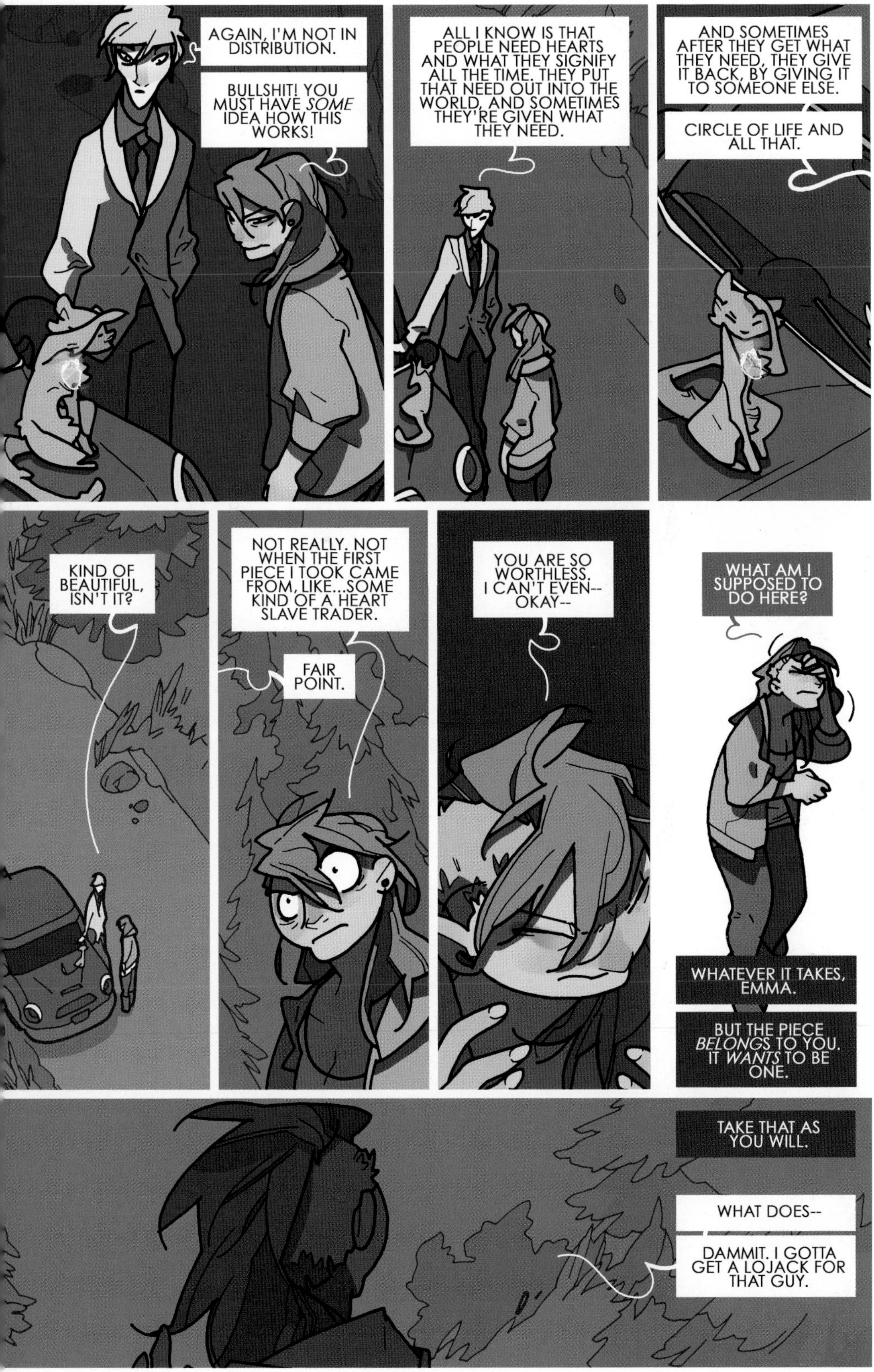
AGAIN, I'M NOT IN DISTRIBUTION.
BULLSHIT! YOU MUST HAVE *SOME* IDEA HOW THIS WORKS!
ALL I KNOW IS THAT PEOPLE NEED HEARTS AND WHAT THEY SIGNIFY ALL THE TIME. THEY PUT THAT NEED OUT INTO THE WORLD, AND SOMETIMES THEY'RE GIVEN WHAT THEY NEED.
AND SOMETIMES AFTER THEY GET WHAT THEY NEED, THEY GIVE IT BACK, BY GIVING IT TO SOMEONE ELSE.
CIRCLE OF LIFE AND ALL THAT.
KIND OF BEAUTIFUL, ISN'T IT?
NOT REALLY. NOT WHEN THE FIRST PIECE I TOOK CAME FROM, LIKE...SOME KIND OF A HEART SLAVE TRADER.
FAIR POINT.
YOU ARE SO WORTHLESS. I CAN'T EVEN-- OKAY--
WHAT AM I SUPPOSED TO DO HERE?
WHATEVER IT TAKES, EMMA.
BUT THE PIECE *BELONGS* TO YOU. IT *WANTS* TO BE ONE.
TAKE THAT AS YOU WILL.
WHAT DOES--
DAMMIT. I GOTTA GET A LOJACK FOR THAT GUY.

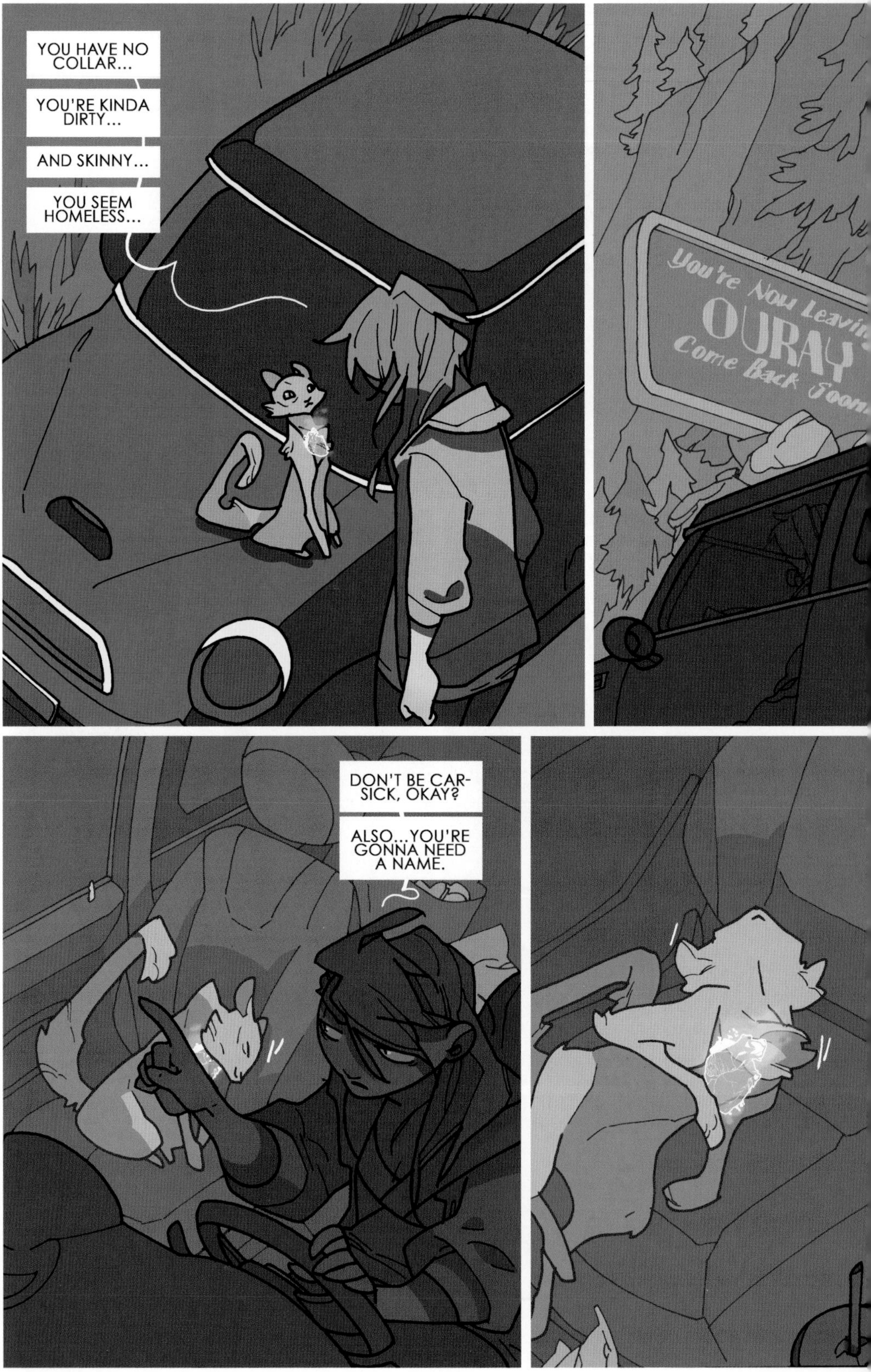
YOU HAVE NO COLLAR...
YOU'RE KINDA DIRTY...
AND SKINNY...
YOU SEEM HOMELESS...
You're Now Leaving OURAY Come Back Soon
DON'T BE CAR-SICK, OKAY?
ALSO...YOU'RE GONNA NEED A NAME.

PIECE no. 4

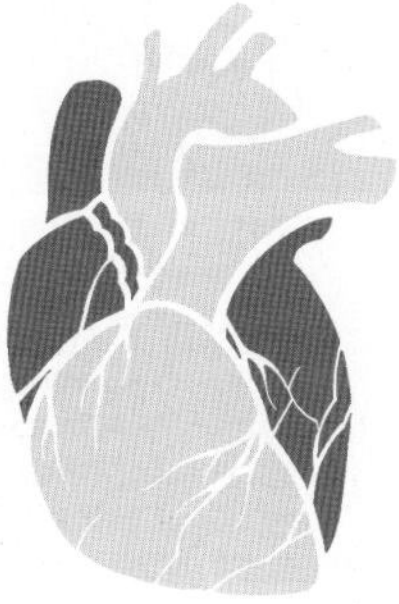

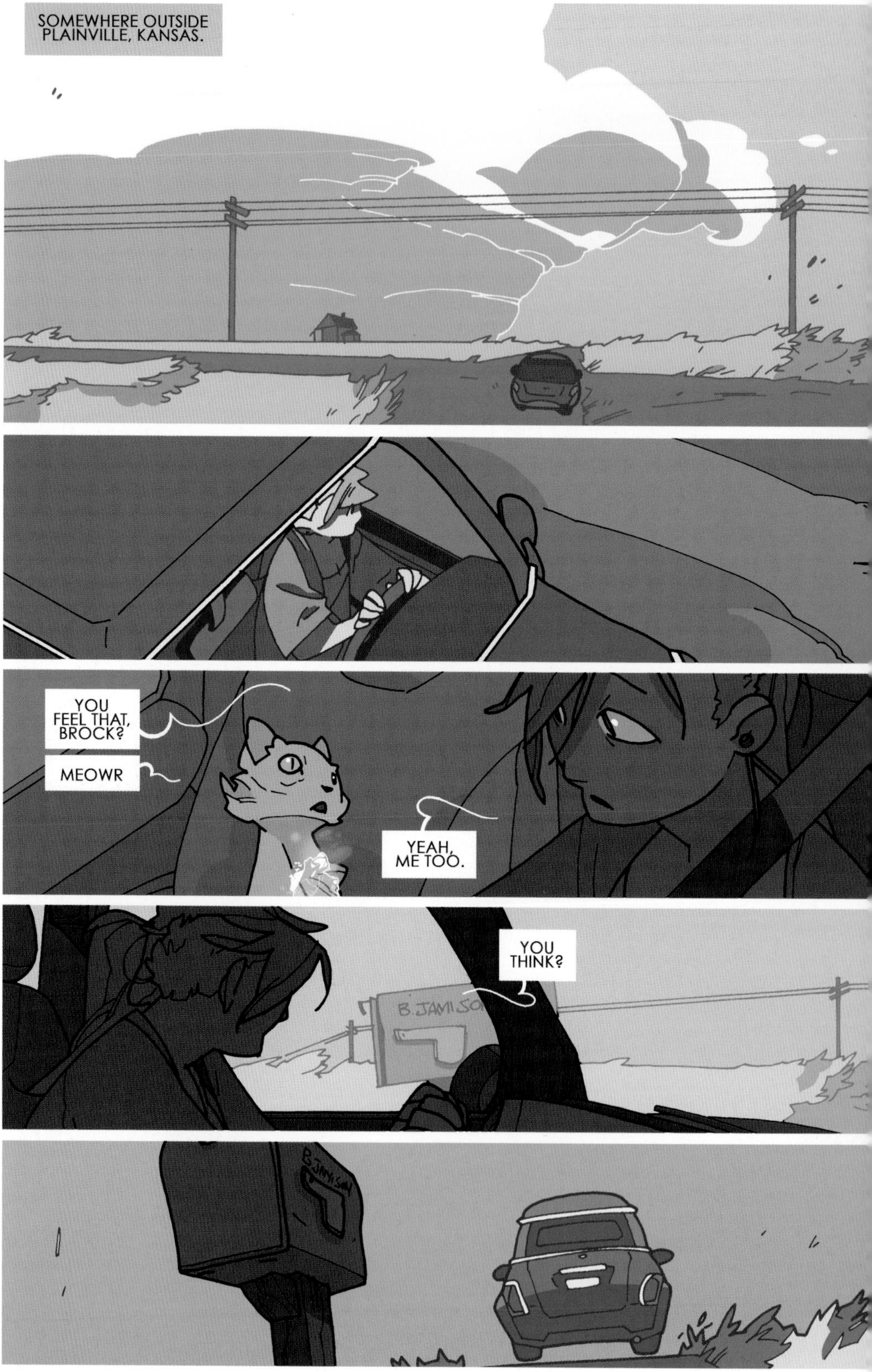
SOMEWHERE OUTSIDE PLAINVILLE, KANSAS.
YOU FEEL THAT, BROCK?
MEOWR
YEAH, ME TOO.
YOU THINK?
B. JAMISON

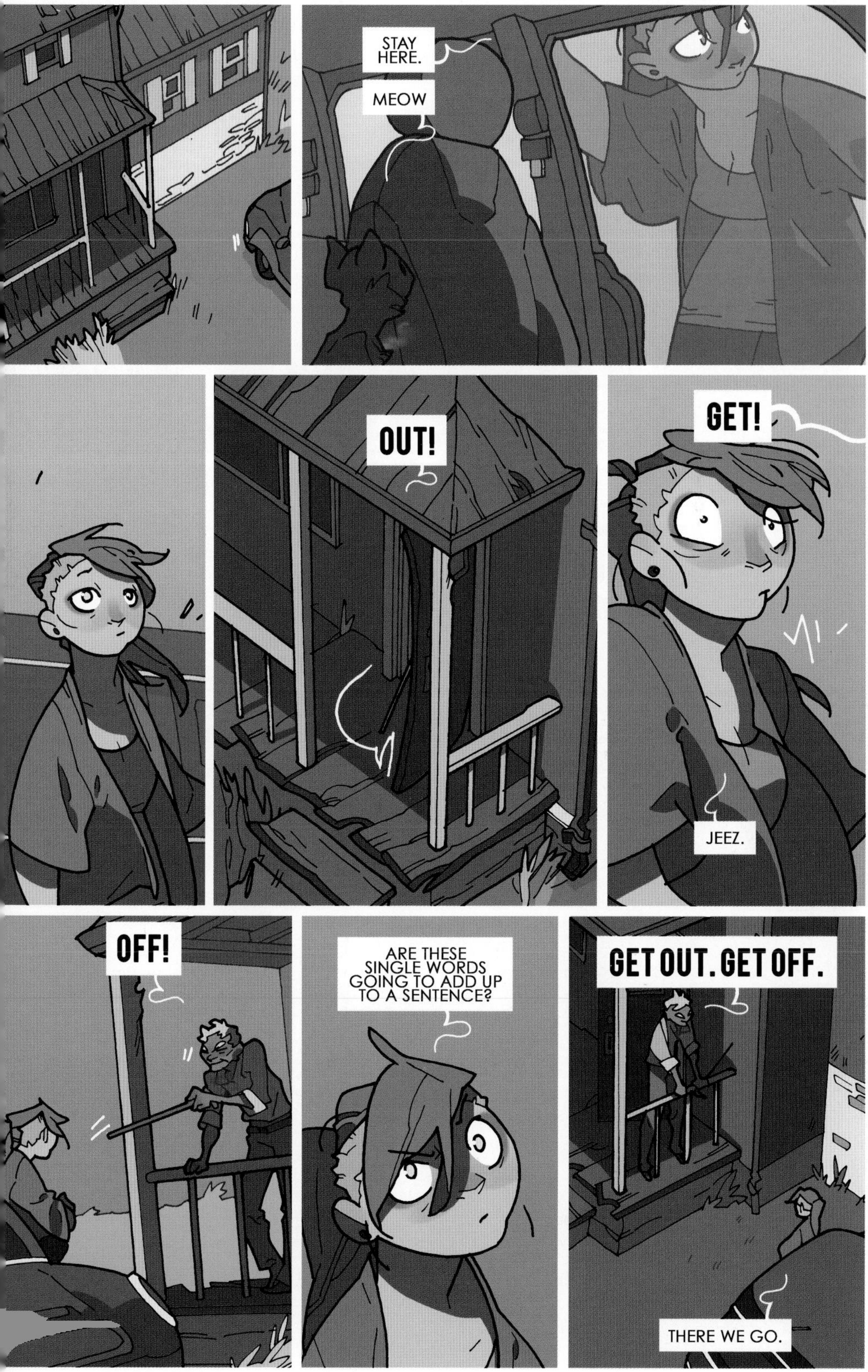
STAY HERE.
MEOW
OUT!
GET!
JEEZ.
OFF!
ARE THESE SINGLE WORDS GOING TO ADD UP TO A SENTENCE?
GET OUT. GET OFF.
THERE WE GO.

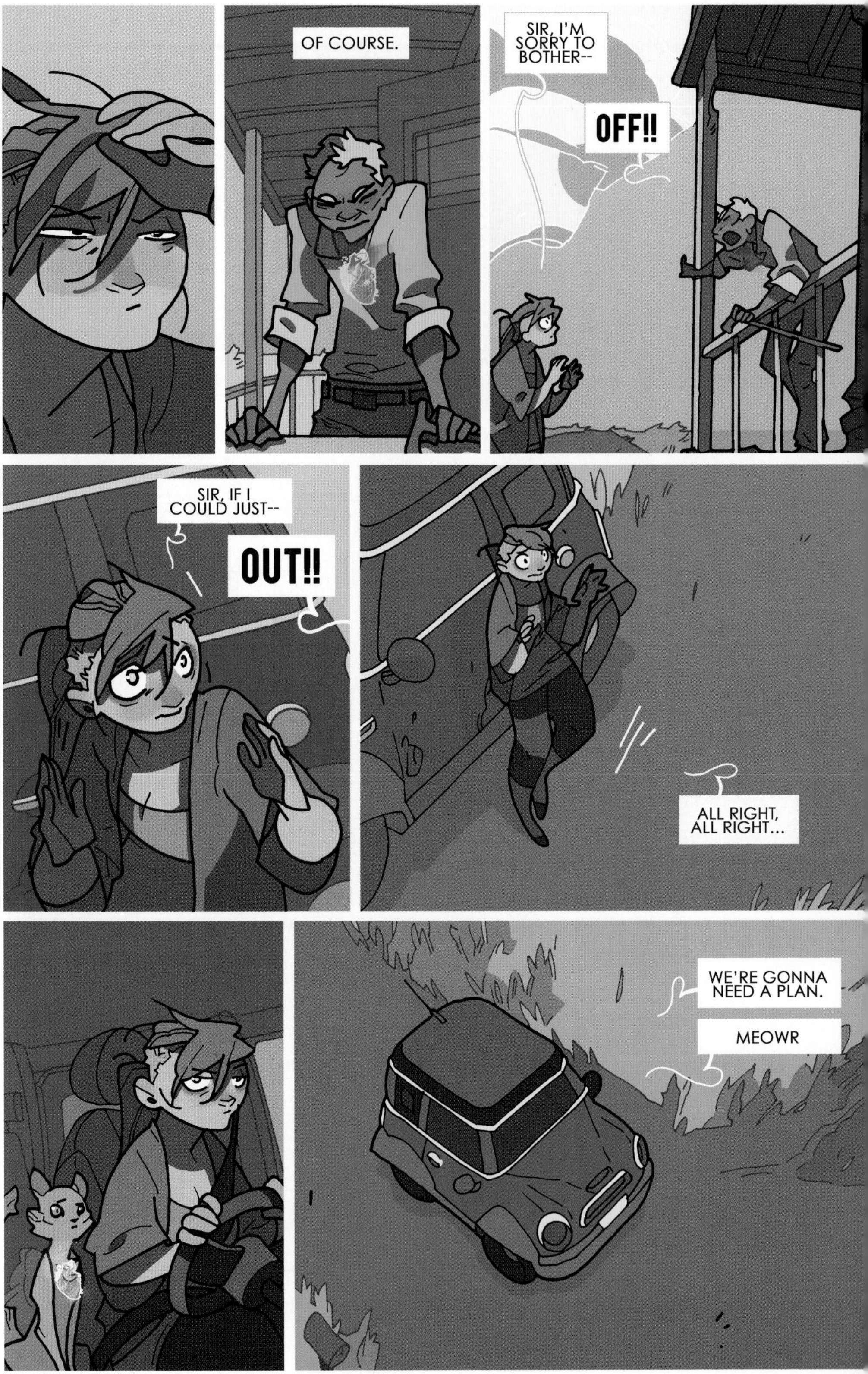
OF COURSE.
SIR, I'M SORRY TO BOTHER--
OFF!!
SIR, IF I COULD JUST--
OUT!!
ALL RIGHT, ALL RIGHT...
WE'RE GONNA NEED A PLAN.
MEOWR

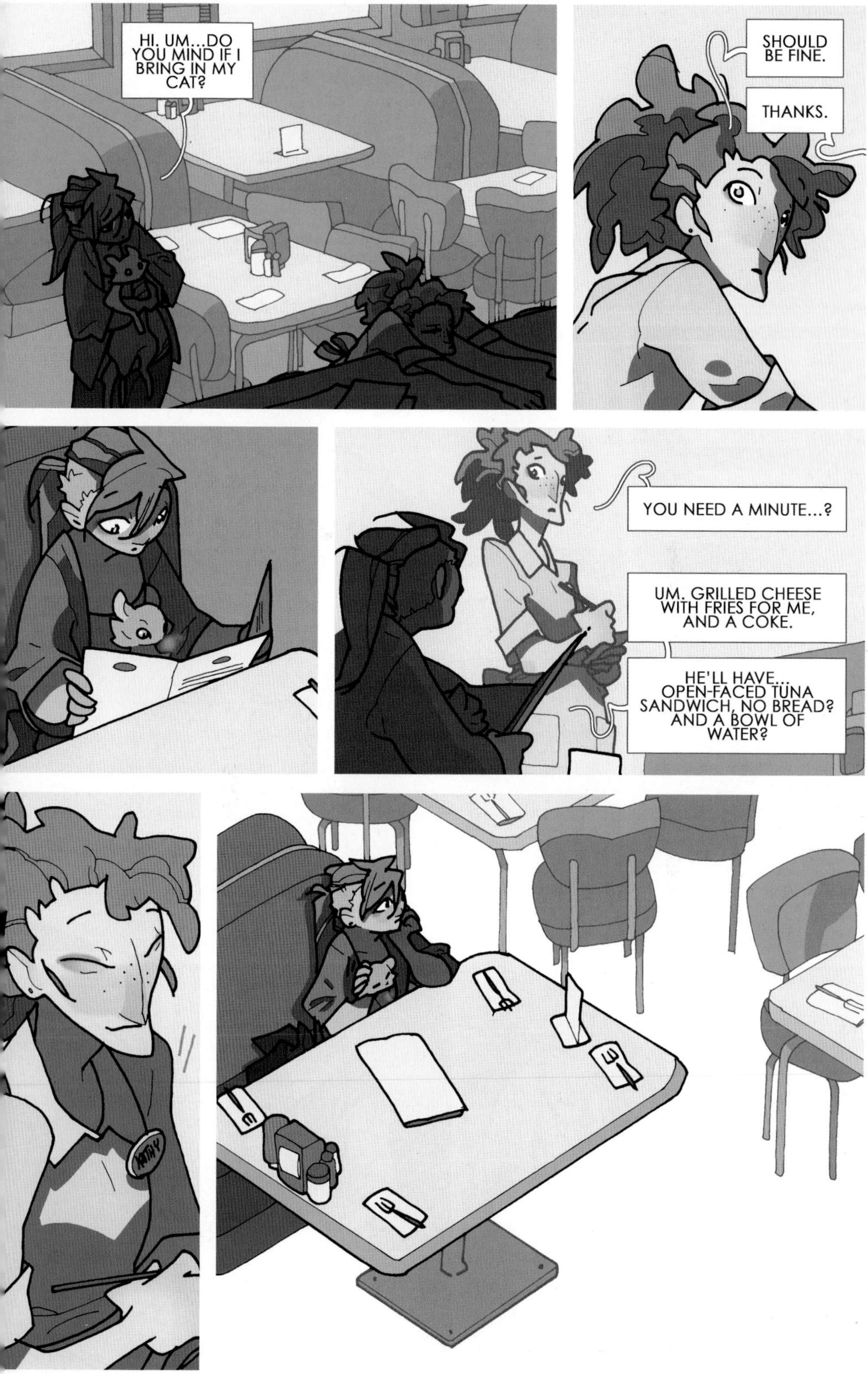
HI. UM...DO YOU MIND IF I BRING IN MY CAT?
SHOULD BE FINE.
THANKS.
YOU NEED A MINUTE...?
UM. GRILLED CHEESE WITH FRIES FOR ME, AND A COKE.
HE'LL HAVE... OPEN-FACED TUNA SANDWICH, NO BREAD? AND A BOWL OF WATER?
KATHY

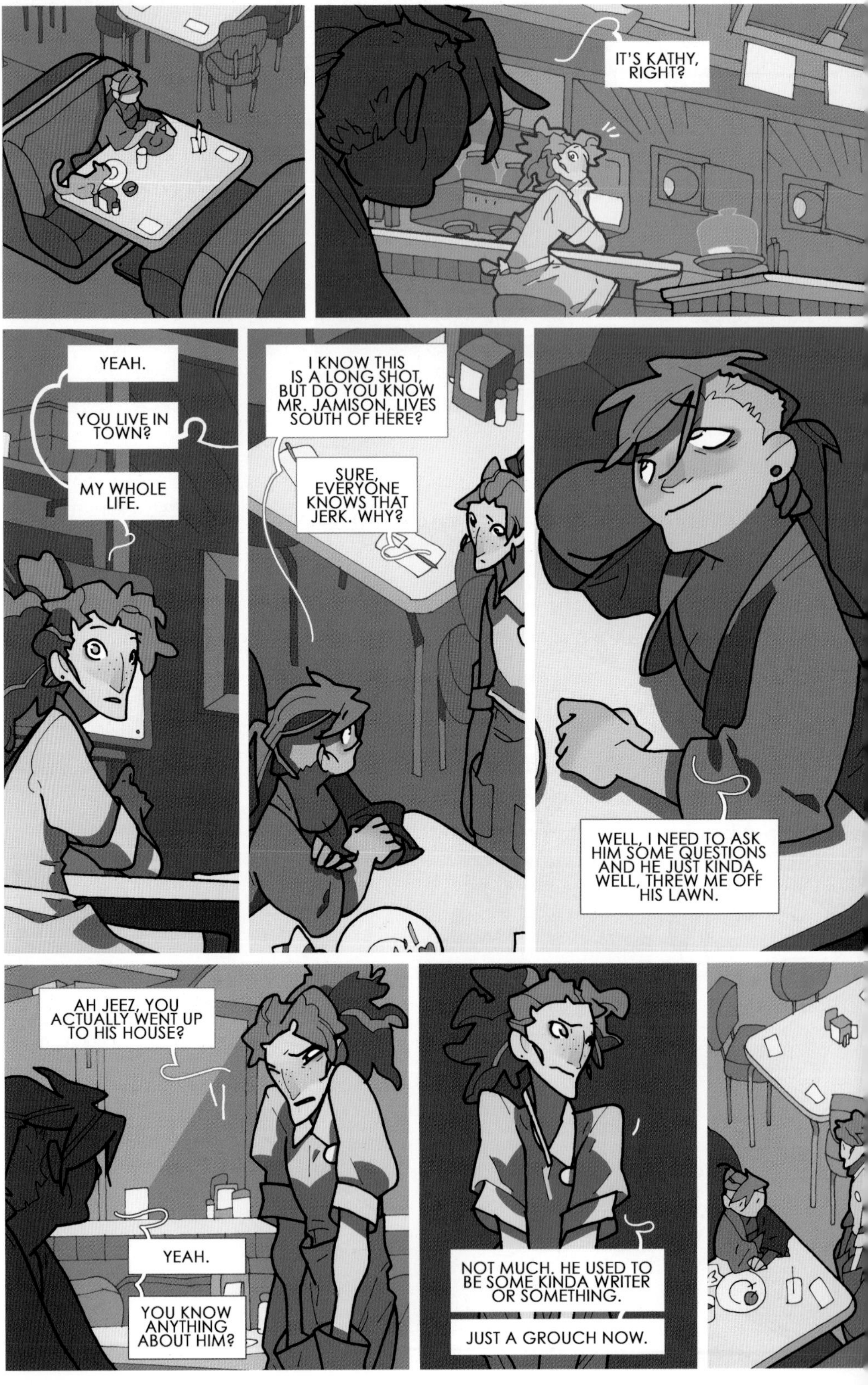
IT'S KATHY, RIGHT?
YEAH.
YOU LIVE IN TOWN?
MY WHOLE LIFE.
I KNOW THIS IS A LONG SHOT, BUT DO YOU KNOW MR. JAMISON, LIVES SOUTH OF HERE?
SURE, EVERYONE KNOWS THAT JERK. WHY?
WELL, I NEED TO ASK HIM SOME QUESTIONS AND HE JUST KINDA, WELL, THREW ME OFF HIS LAWN.
AH JEEZ, YOU ACTUALLY WENT UP TO HIS HOUSE?
YEAH.
YOU KNOW ANYTHING ABOUT HIM?
NOT MUCH. HE USED TO BE SOME KINDA WRITER OR SOMETHING.
JUST A GROUCH NOW.

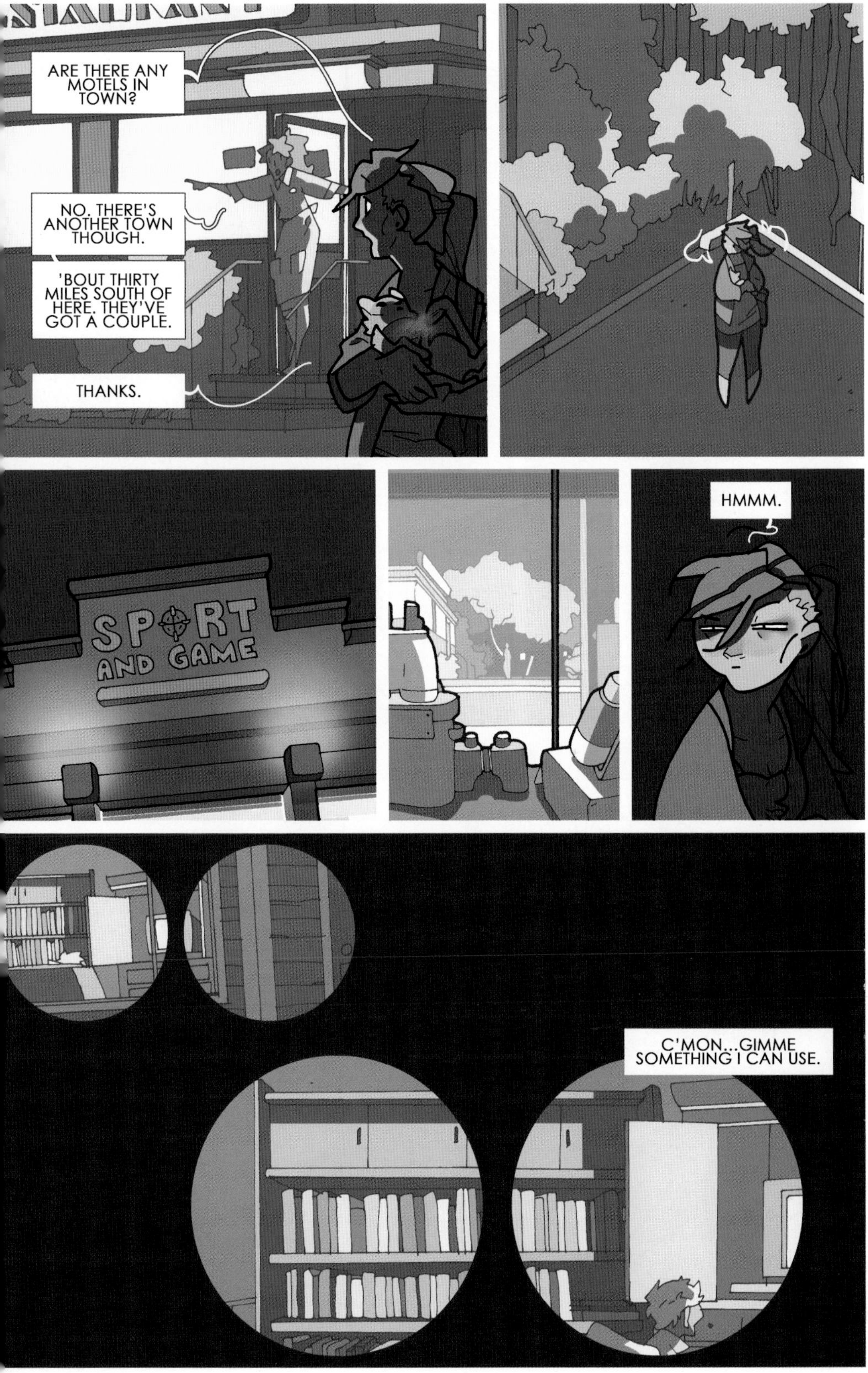
ARE THERE ANY MOTELS IN TOWN?
NO. THERE'S ANOTHER TOWN THOUGH.
'BOUT THIRTY MILES SOUTH OF HERE. THEY'VE GOT A COUPLE.
THANKS.
SPORT AND GAME
HMMM.
C'MON...GIMME SOMETHING I CAN USE.

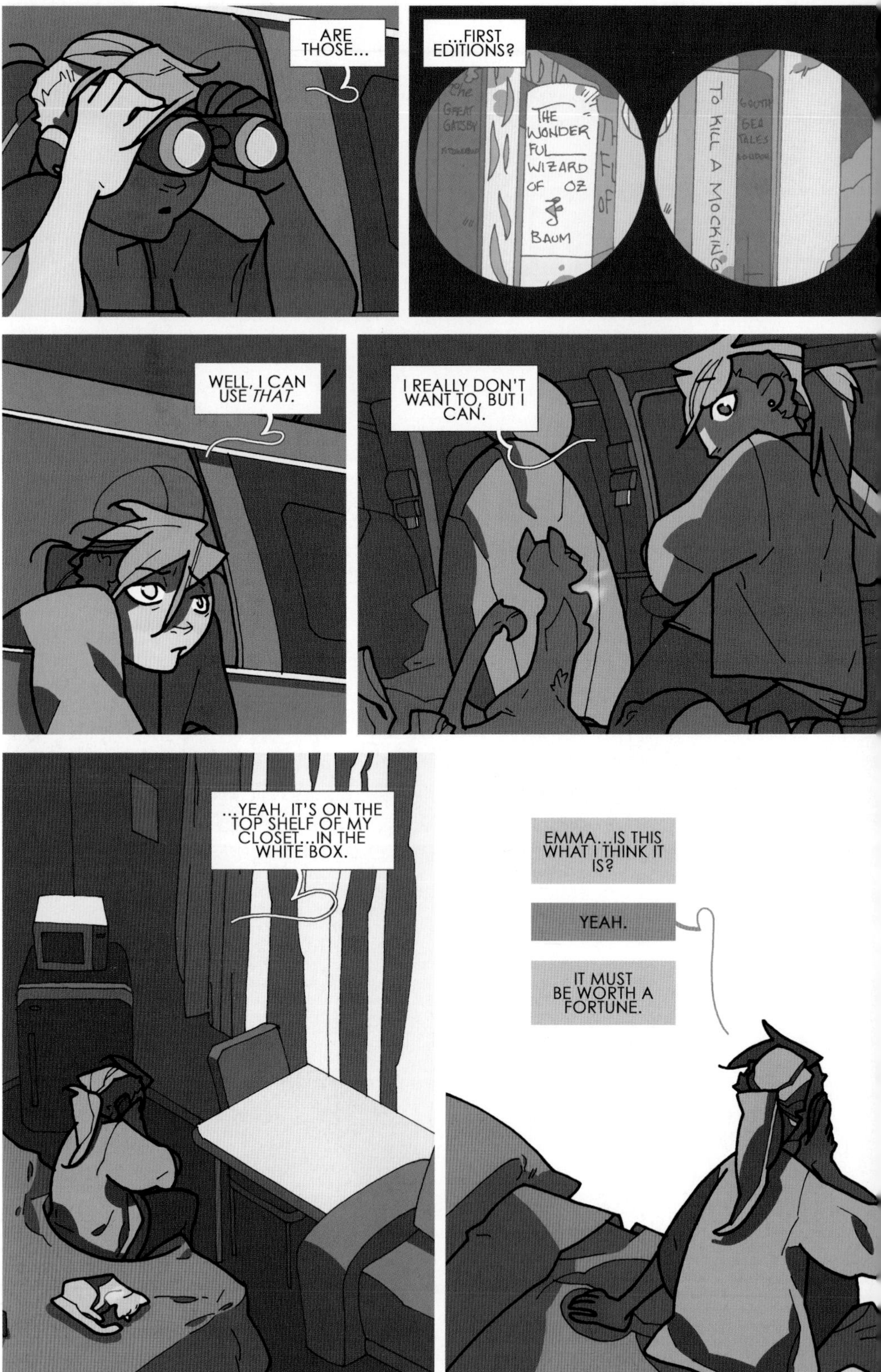
ARE THOSE...
...FIRST EDITIONS?
The GREAT GATSBY
THE WONDER FUL WIZARD OF OZ
BAUM
TO KILL A MOCKING
WELL, I CAN USE *THAT.*
I REALLY DON'T WANT TO, BUT I CAN.
...YEAH, IT'S ON THE TOP SHELF OF MY CLOSET...IN THE WHITE BOX.
EMMA...IS THIS WHAT I THINK IT IS?
YEAH.
IT MUST BE WORTH A FORTUNE.

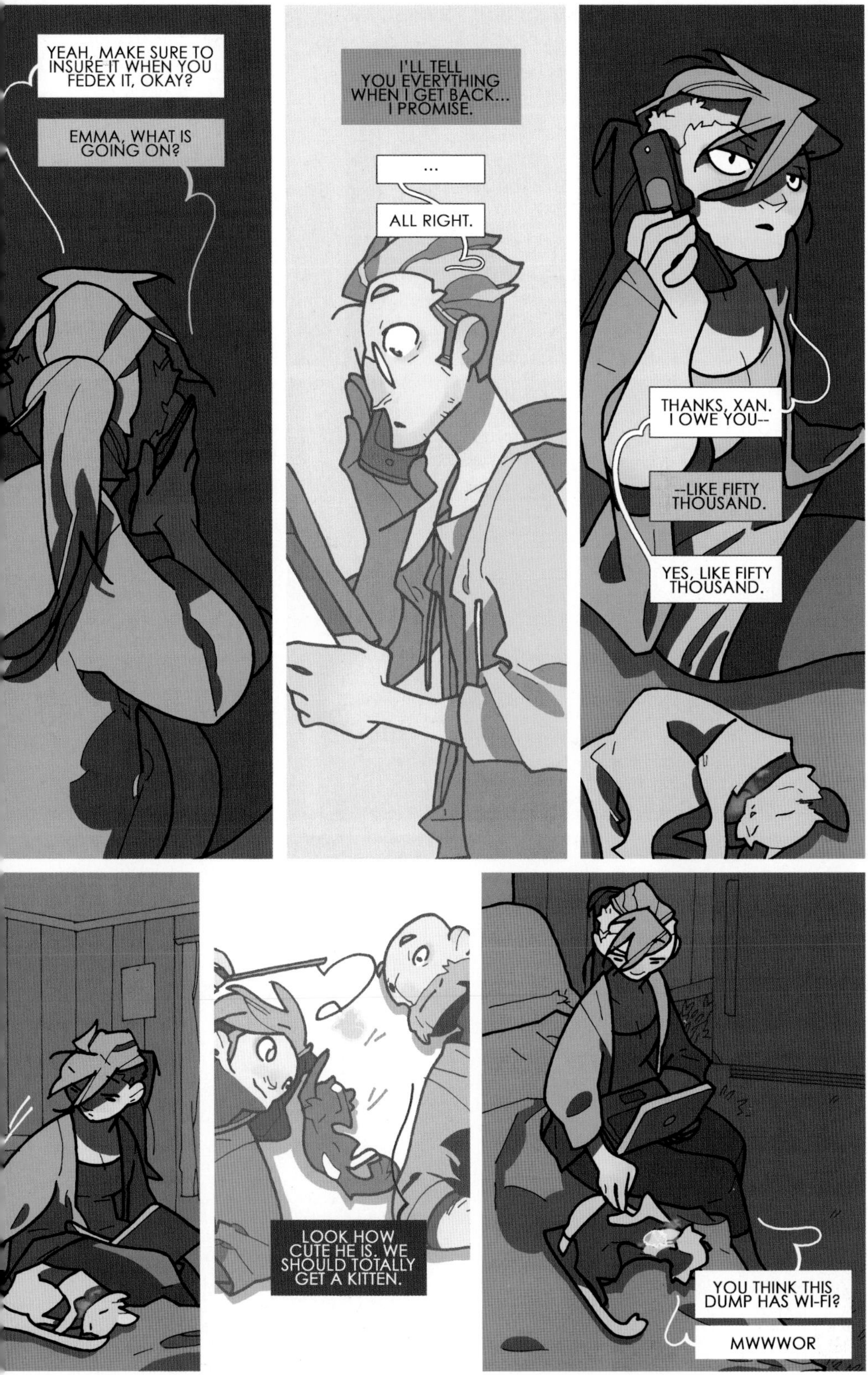
YEAH, MAKE SURE TO INSURE IT WHEN YOU FEDEX IT, OKAY?
EMMA, WHAT IS GOING ON?
I'LL TELL YOU EVERYTHING WHEN I GET BACK... I PROMISE.
...
ALL RIGHT.
THANKS, XAN. I OWE YOU--
--LIKE FIFTY THOUSAND.
YES, LIKE FIFTY THOUSAND.
LOOK HOW CUTE HE IS. WE SHOULD TOTALLY GET A KITTEN.
YOU THINK THIS DUMP HAS WI-FI?
MWWWOR

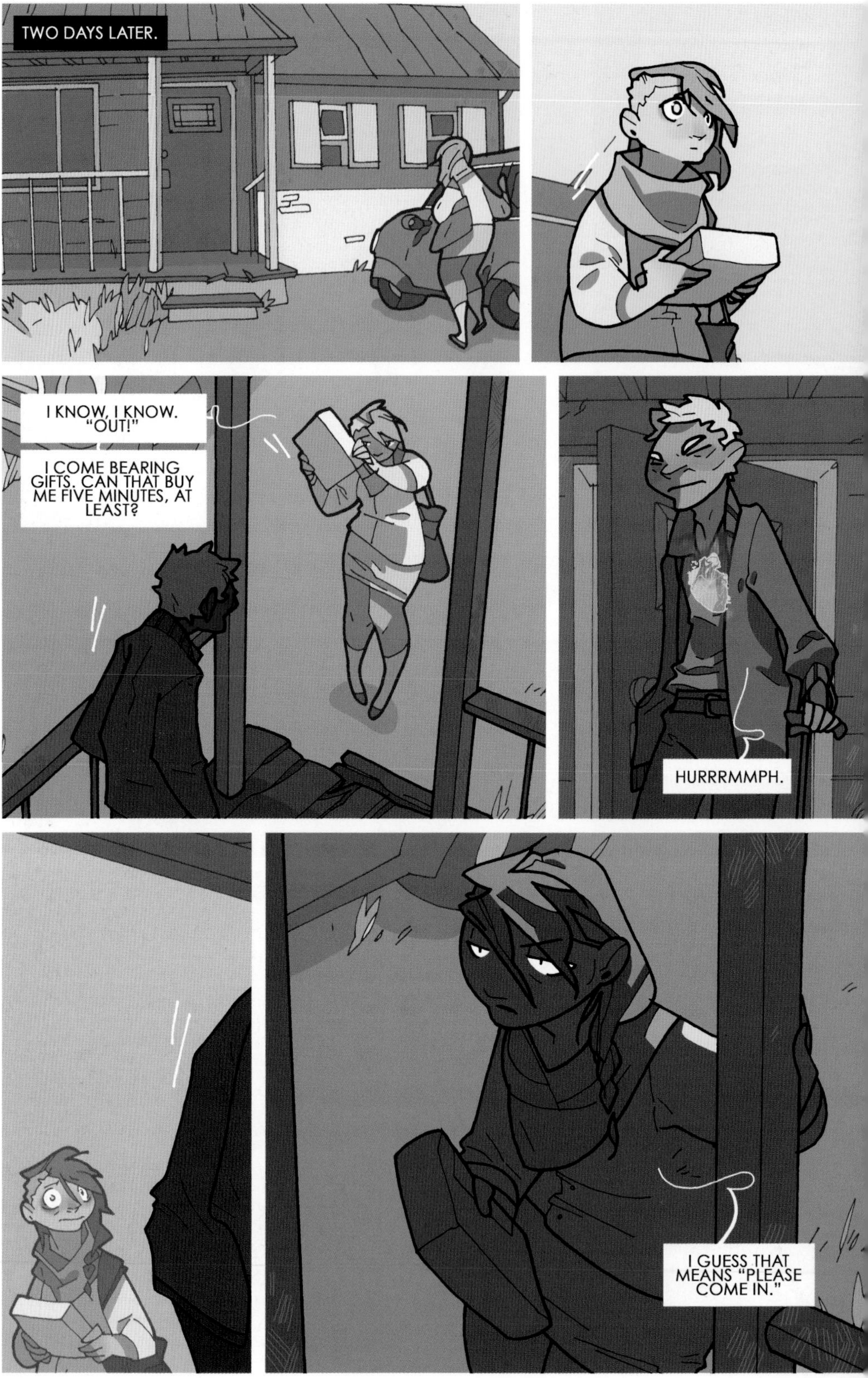
TWO DAYS LATER.
I KNOW, I KNOW. "OUT!"
I COME BEARING GIFTS. CAN THAT BUY ME FIVE MINUTES, AT LEAST?
HURRRMMPH.
I GUESS THAT MEANS "PLEASE COME IN."

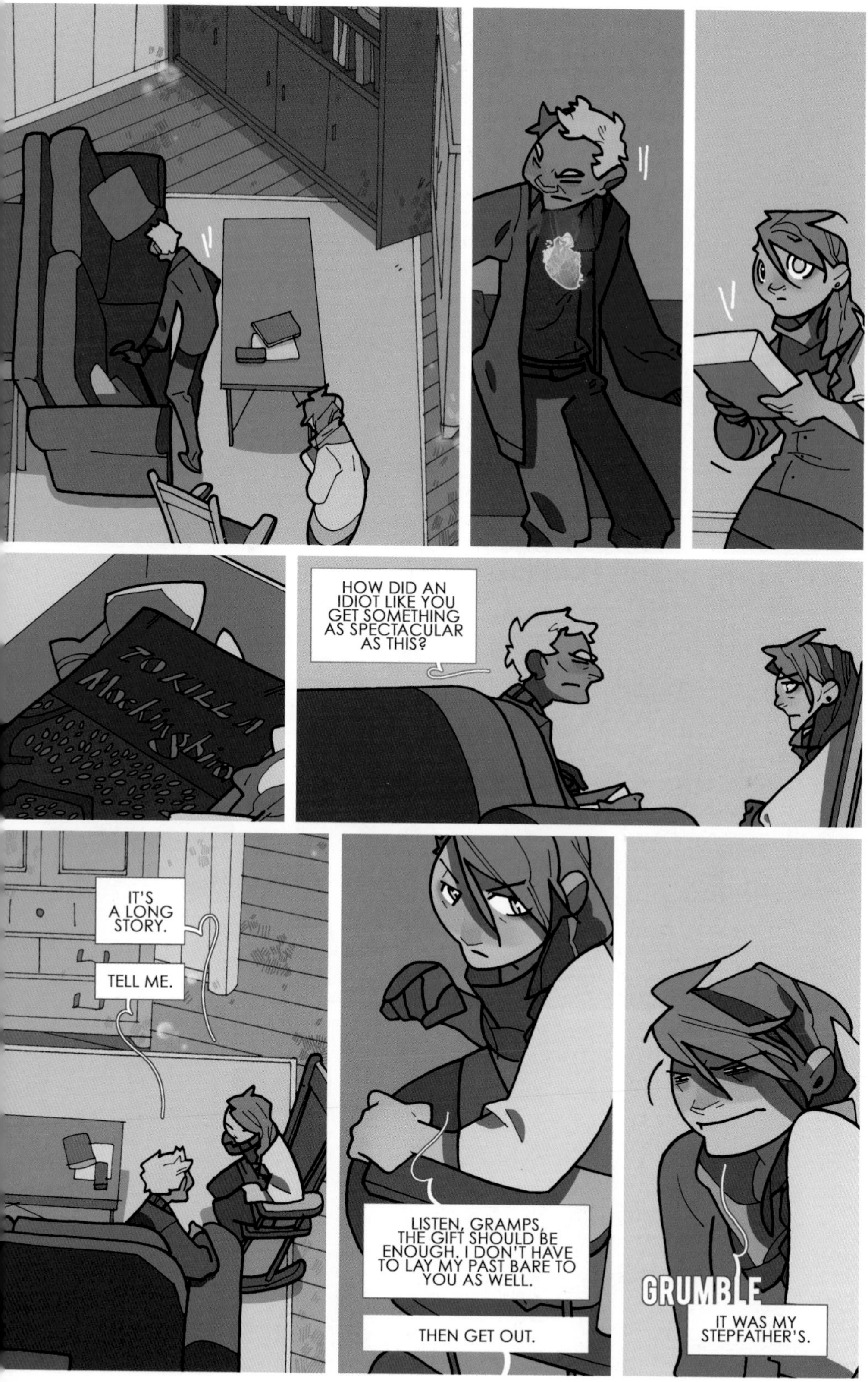
TO KILL A Mockingbird
HOW DID AN IDIOT LIKE YOU GET SOMETHING AS SPECTACULAR AS THIS?
IT'S A LONG STORY.
TELL ME.
LISTEN, GRAMPS, THE GIFT SHOULD BE ENOUGH. I DON'T HAVE TO LAY MY PAST BARE TO YOU AS WELL.
THEN GET OUT.
GRUMBLE
IT WAS MY STEPFATHER'S.

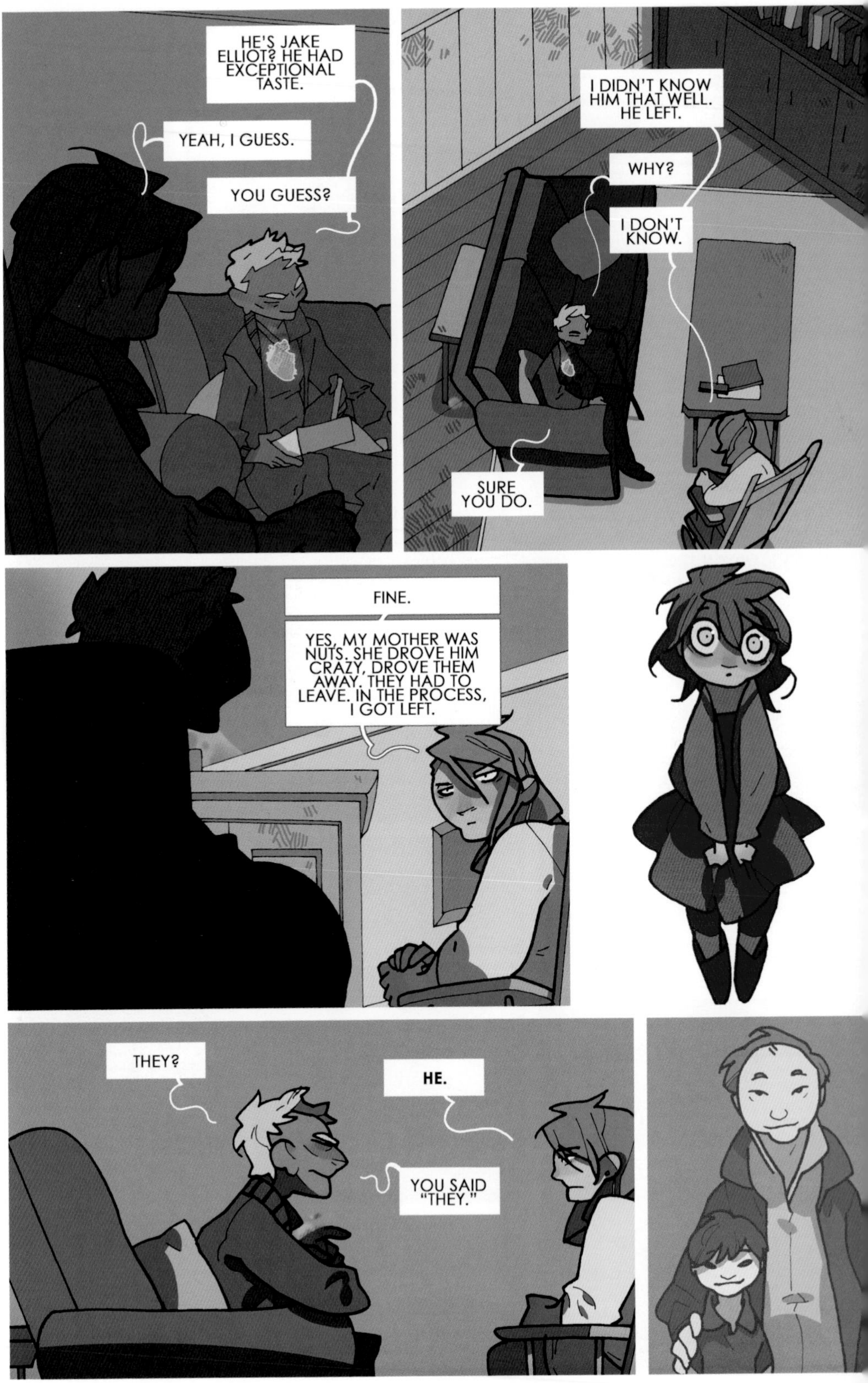
HE'S JAKE ELLIOT? HE HAD EXCEPTIONAL TASTE.
YEAH, I GUESS.
YOU GUESS?
I DIDN'T KNOW HIM THAT WELL. HE LEFT.
WHY?
I DON'T KNOW.
SURE YOU DO.
FINE.
YES, MY MOTHER WAS NUTS. SHE DROVE HIM CRAZY, DROVE THEM AWAY. THEY HAD TO LEAVE. IN THE PROCESS, I GOT LEFT.
THEY?
HE.
YOU SAID "THEY."

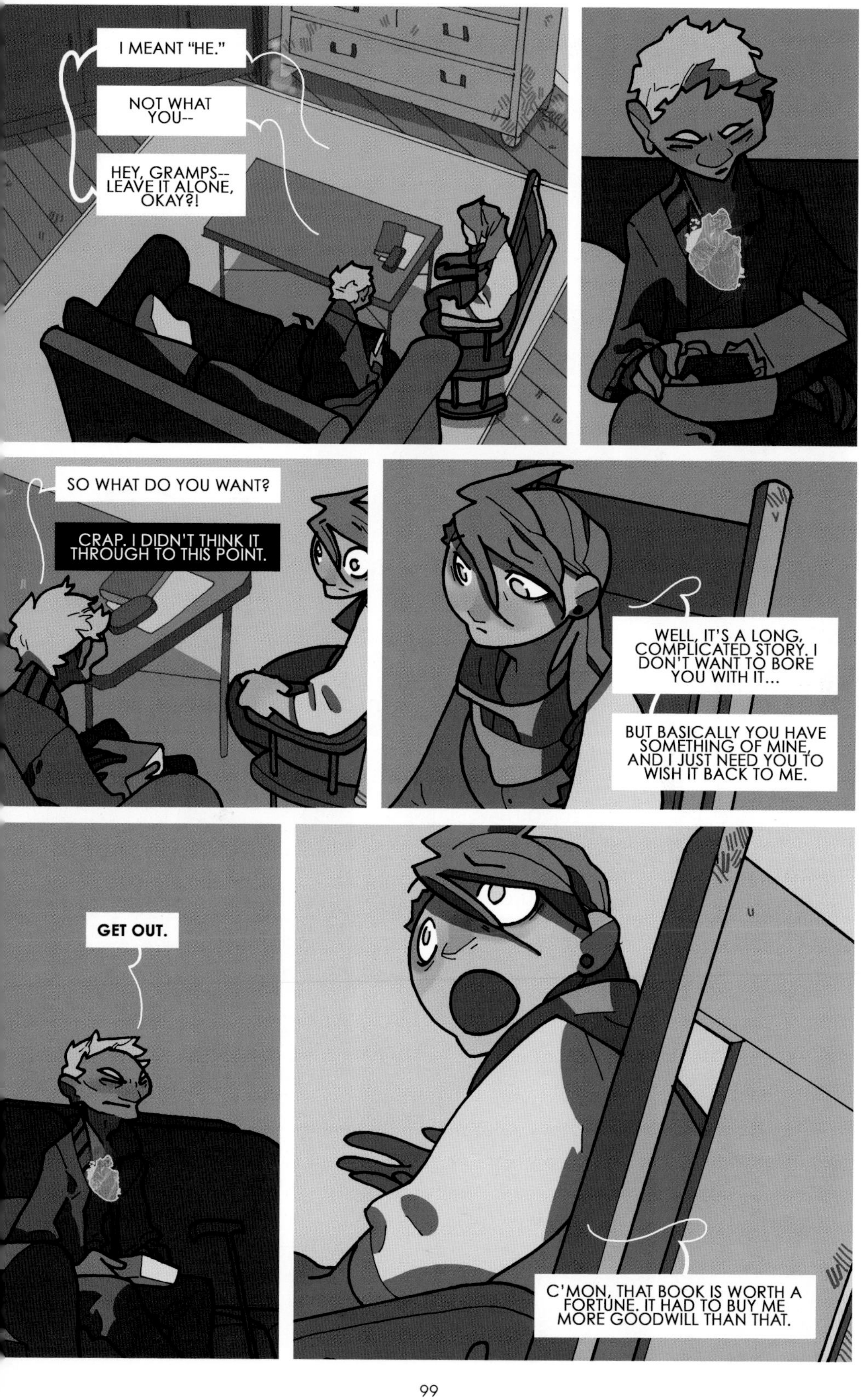
I MEANT "HE."
NOT WHAT YOU--
HEY, GRAMPS-- LEAVE IT ALONE, OKAY?!
SO WHAT DO YOU WANT?
CRAP. I DIDN'T THINK IT THROUGH TO THIS POINT.
WELL, IT'S A LONG, COMPLICATED STORY. I DON'T WANT TO BORE YOU WITH IT...
BUT BASICALLY YOU HAVE SOMETHING OF MINE, AND I JUST NEED YOU TO WISH IT BACK TO ME.
GET OUT.
C'MON, THAT BOOK IS WORTH A FORTUNE. IT HAD TO BUY ME MORE GOODWILL THAN THAT.

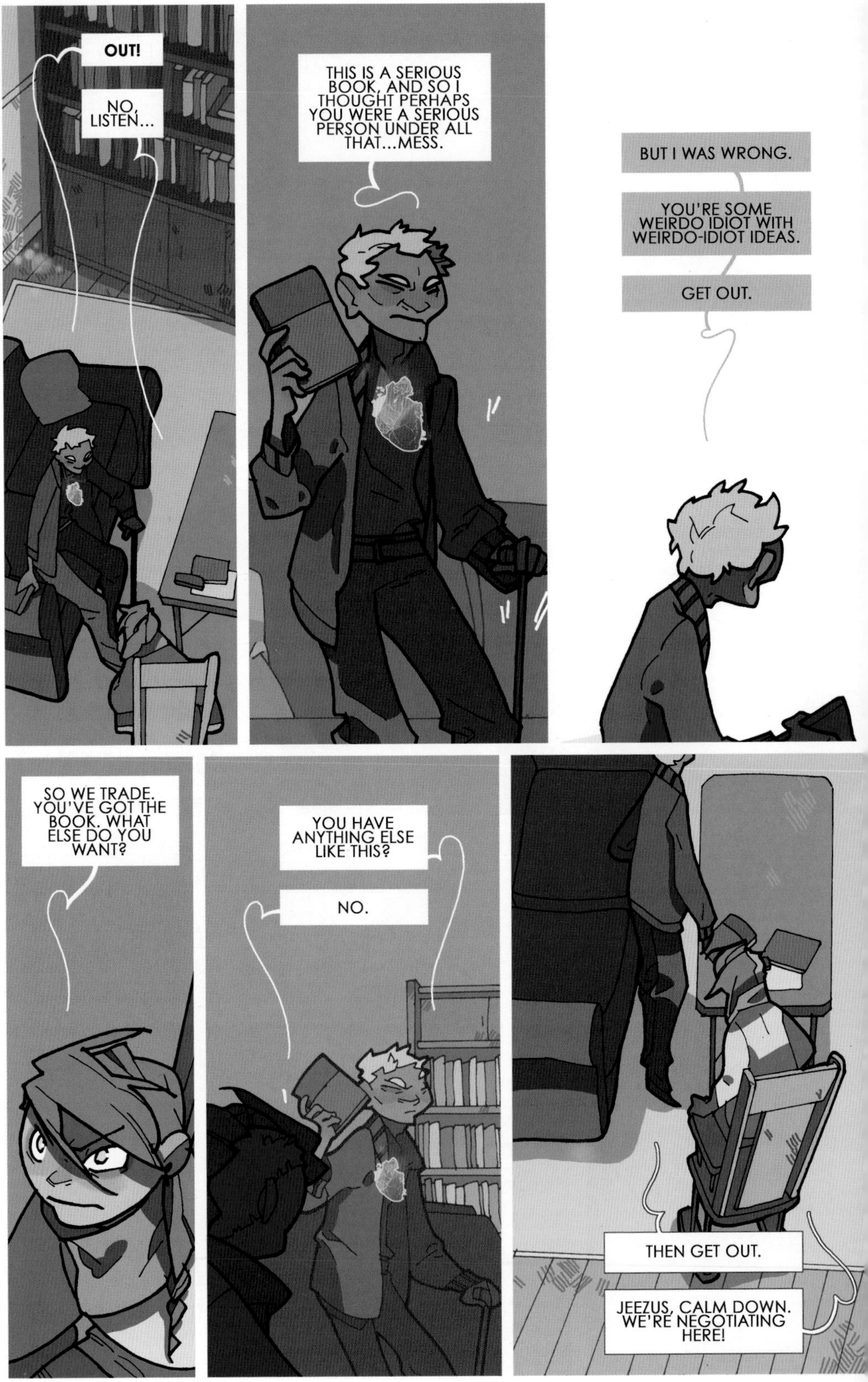

OUT!
NO, LISTEN...
THIS IS A SERIOUS BOOK, AND SO I THOUGHT PERHAPS YOU WERE A SERIOUS PERSON UNDER ALL THAT...MESS.
BUT I WAS WRONG.
YOU'RE SOME WEIRDO IDIOT WITH WEIRDO-IDIOT IDEAS.
GET OUT.
SO WE TRADE. YOU'VE GOT THE BOOK. WHAT ELSE DO YOU WANT?
YOU HAVE ANYTHING ELSE LIKE THIS?
NO.
THEN GET OUT.
JEEZUS, CALM DOWN. WE'RE NEGOTIATING HERE!

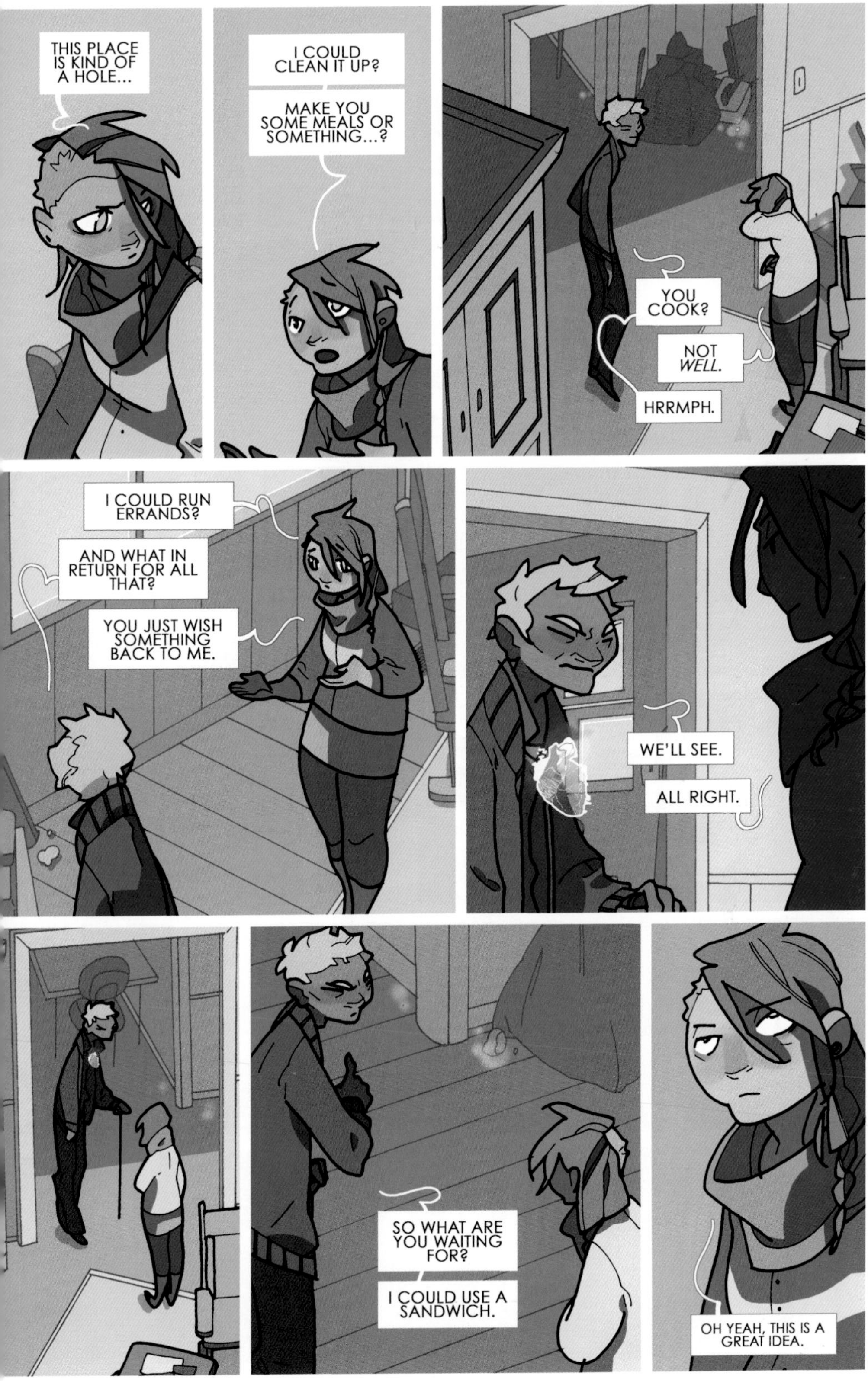
THIS PLACE IS KIND OF A HOLE...
I COULD CLEAN IT UP?
MAKE YOU SOME MEALS OR SOMETHING...?
YOU COOK?
NOT *WELL*.
HRRMPH.
I COULD RUN ERRANDS?
AND WHAT IN RETURN FOR ALL THAT?
YOU JUST WISH SOMETHING BACK TO ME.
WE'LL SEE.
ALL RIGHT.
SO WHAT ARE YOU WAITING FOR?
I COULD USE A SANDWICH.
OH YEAH, THIS IS A GREAT IDEA.

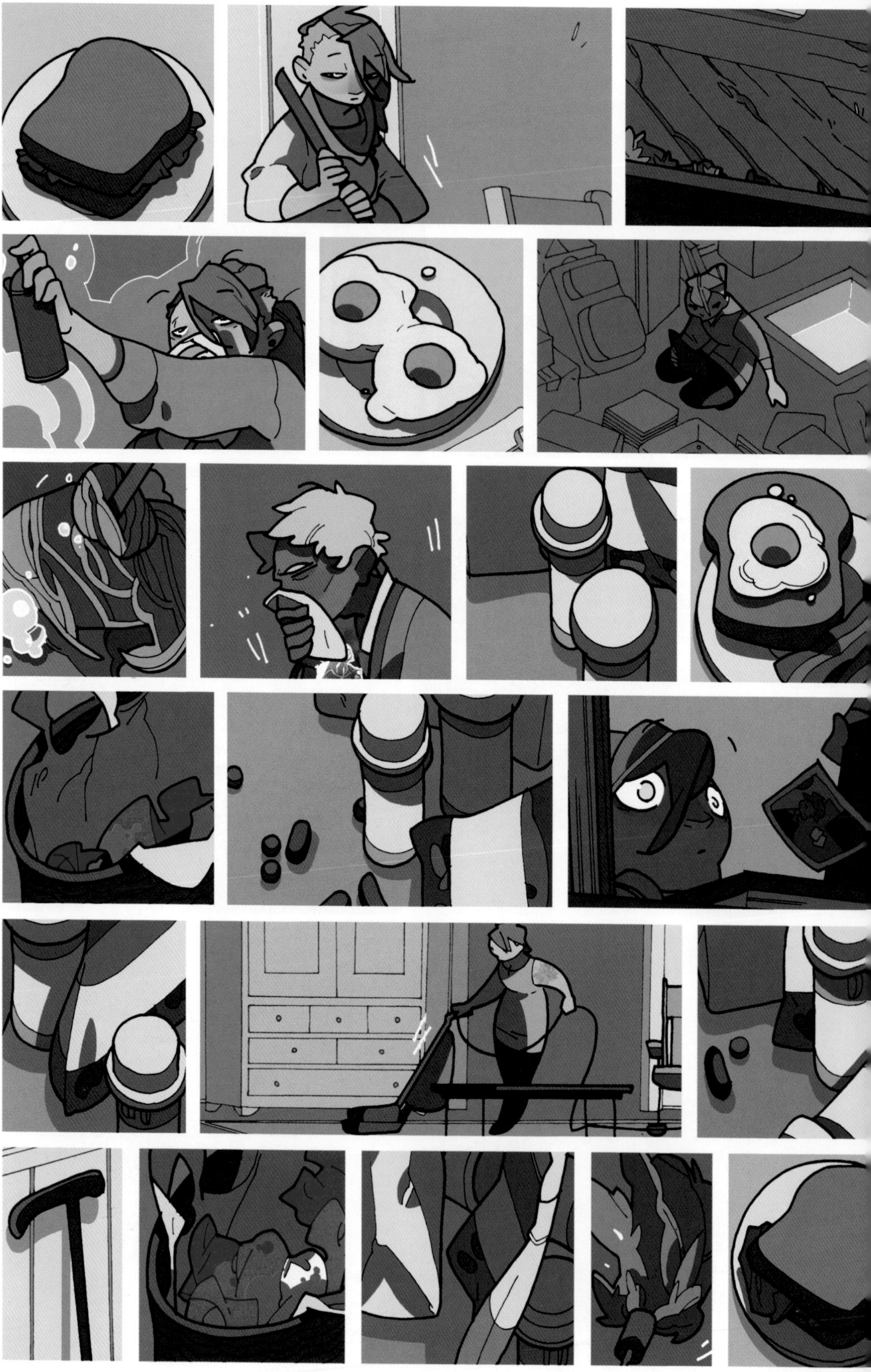

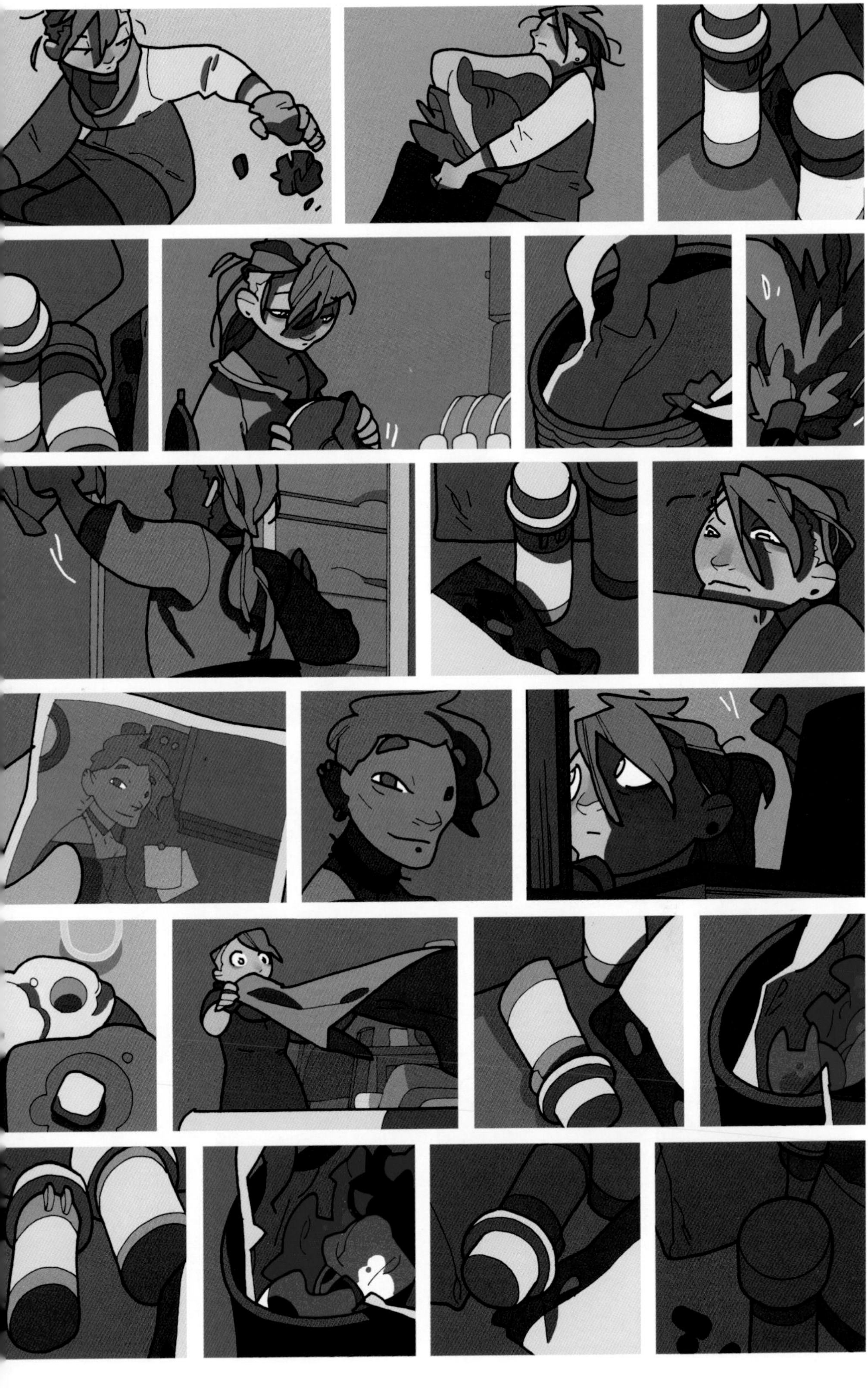

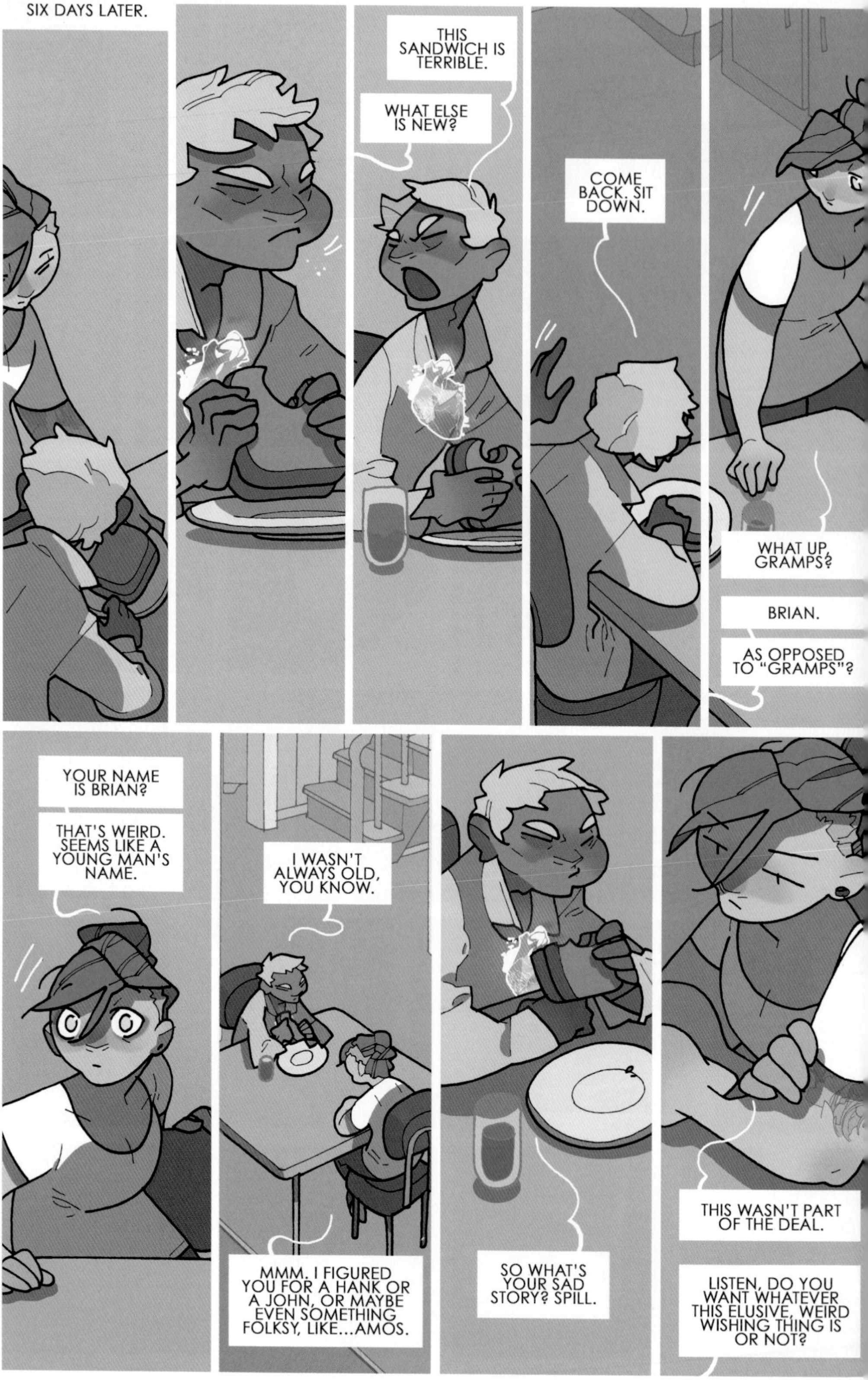
SIX DAYS LATER.
THIS SANDWICH IS TERRIBLE.
WHAT ELSE IS NEW?
COME BACK. SIT DOWN.
WHAT UP, GRAMPS?
BRIAN.
AS OPPOSED TO "GRAMPS"?
YOUR NAME IS BRIAN?
THAT'S WEIRD. SEEMS LIKE A YOUNG MAN'S NAME.
I WASN'T ALWAYS OLD, YOU KNOW.
MMM. I FIGURED YOU FOR A HANK OR A JOHN, OR MAYBE EVEN SOMETHING FOLKSY, LIKE...AMOS.
SO WHAT'S YOUR SAD STORY? SPILL.
THIS WASN'T PART OF THE DEAL.
LISTEN, DO YOU WANT WHATEVER THIS ELUSIVE, WEIRD WISHING THING IS OR NOT?

SIGH

FINE.

WHAT DO YOU WANT TO KNOW?

TELL ME ABOUT THIS STEPFATHER OF YOURS.

C'MON, EM!

MY MOTHER WAS KIND OF A NIGHTMARE. BUT SHE DID GET IT TOGETHER LONG ENOUGH TO SNAG A NEW HUSBAND.

JAKE. I LIKED HIM. HE WAS A GOOD DAD. HE HAD A SON, MILES, OLDER THAN ME BY A FEW YEARS.

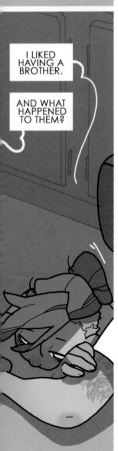

I LIKED HAVING A BROTHER.

AND WHAT HAPPENED TO THEM?

MY MOTHER HAPPENED.

EVENTUALLY JAKE COULDN'T HANDLE IT. HE LEFT, AND MILES WITH HIM.

I LEFT HER AS SOON AS I COULD TOO.

SEVENTEEN AND DUMB AS A BOX OF HAIR, BUT JUST GLAD TO BE FREE OF HER.

SHE DIED LAST YEAR.

I DIDN'T GO.

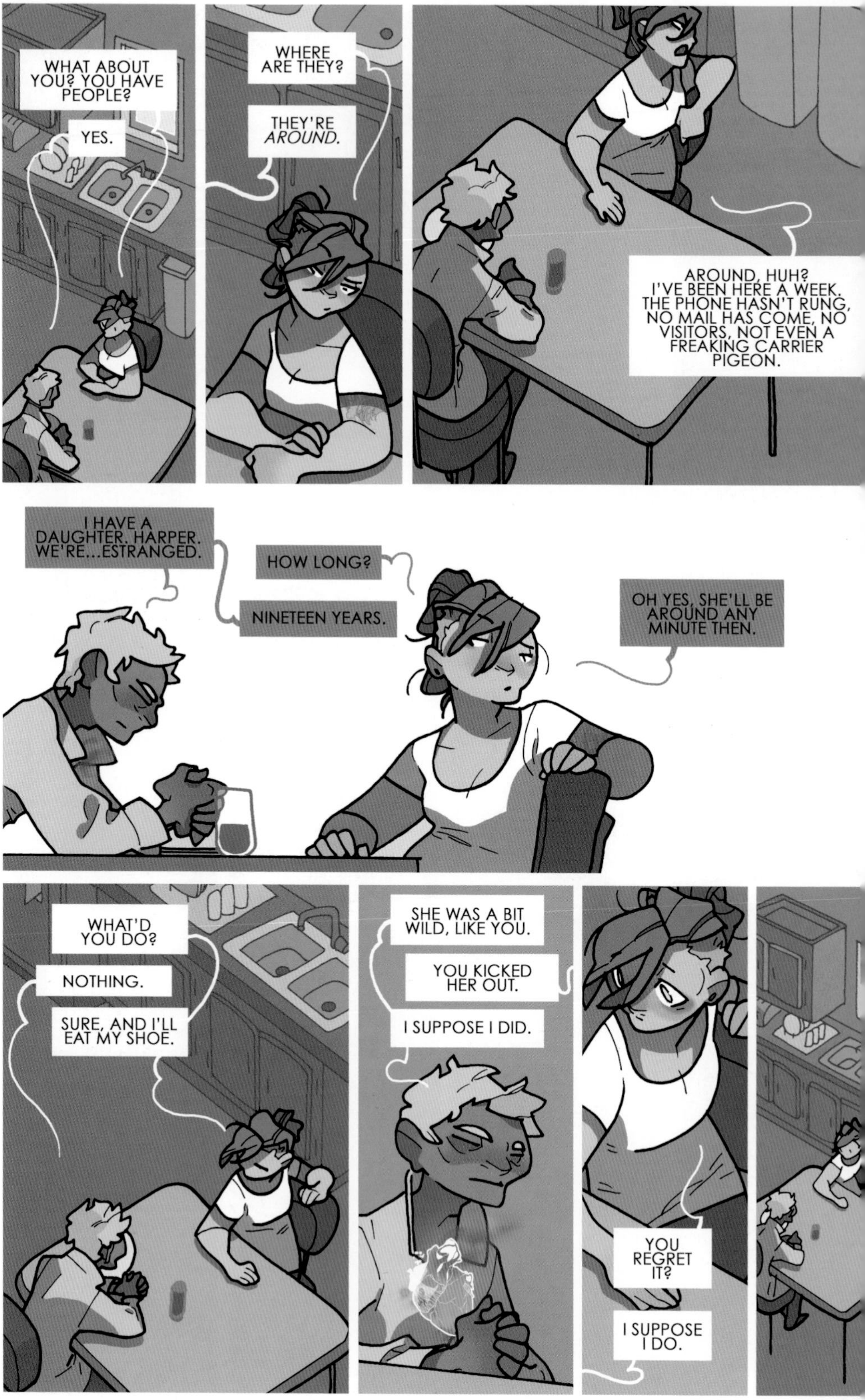
WHAT ABOUT YOU? YOU HAVE PEOPLE?
YES.
WHERE ARE THEY?
THEY'RE *AROUND.*
AROUND, HUH? I'VE BEEN HERE A WEEK. THE PHONE HASN'T RUNG, NO MAIL HAS COME, NO VISITORS, NOT EVEN A FREAKING CARRIER PIGEON.
I HAVE A DAUGHTER. HARPER. WE'RE...ESTRANGED.
HOW LONG?
NINETEEN YEARS.
OH YES, SHE'LL BE AROUND ANY MINUTE THEN.
WHAT'D YOU DO?
NOTHING.
SURE, AND I'LL EAT MY SHOE.
SHE WAS A BIT WILD, LIKE YOU.
YOU KICKED HER OUT.
I SUPPOSE I DID.
YOU REGRET IT?
I SUPPOSE I DO.

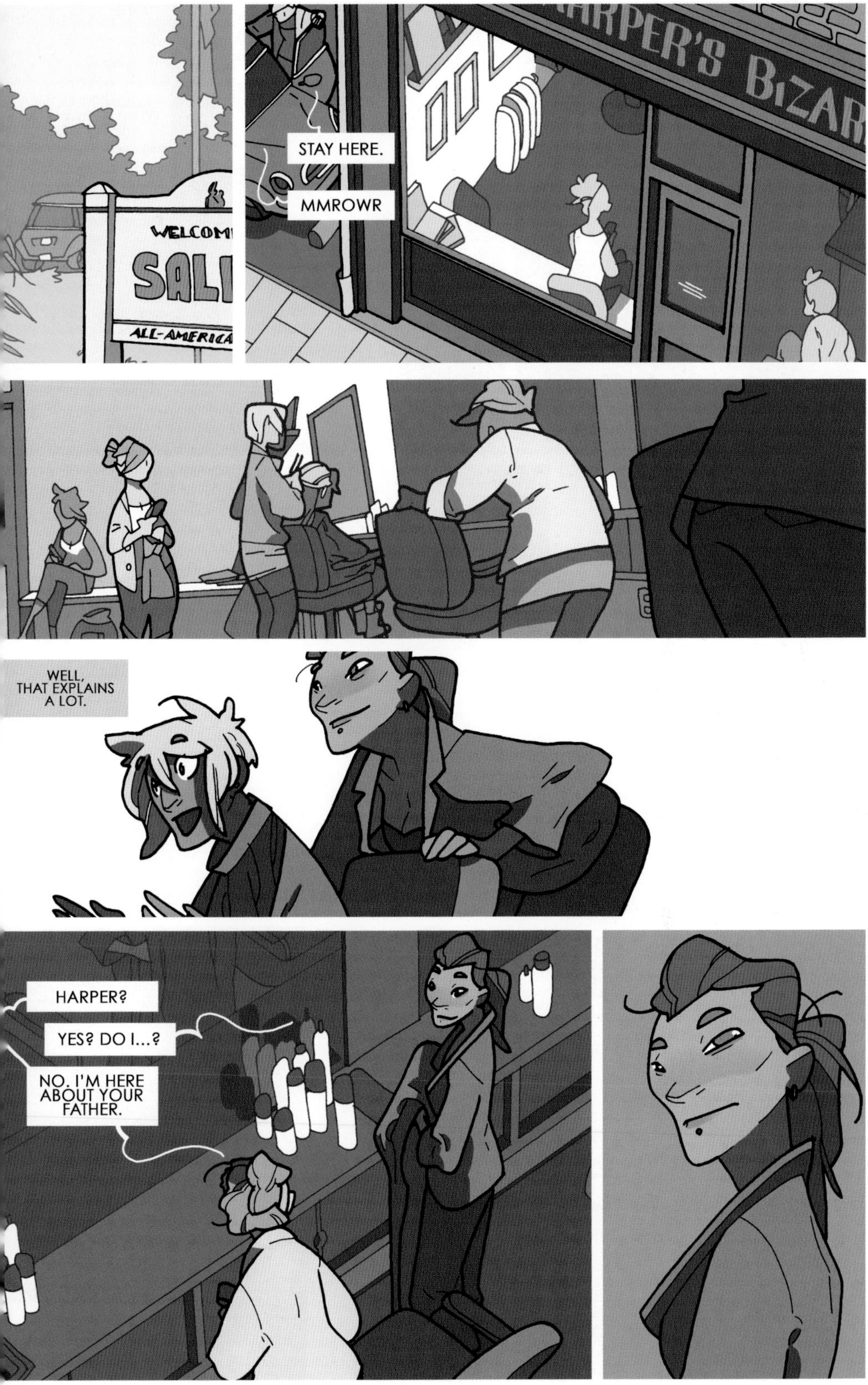
WELCOM
SAL
ALL-AMERICA
HARPER'S BIZAR
STAY HERE.
MMROWR
WELL, THAT EXPLAINS A LOT.
HARPER?
YES? DO I...?
NO. I'M HERE ABOUT YOUR FATHER.

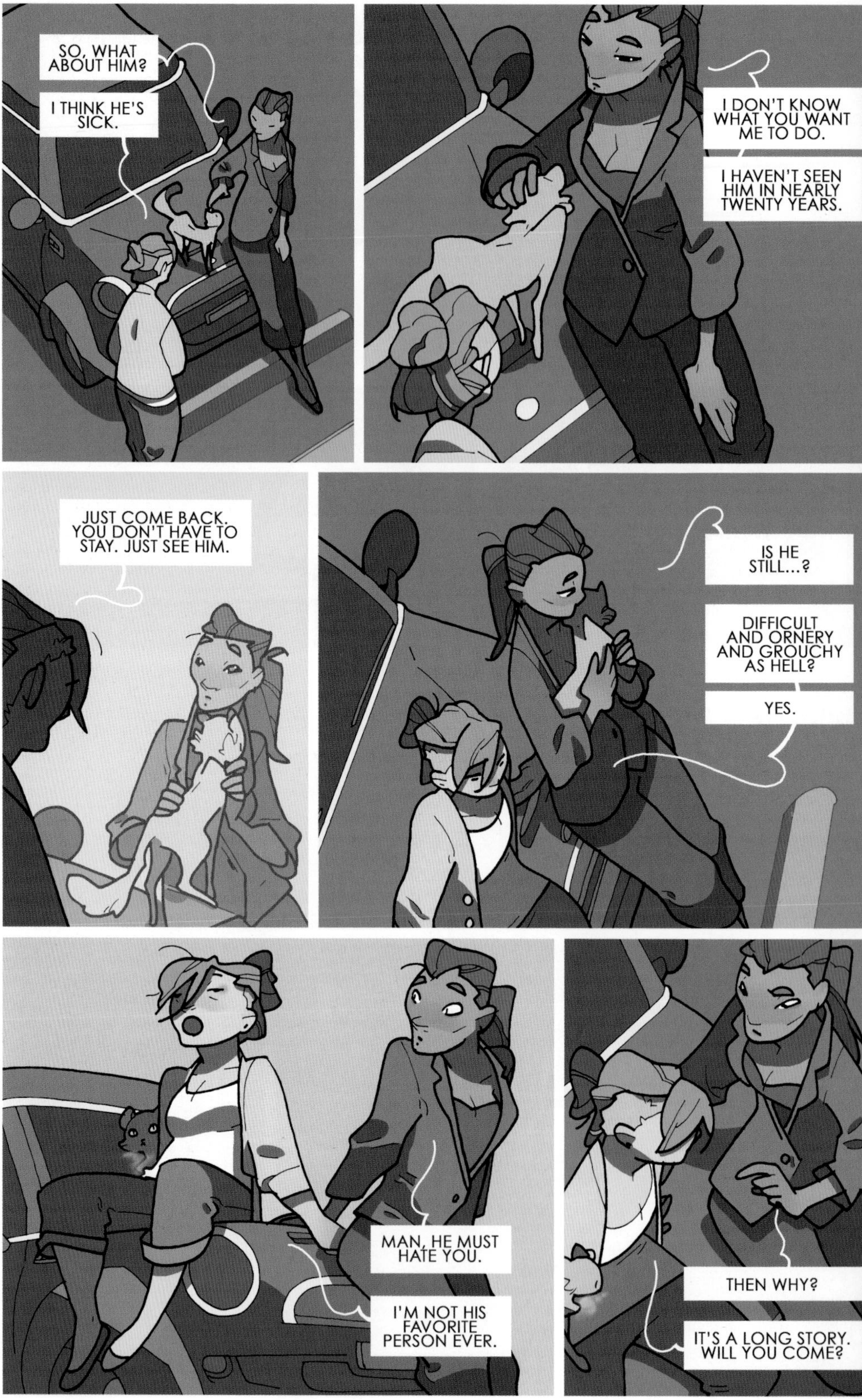
SO, WHAT ABOUT HIM?
I THINK HE'S SICK.
I DON'T KNOW WHAT YOU WANT ME TO DO.
I HAVEN'T SEEN HIM IN NEARLY TWENTY YEARS.
JUST COME BACK. YOU DON'T HAVE TO STAY. JUST SEE HIM.
IS HE STILL...?
DIFFICULT AND ORNERY AND GROUCHY AS HELL?
YES.
MAN, HE MUST HATE YOU.
I'M NOT HIS FAVORITE PERSON EVER.
THEN WHY?
IT'S A LONG STORY. WILL YOU COME?

PLEASE
COME,
HARPER.

NO.

BUT--

I'M SORRY.

IT'S TOO LATE.

IT TOOK ME A LOT
OF YEARS TO FIX
MYSELF.

I'M NOT GOING TO
LET HIM UNDO
WHAT I'VE DONE.

I UNDERSTAND.

WHAT ARE
YOU GOING
TO DO?

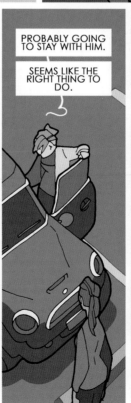

PROBABLY GOING
TO STAY WITH HIM.

SEEMS LIKE THE
RIGHT THING TO
DO.

THANKS.

SURE.

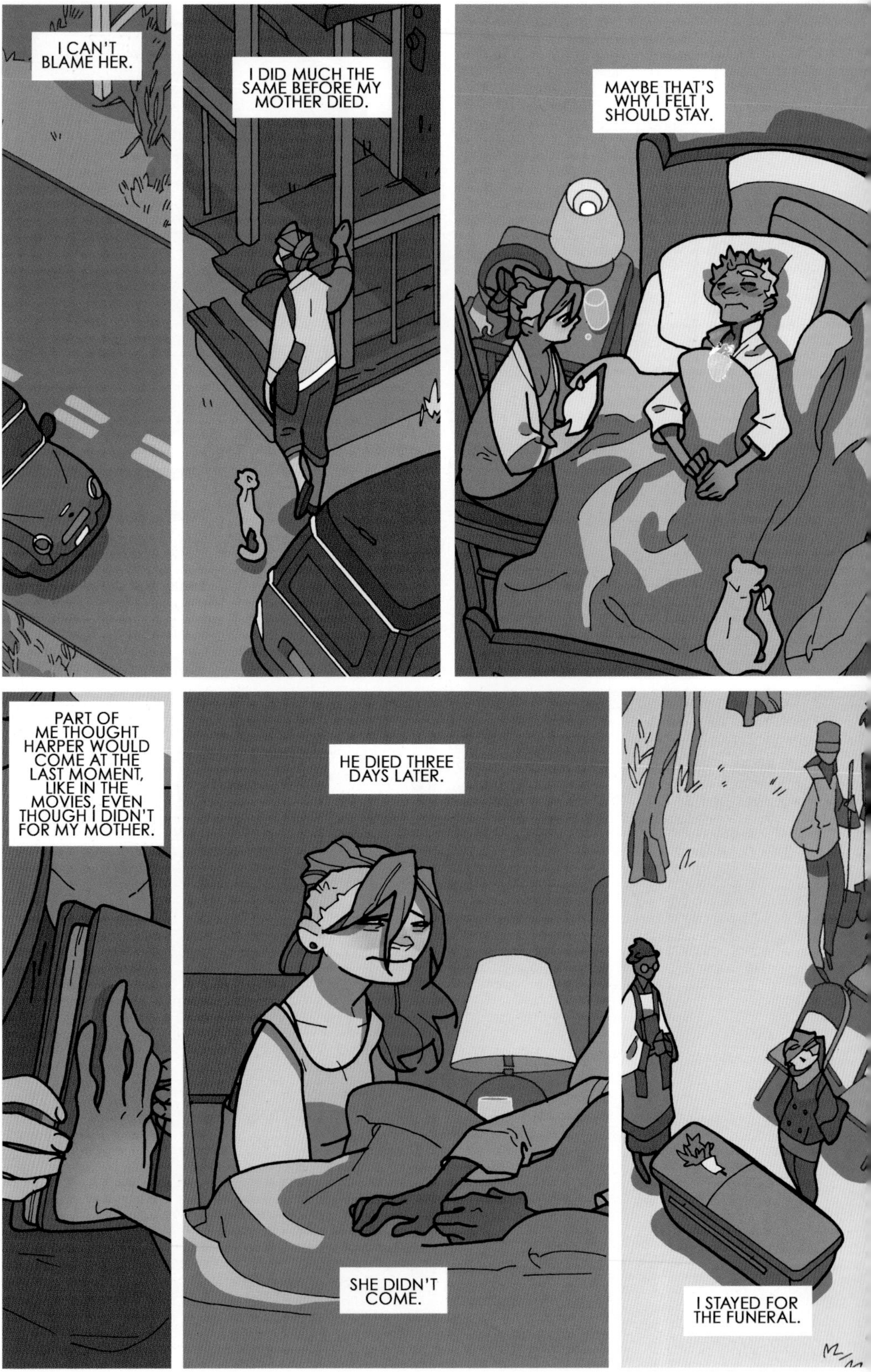
I CAN'T BLAME HER.
I DID MUCH THE SAME BEFORE MY MOTHER DIED.
MAYBE THAT'S WHY I FELT I SHOULD STAY.
PART OF ME THOUGHT HARPER WOULD COME AT THE LAST MOMENT, LIKE IN THE MOVIES, EVEN THOUGH I DIDN'T FOR MY MOTHER.
HE DIED THREE DAYS LATER.
SHE DIDN'T COME.
I STAYED FOR THE FUNERAL.

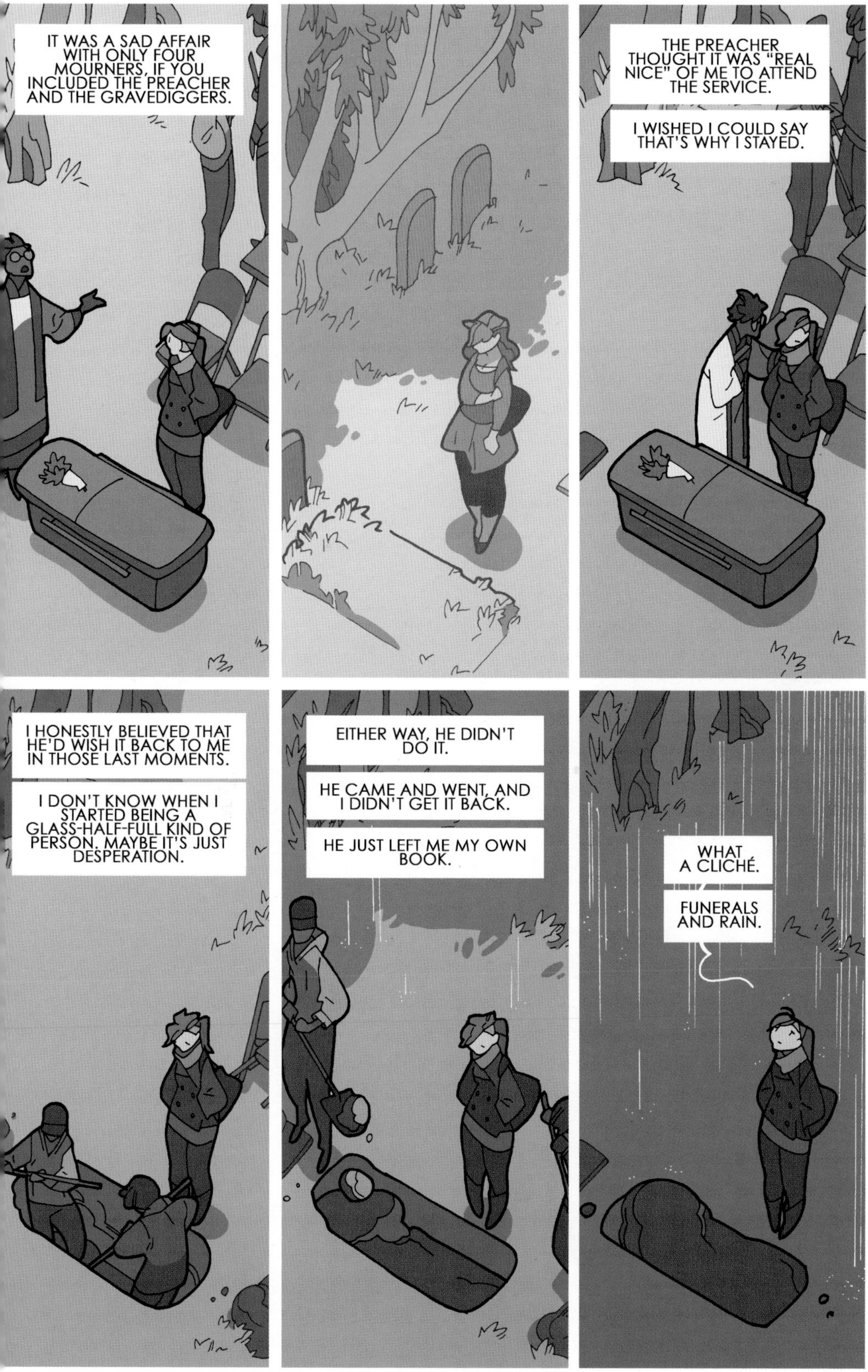
IT WAS A SAD AFFAIR WITH ONLY FOUR MOURNERS, IF YOU INCLUDED THE PREACHER AND THE GRAVEDIGGERS.
THE PREACHER THOUGHT IT WAS "REAL NICE" OF ME TO ATTEND THE SERVICE.
I WISHED I COULD SAY THAT'S WHY I STAYED.
I HONESTLY BELIEVED THAT HE'D WISH IT BACK TO ME IN THOSE LAST MOMENTS.
I DON'T KNOW WHEN I STARTED BEING A GLASS-HALF-FULL KIND OF PERSON. MAYBE IT'S JUST DESPERATION.
EITHER WAY, HE DIDN'T DO IT.
HE CAME AND WENT, AND I DIDN'T GET IT BACK.
HE JUST LEFT ME MY OWN BOOK.
WHAT A CLICHÉ.
FUNERALS AND RAIN.

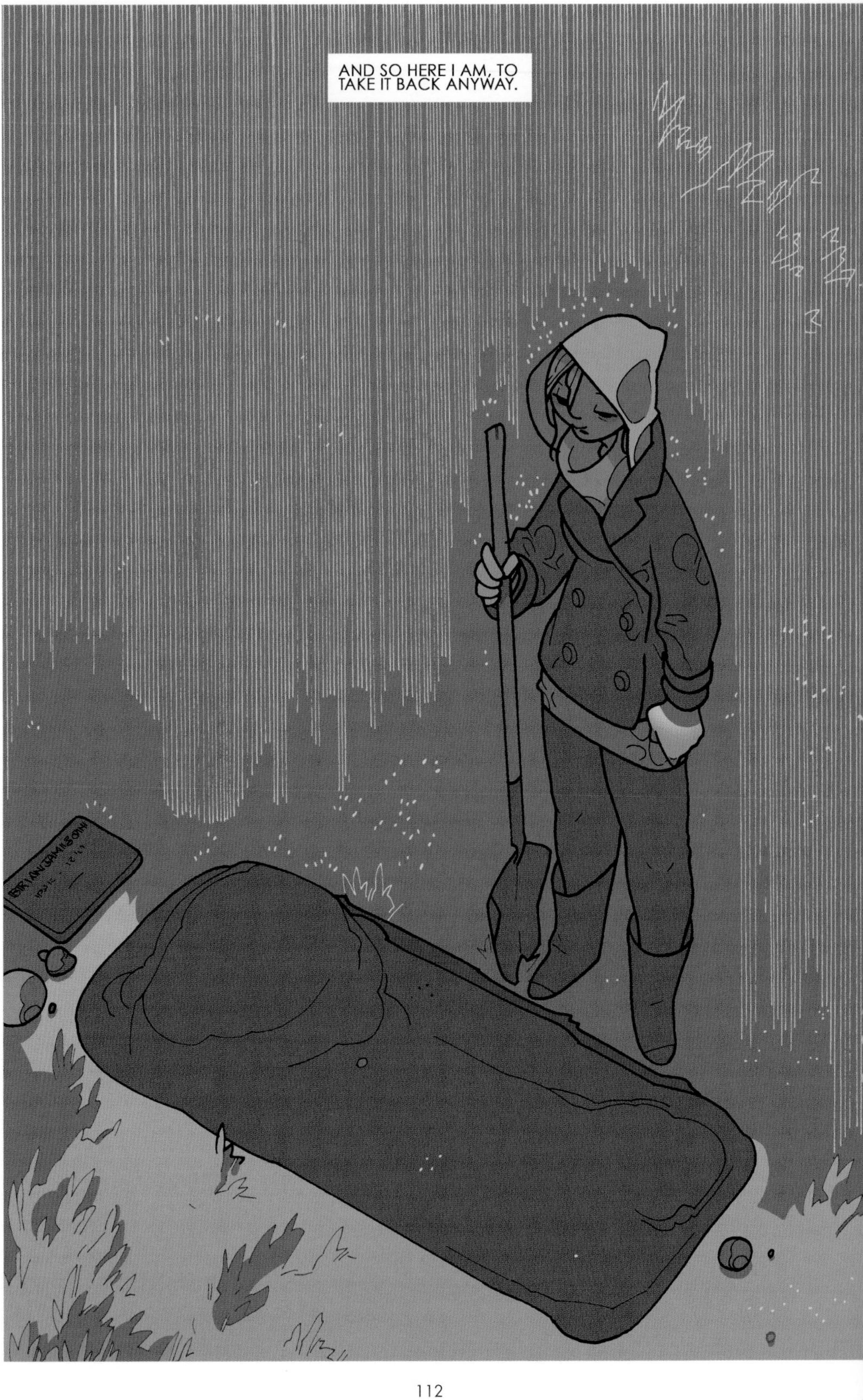
AND SO HERE I AM, TO TAKE IT BACK ANYWAY.

PIECE no. 5

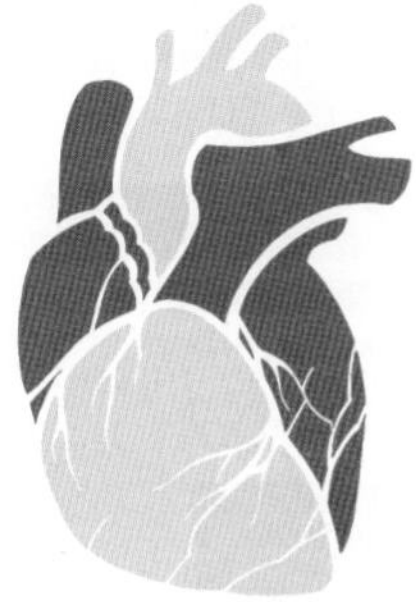

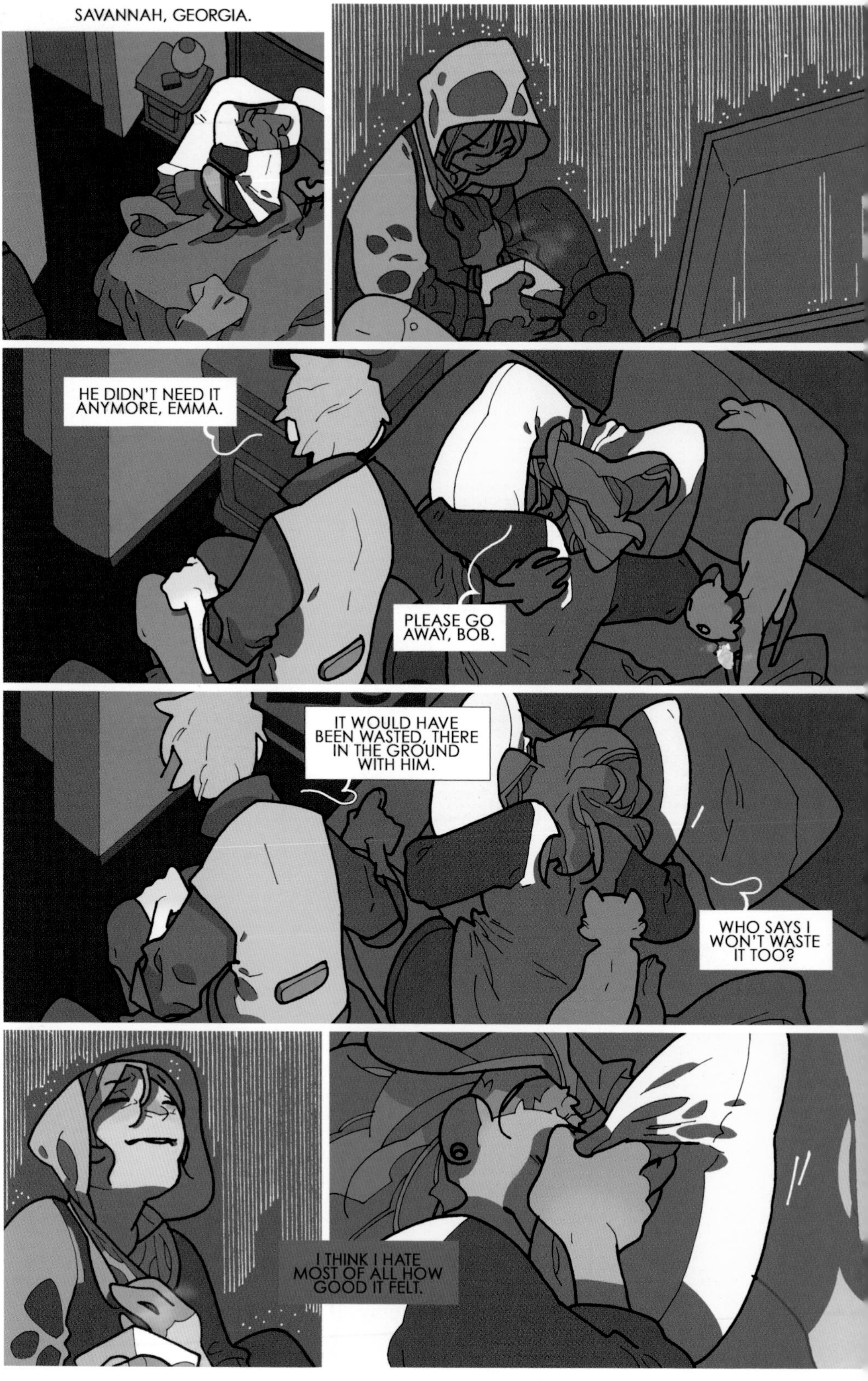
SAVANNAH, GEORGIA.
HE DIDN'T NEED IT ANYMORE, EMMA.
PLEASE GO AWAY, BOB.
IT WOULD HAVE BEEN WASTED, THERE IN THE GROUND WITH HIM.
WHO SAYS I WON'T WASTE IT TOO?
I THINK I HATE MOST OF ALL HOW GOOD IT FELT.

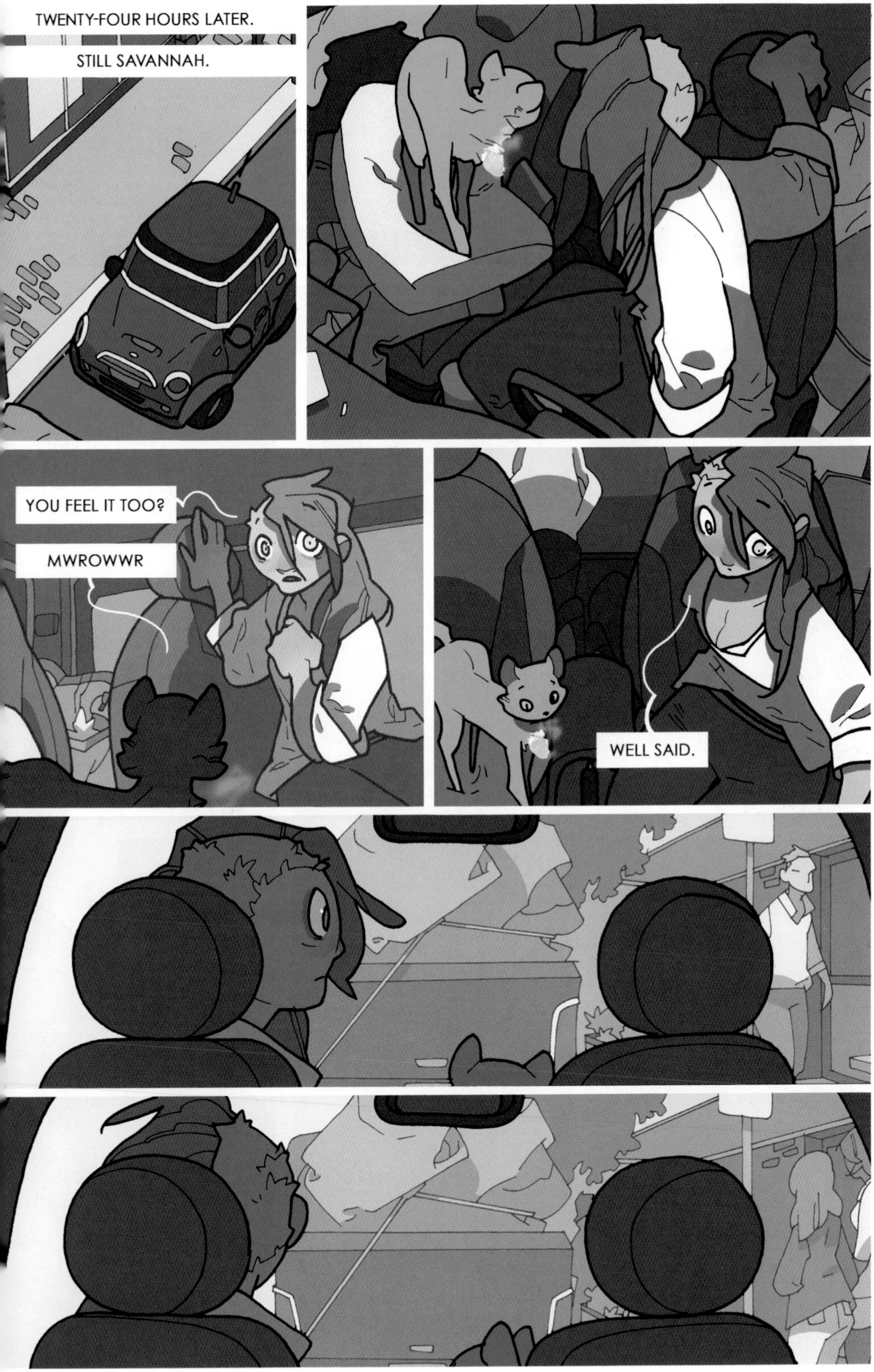
TWENTY-FOUR HOURS LATER.
STILL SAVANNAH.
YOU FEEL IT TOO?
MWROWWR
WELL SAID.

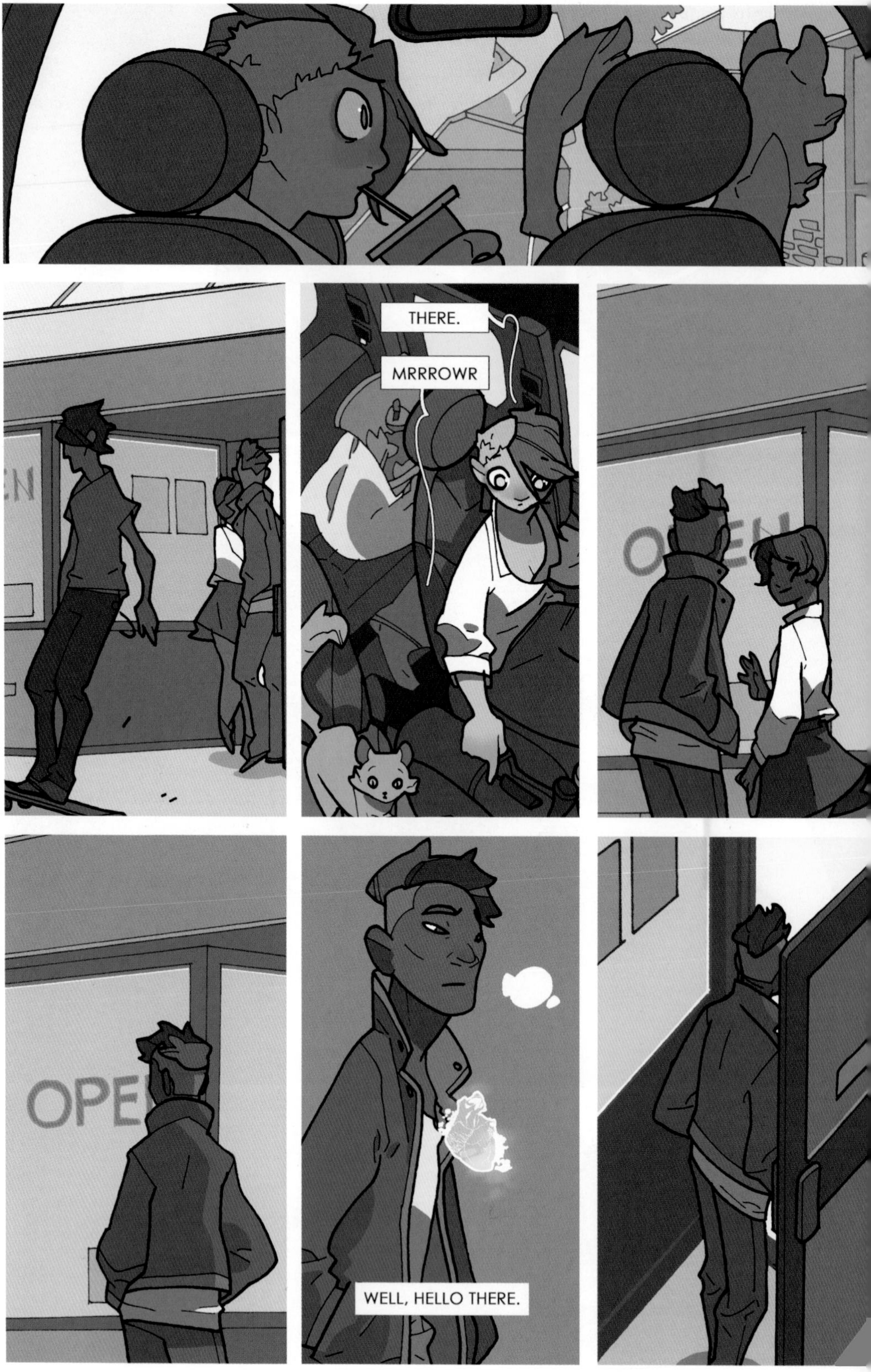
THERE.
MRRROWR
OPEN
WELL, HELLO THERE.

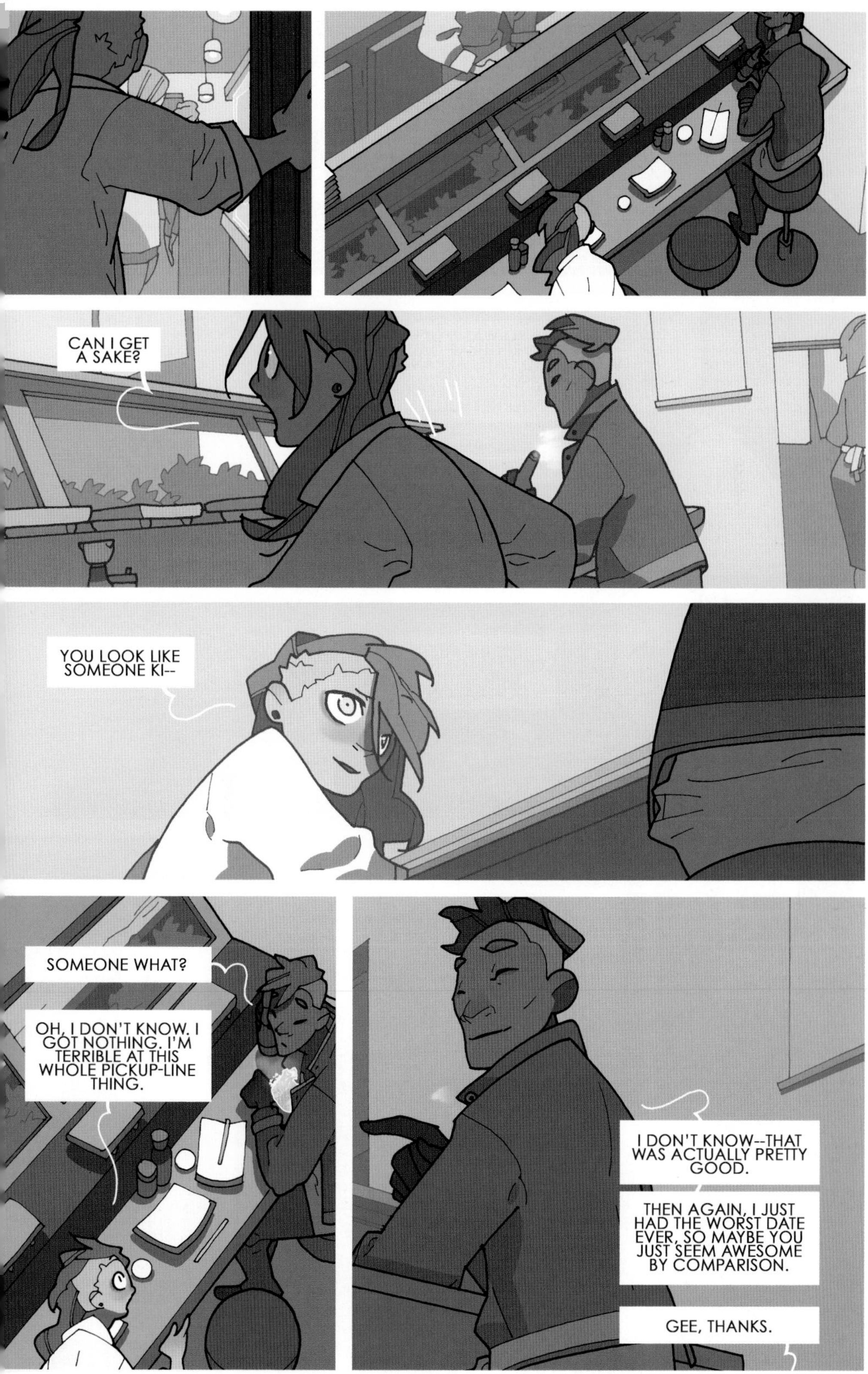
CAN I GET A SAKE?
YOU LOOK LIKE SOMEONE KI--
SOMEONE WHAT?
OH, I DON'T KNOW. I GOT NOTHING. I'M TERRIBLE AT THIS WHOLE PICKUP-LINE THING.
I DON'T KNOW--THAT WAS ACTUALLY PRETTY GOOD.
THEN AGAIN, I JUST HAD THE WORST DATE EVER, SO MAYBE YOU JUST SEEM AWESOME BY COMPARISON.
GEE, THANKS.

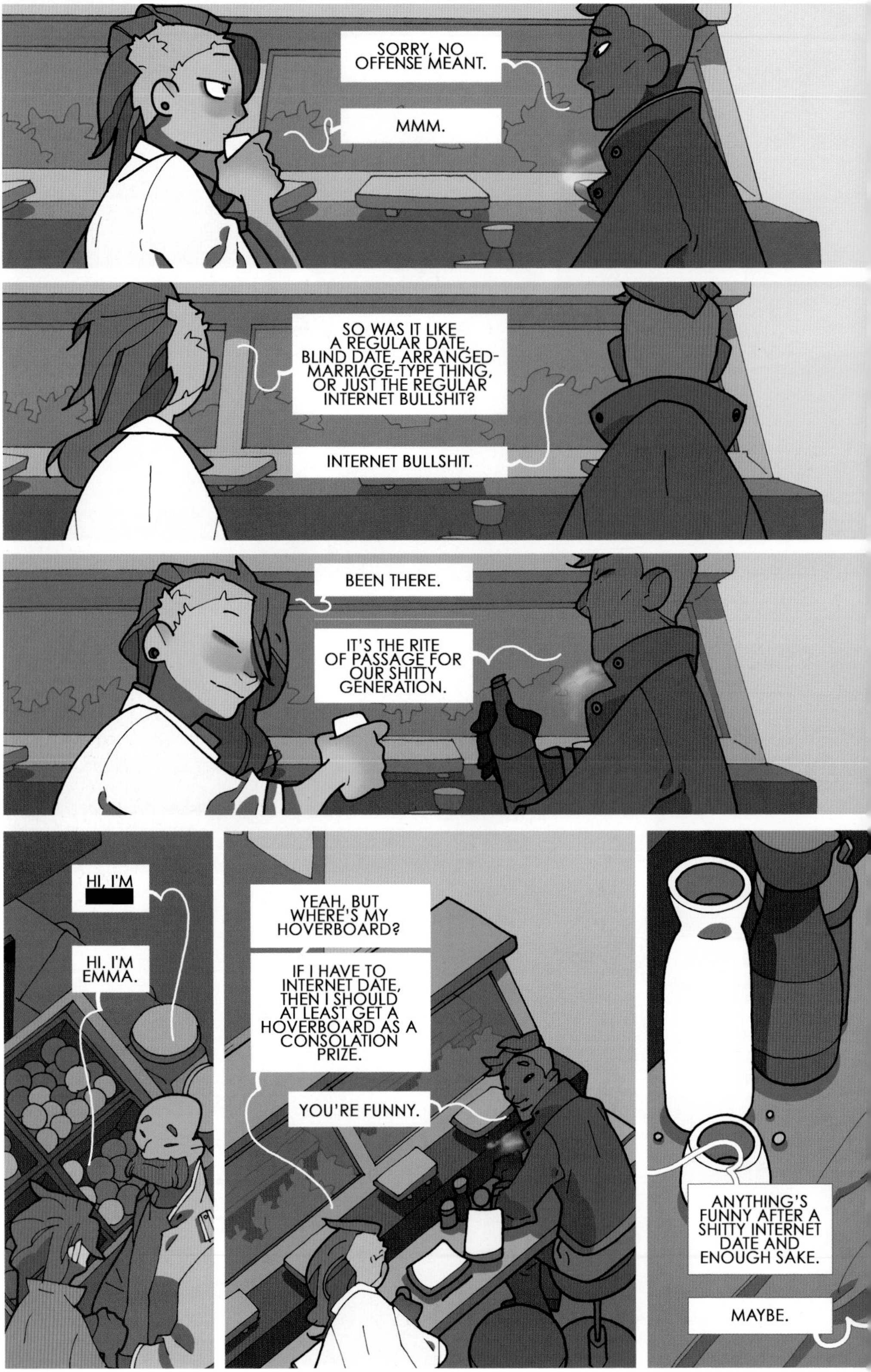
SORRY, NO OFFENSE MEANT.
MMM.
SO WAS IT LIKE A REGULAR DATE, BLIND DATE, ARRANGED-MARRIAGE-TYPE THING, OR JUST THE REGULAR INTERNET BULLSHIT?
INTERNET BULLSHIT.
BEEN THERE.
IT'S THE RITE OF PASSAGE FOR OUR SHITTY GENERATION.
HI, I'M [redacted]
HI. I'M EMMA.
YEAH, BUT WHERE'S MY HOVERBOARD?
IF I HAVE TO INTERNET DATE, THEN I SHOULD AT LEAST GET A HOVERBOARD AS A CONSOLATION PRIZE.
YOU'RE FUNNY.
ANYTHING'S FUNNY AFTER A SHITTY INTERNET DATE AND ENOUGH SAKE.
MAYBE.

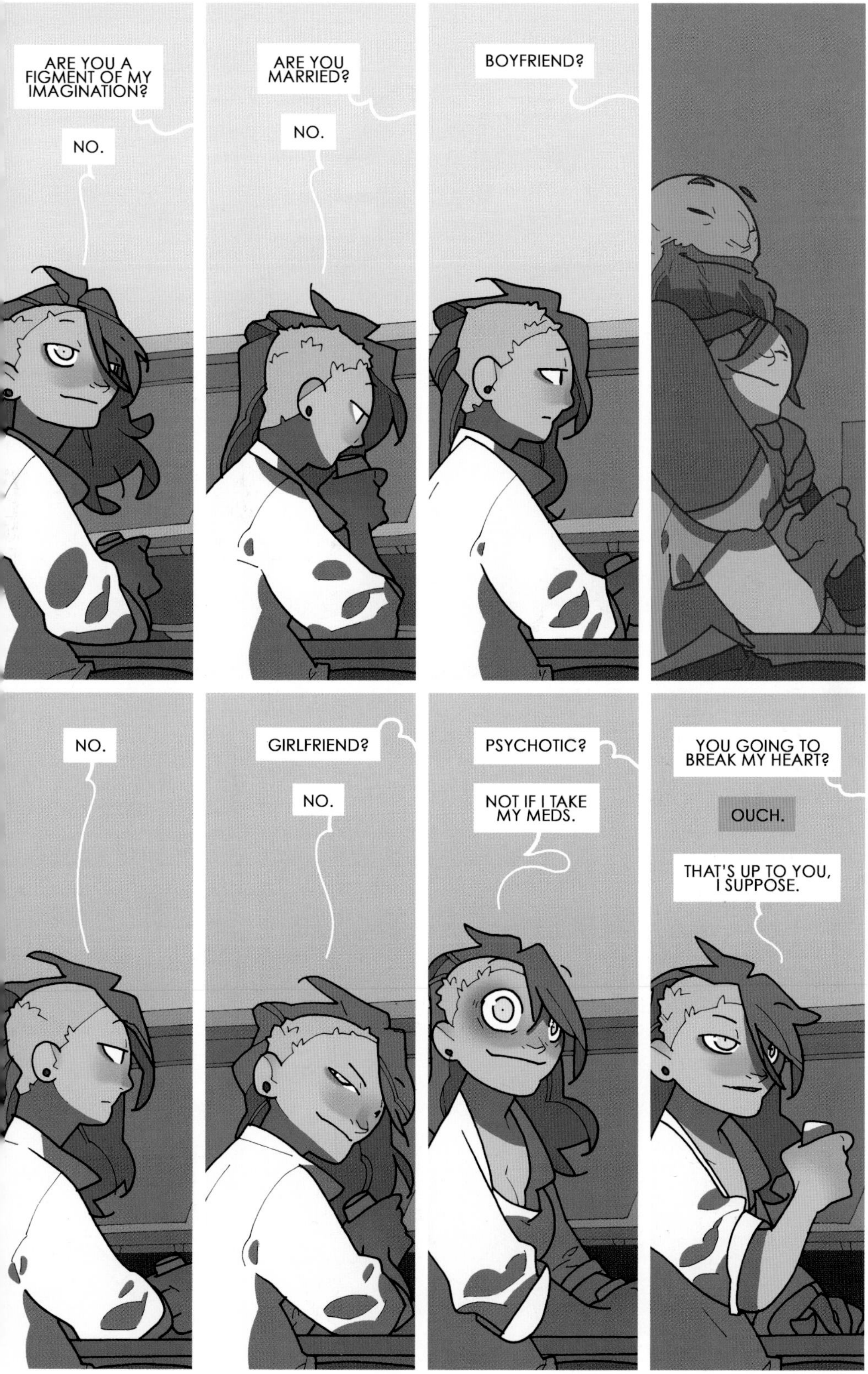
ARE YOU A FIGMENT OF MY IMAGINATION?
NO.
ARE YOU MARRIED?
NO.
BOYFRIEND?
NO.
GIRLFRIEND?
NO.
PSYCHOTIC?
NOT IF I TAKE MY MEDS.
YOU GOING TO BREAK MY HEART?
OUCH.
THAT'S UP TO YOU, I SUPPOSE.

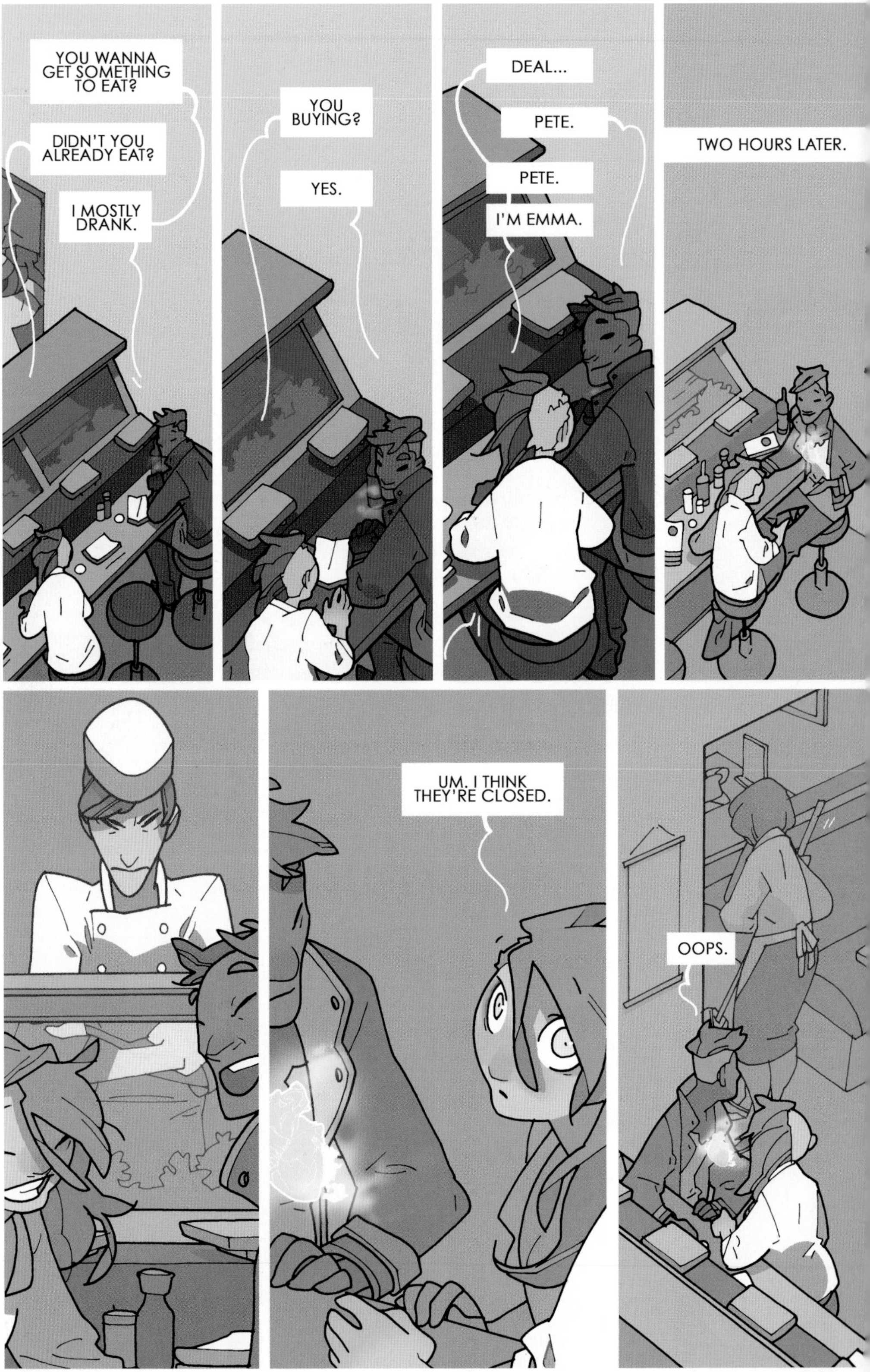
YOU WANNA GET SOMETHING TO EAT?
DIDN'T YOU ALREADY EAT?
I MOSTLY DRANK.
YOU BUYING?
YES.
DEAL...
PETE.
PETE.
I'M EMMA.
TWO HOURS LATER.
UM. I THINK THEY'RE CLOSED.
OOPS.

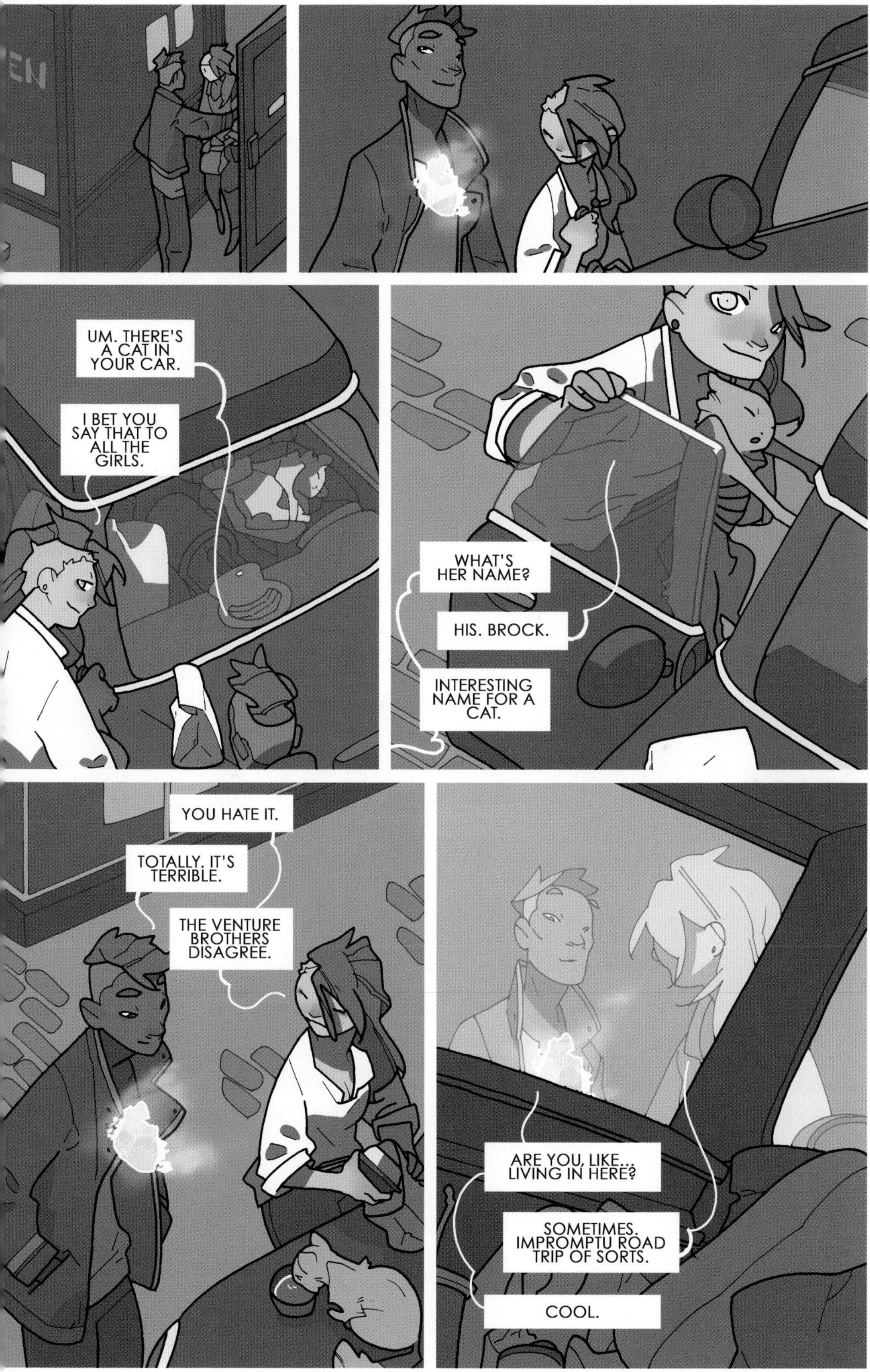
UM. THERE'S A CAT IN YOUR CAR.
I BET YOU SAY THAT TO ALL THE GIRLS.
WHAT'S HER NAME?
HIS. BROCK.
INTERESTING NAME FOR A CAT.
YOU HATE IT.
TOTALLY. IT'S TERRIBLE.
THE VENTURE BROTHERS DISAGREE.
ARE YOU, LIKE... LIVING IN HERE?
SOMETIMES. IMPROMPTU ROAD TRIP OF SORTS.
COOL.

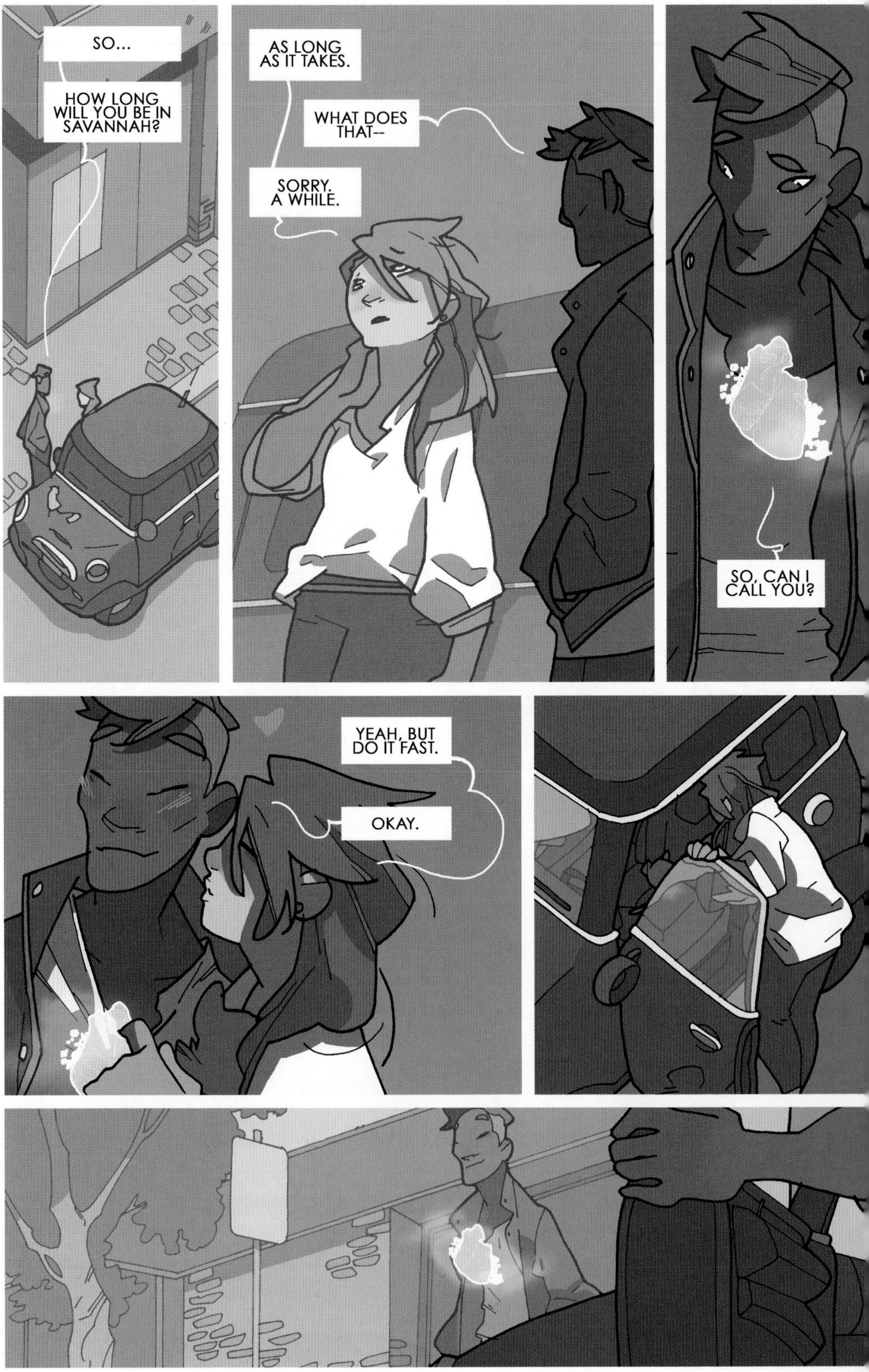
SO...
HOW LONG WILL YOU BE IN SAVANNAH?
AS LONG AS IT TAKES.
WHAT DOES THAT--
SORRY. A WHILE.
SO, CAN I CALL YOU?
YEAH, BUT DO IT FAST.
OKAY.

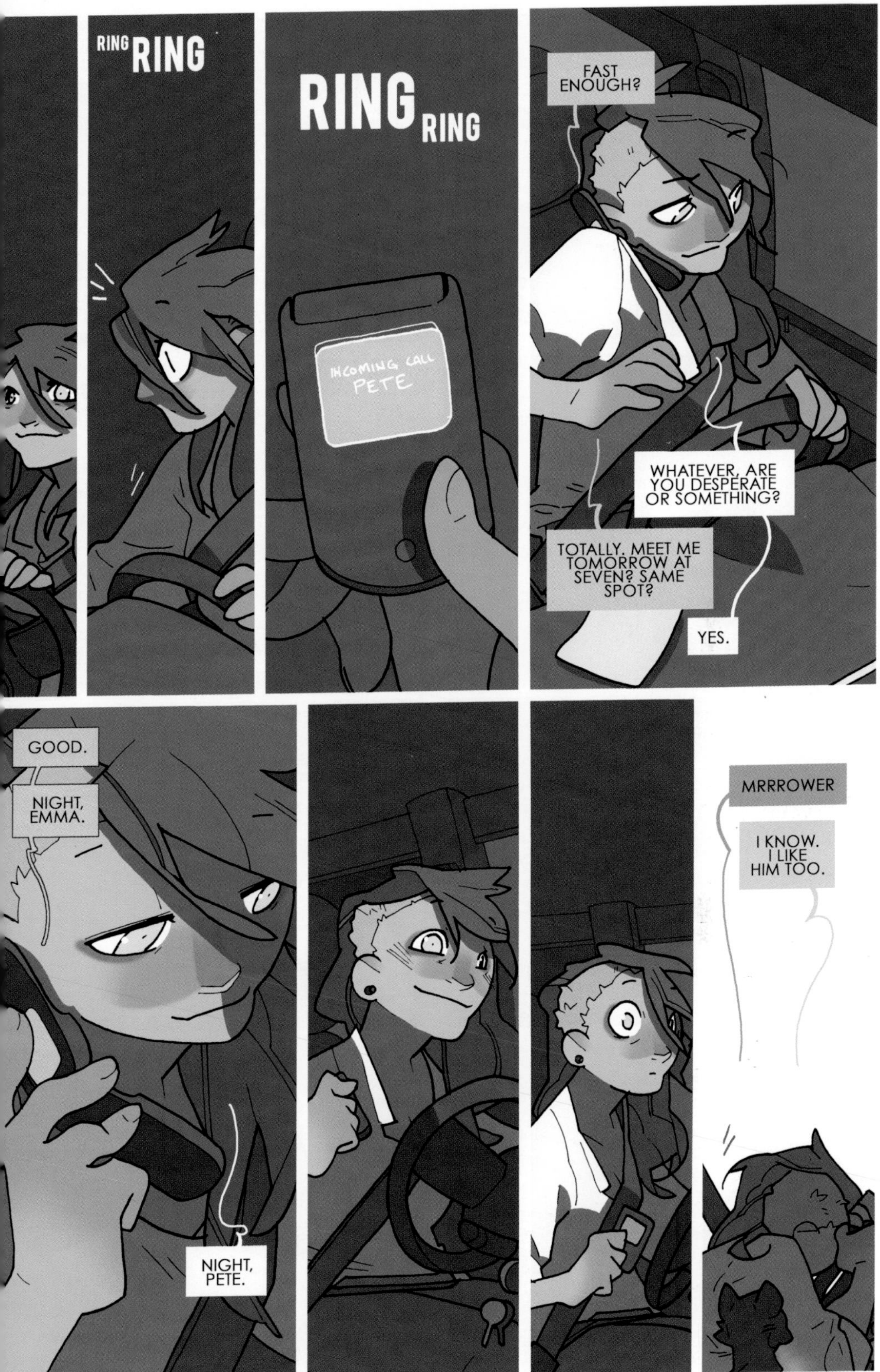
RING RING
RING RING
INCOMING CALL
PETE
FAST ENOUGH?
WHATEVER, ARE YOU DESPERATE OR SOMETHING?
TOTALLY. MEET ME TOMORROW AT SEVEN? SAME SPOT?
YES.
GOOD.
NIGHT, EMMA.
NIGHT, PETE.
MRRROWER
I KNOW. I LIKE HIM TOO.

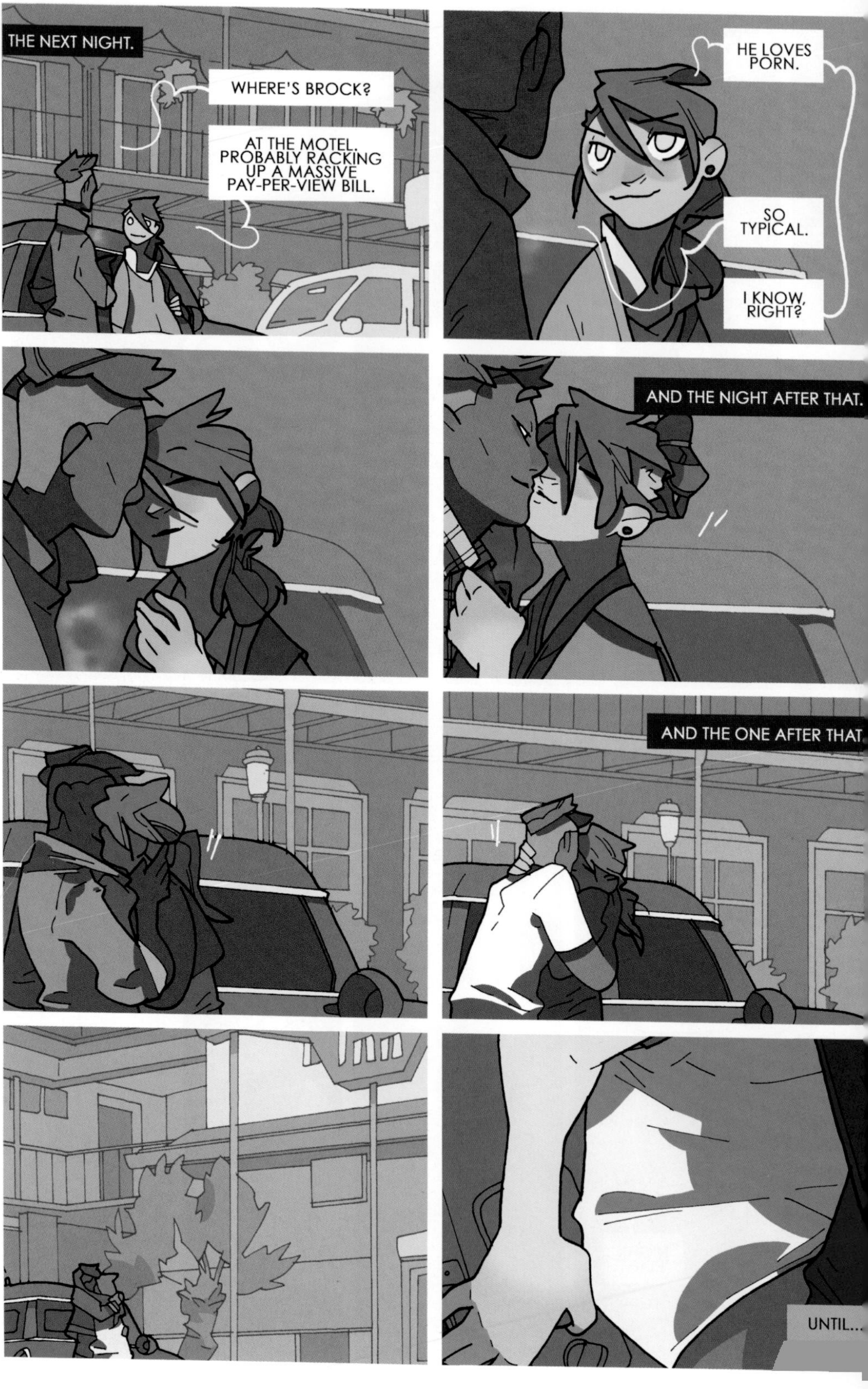
THE NEXT NIGHT.
WHERE'S BROCK?
AT THE MOTEL. PROBABLY RACKING UP A MASSIVE PAY-PER-VIEW BILL.
HE LOVES PORN.
SO TYPICAL.
I KNOW, RIGHT?
AND THE NIGHT AFTER THAT.
AND THE ONE AFTER THAT
UNTIL...

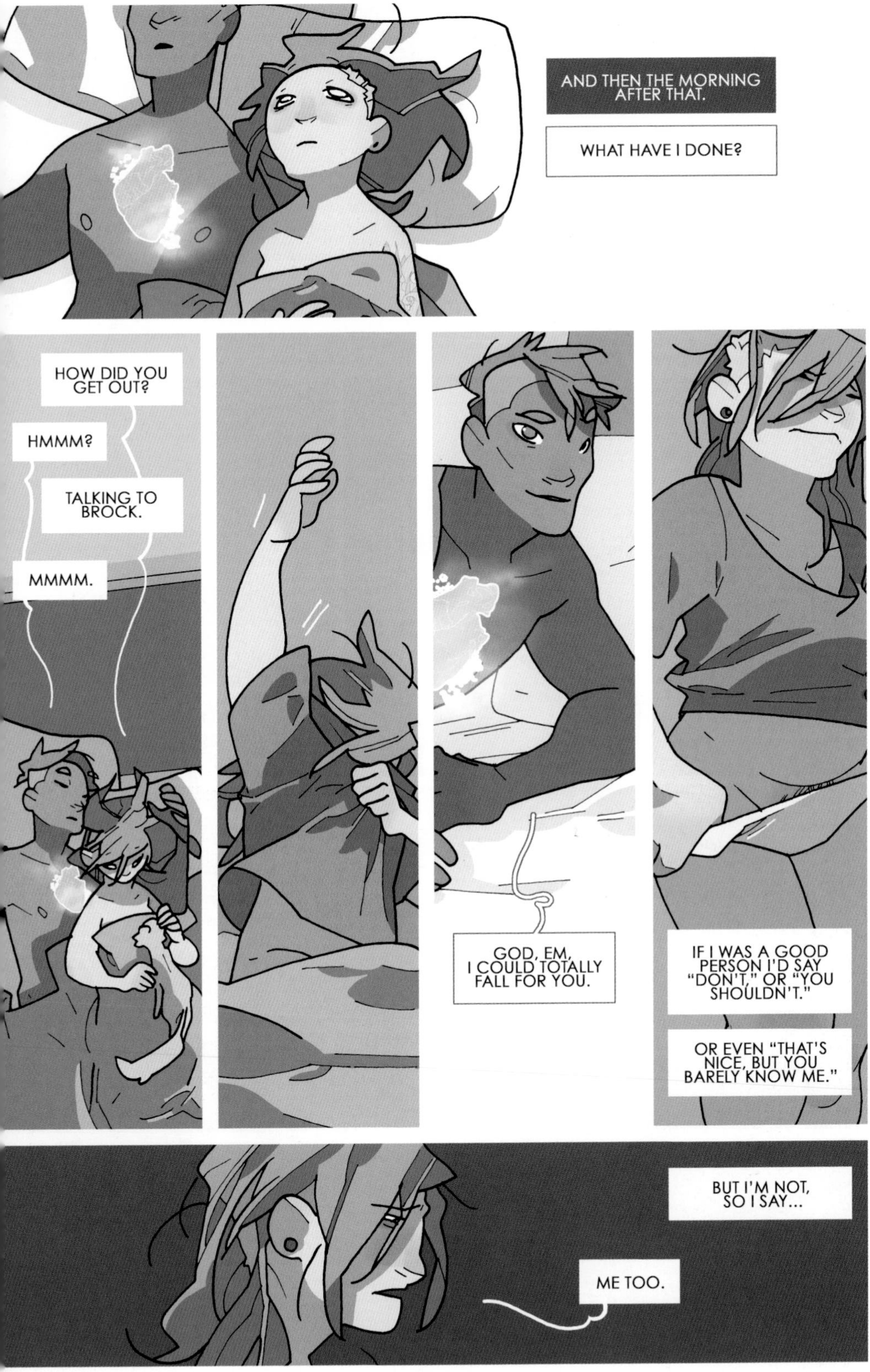
AND THEN THE MORNING AFTER THAT.
WHAT HAVE I DONE?
HOW DID YOU GET OUT?
HMMM?
TALKING TO BROCK.
MMMM.
GOD, EM, I COULD TOTALLY FALL FOR YOU.
IF I WAS A GOOD PERSON I'D SAY "DON'T," OR "YOU SHOULDN'T."
OR EVEN "THAT'S NICE, BUT YOU BARELY KNOW ME."
BUT I'M NOT, SO I SAY...
ME TOO.

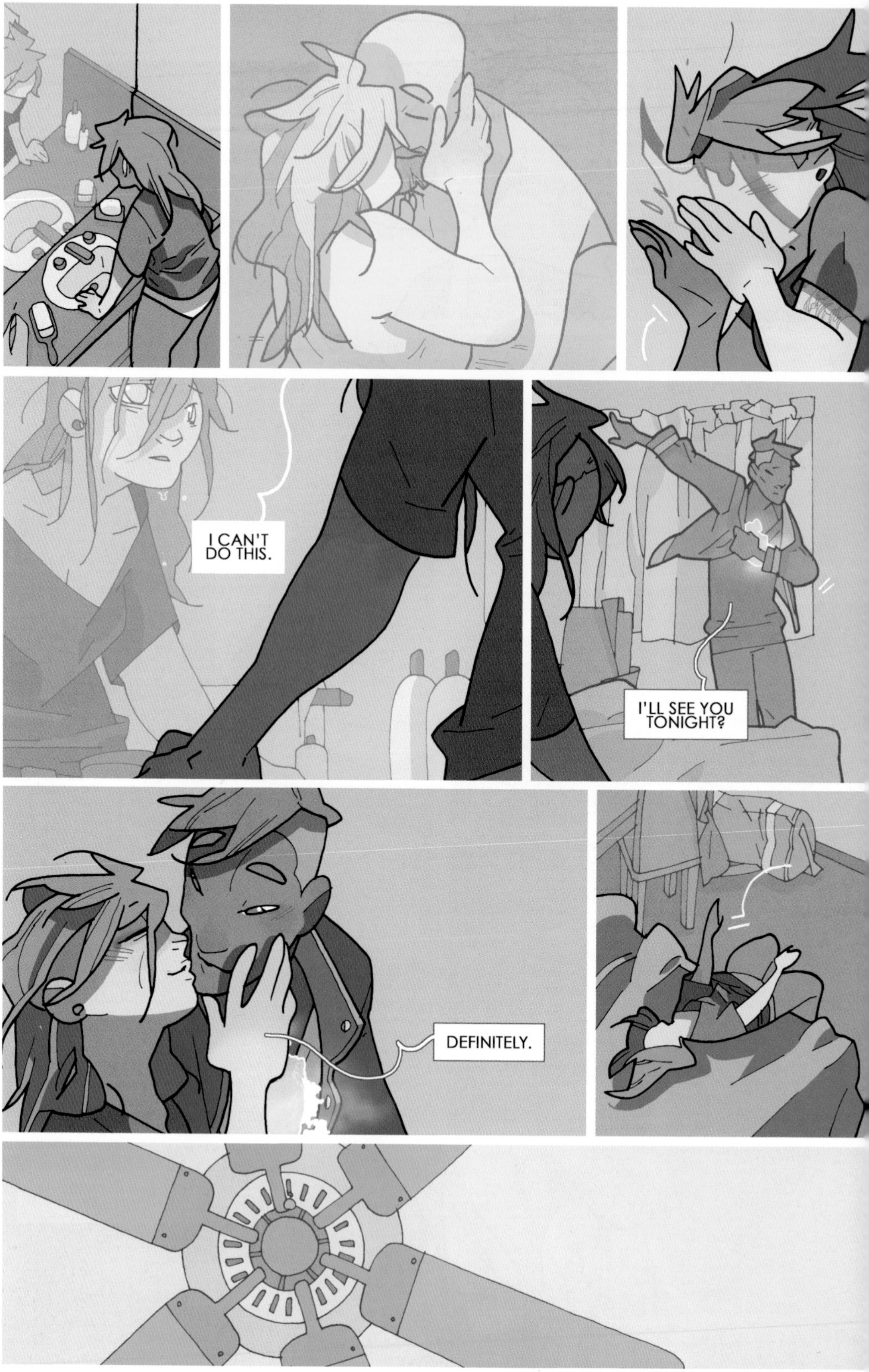
I CAN'T DO THIS.
I'LL SEE YOU TONIGHT?
DEFINITELY.

SSSSSSSSSSSSSSS

YOUR CAT HATES ME.

HE HAS GREAT TASTE.

BOB, I CAN'T BREAK THIS GUY'S HEART.

THEN YOU WON'T EVER BE WHOLE AGAIN.

IS THAT REALLY SO BAD?

DEPENDS ON YOUR PERSPECTIVE, I GUESS.

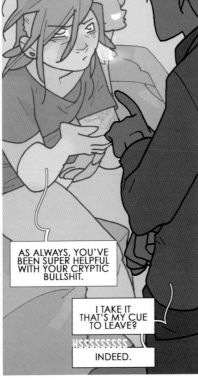

AS ALWAYS, YOU'VE BEEN SUPER HELPFUL WITH YOUR CRYPTIC BULLSHIT.

I TAKE IT THAT'S MY CUE TO LEAVE?

HSSSSSSSSS

INDEED.

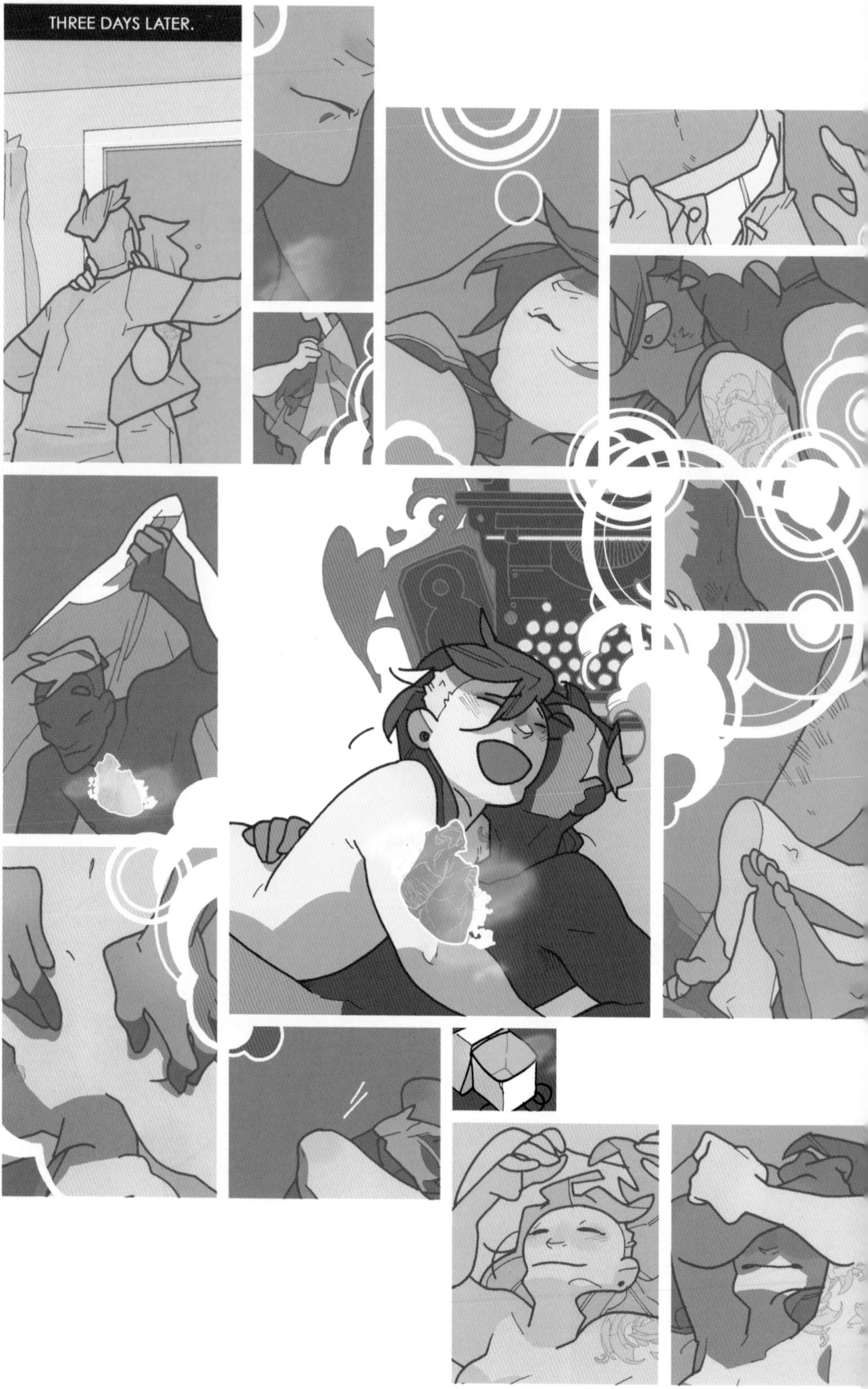
THREE DAYS LATER.

PIECE no. 6

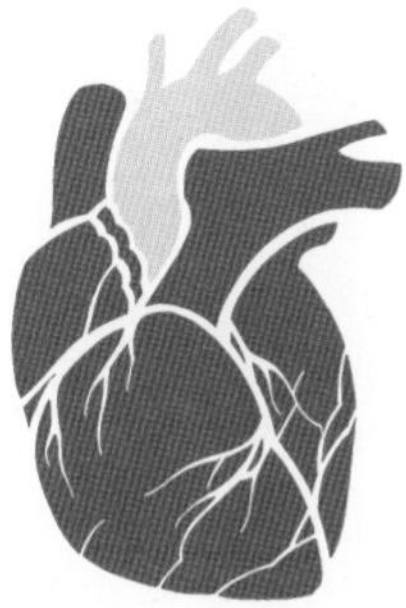

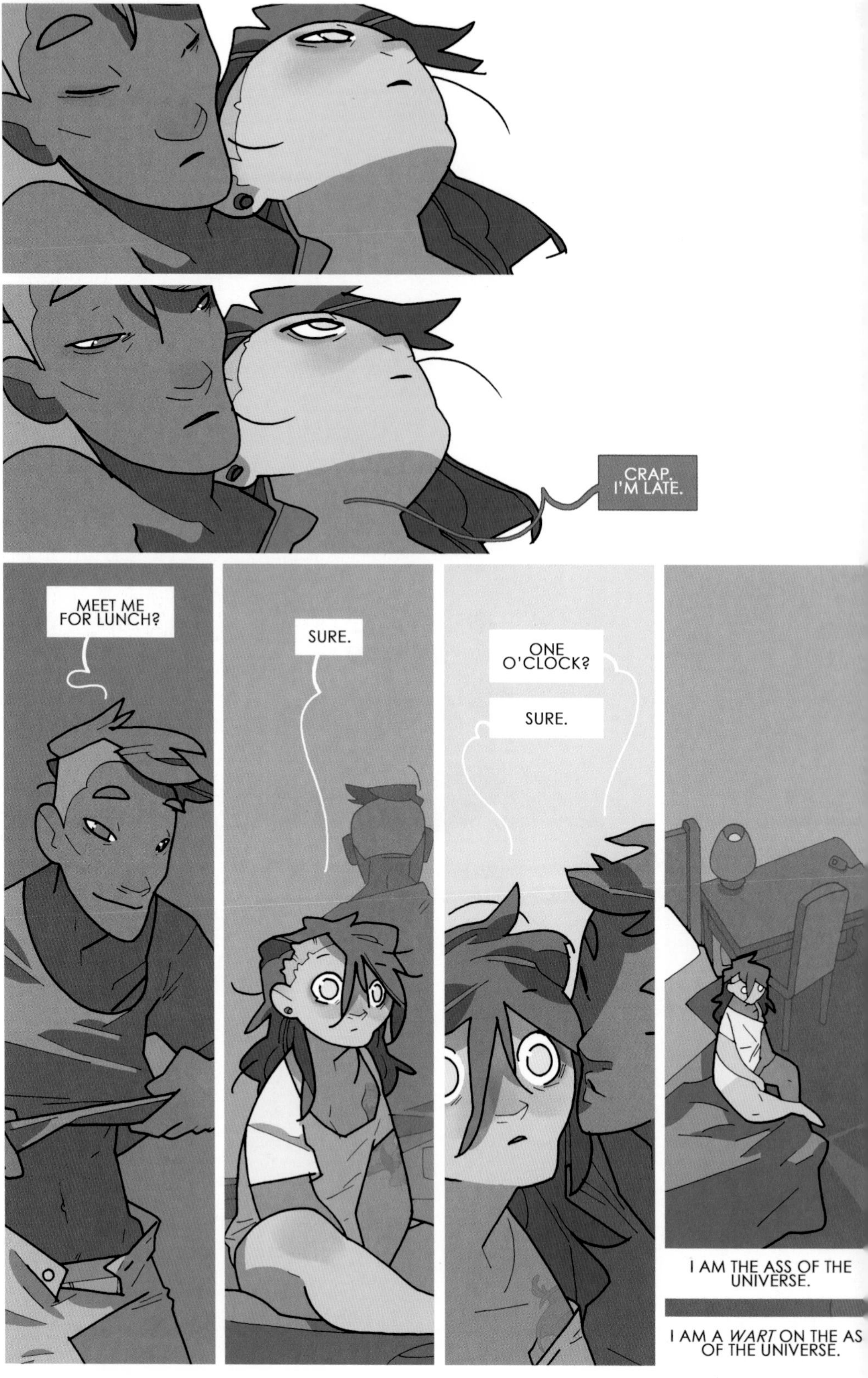
CRAP. I'M LATE.
MEET ME FOR LUNCH?
SURE.
ONE O'CLOCK?
SURE.
I AM THE ASS OF THE UNIVERSE.
I AM A *WART* ON THE AS OF THE UNIVERSE.

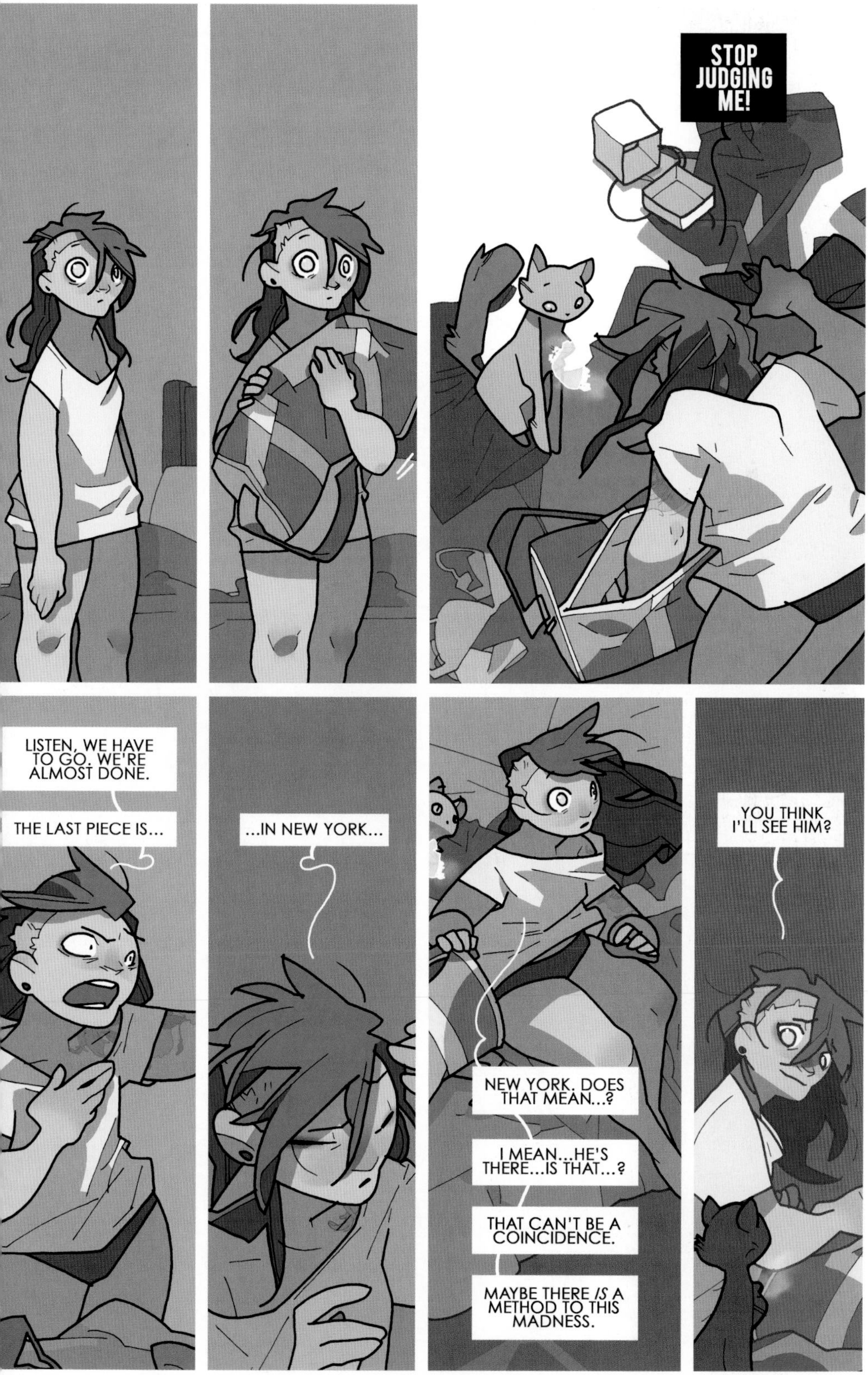
STOP JUDGING ME!
LISTEN, WE HAVE TO GO. WE'RE ALMOST DONE.
THE LAST PIECE IS...
...IN NEW YORK...
NEW YORK. DOES THAT MEAN...?
I MEAN...HE'S THERE...IS THAT...?
THAT CAN'T BE A COINCIDENCE.
MAYBE THERE *IS* A METHOD TO THIS MADNESS.
YOU THINK I'LL SEE HIM?

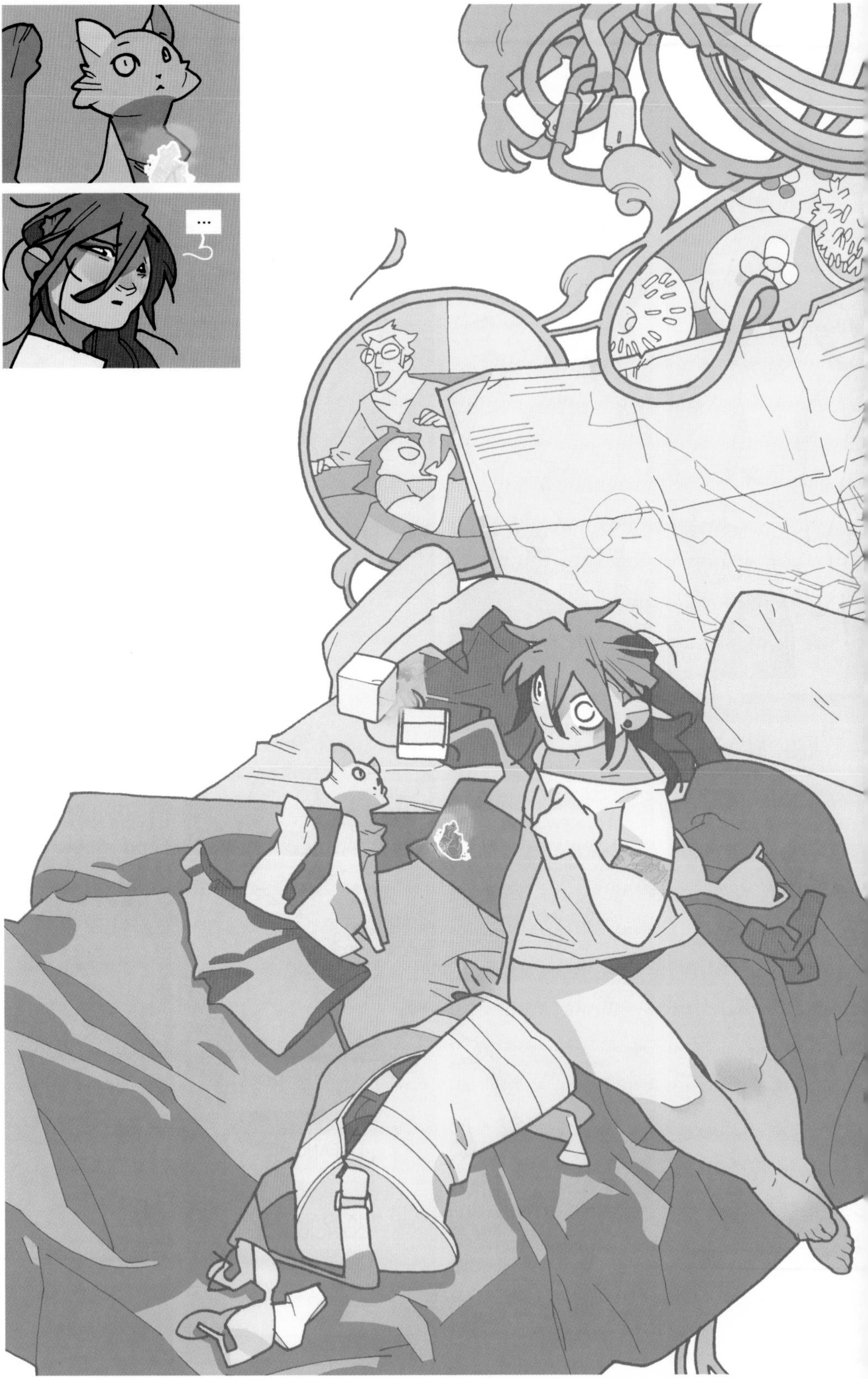
...

PIECE
no.
4

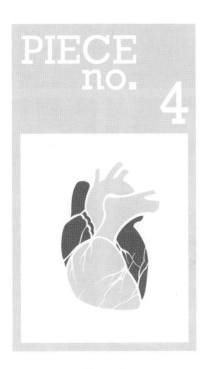

(officially)

THANK YOU.

BROCK!

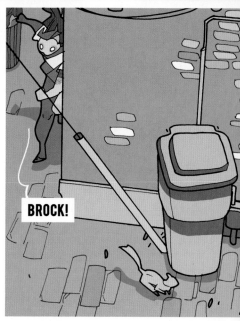

BROCK!

COME BACK!

BROCK!

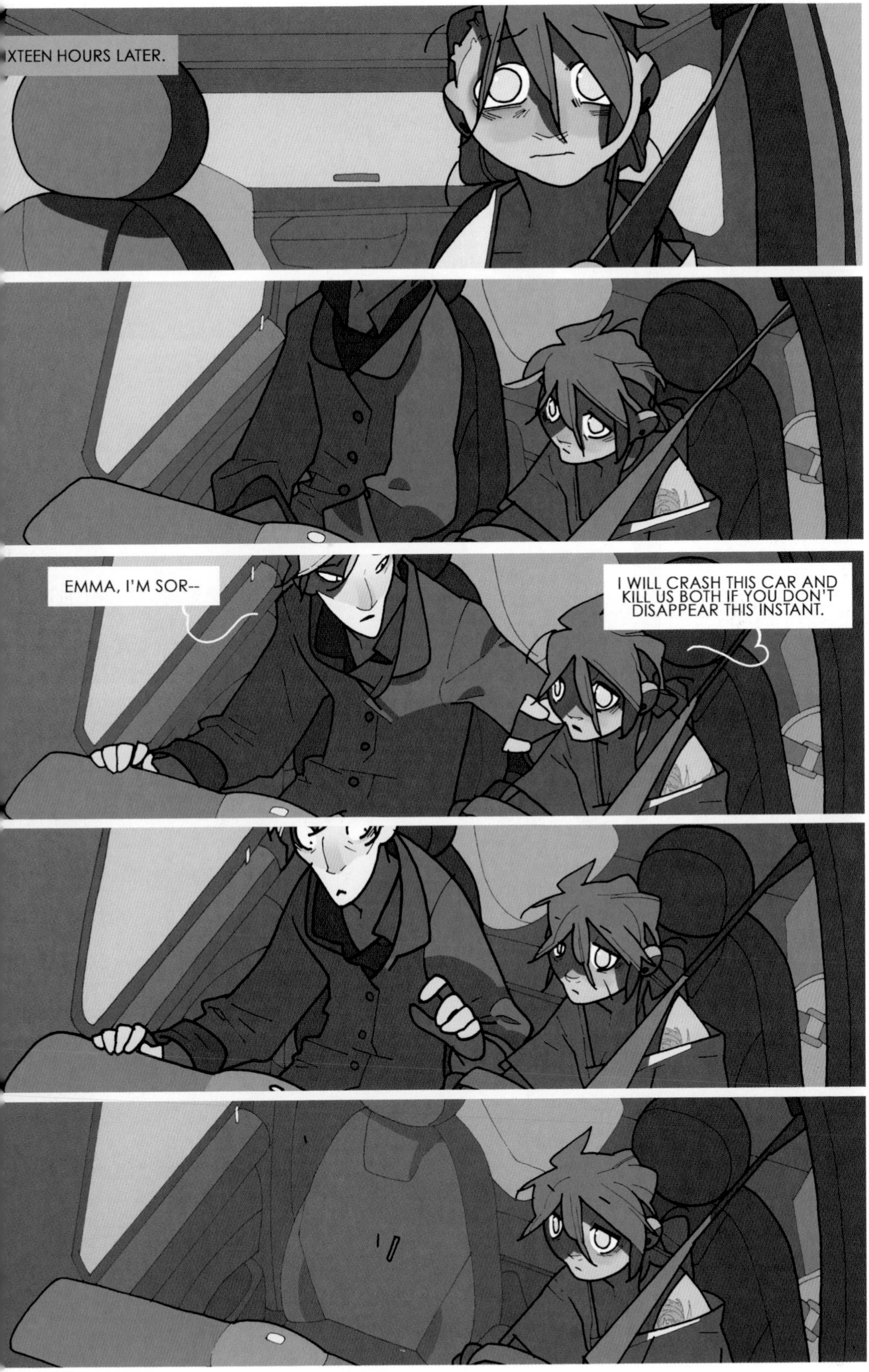
XTEEN HOURS LATER.
EMMA, I'M SOR--
I WILL CRASH THIS CAR AND KILL US BOTH IF YOU DON'T DISAPPEAR THIS INSTANT.

NEW YORK, NEW YORK.

THREE DAYS LATER.

22
MISSED
CALLS

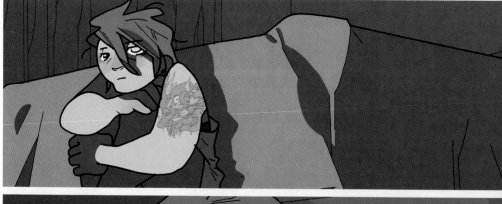

136

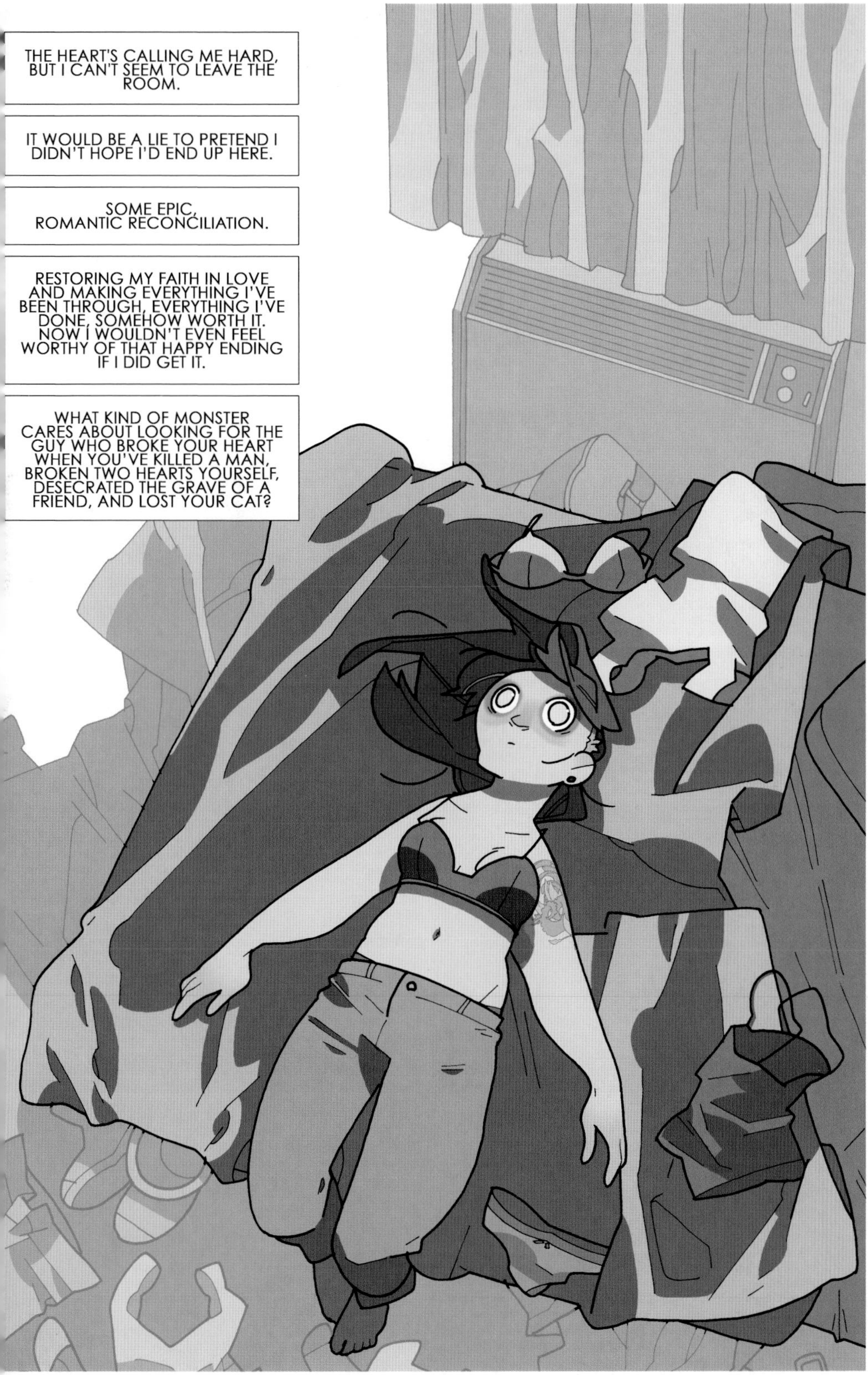
THE HEART'S CALLING ME HARD, BUT I CAN'T SEEM TO LEAVE THE ROOM.
IT WOULD BE A LIE TO PRETEND I DIDN'T HOPE I'D END UP HERE.
SOME EPIC, ROMANTIC RECONCILIATION.
RESTORING MY FAITH IN LOVE AND MAKING EVERYTHING I'VE BEEN THROUGH, EVERYTHING I'VE DONE, SOMEHOW WORTH IT. NOW I WOULDN'T EVEN FEEL WORTHY OF THAT HAPPY ENDING IF I DID GET IT.
WHAT KIND OF MONSTER CARES ABOUT LOOKING FOR THE GUY WHO BROKE YOUR HEART WHEN YOU'VE KILLED A MAN, BROKEN TWO HEARTS YOURSELF, DESECRATED THE GRAVE OF A FRIEND, AND LOST YOUR CAT?

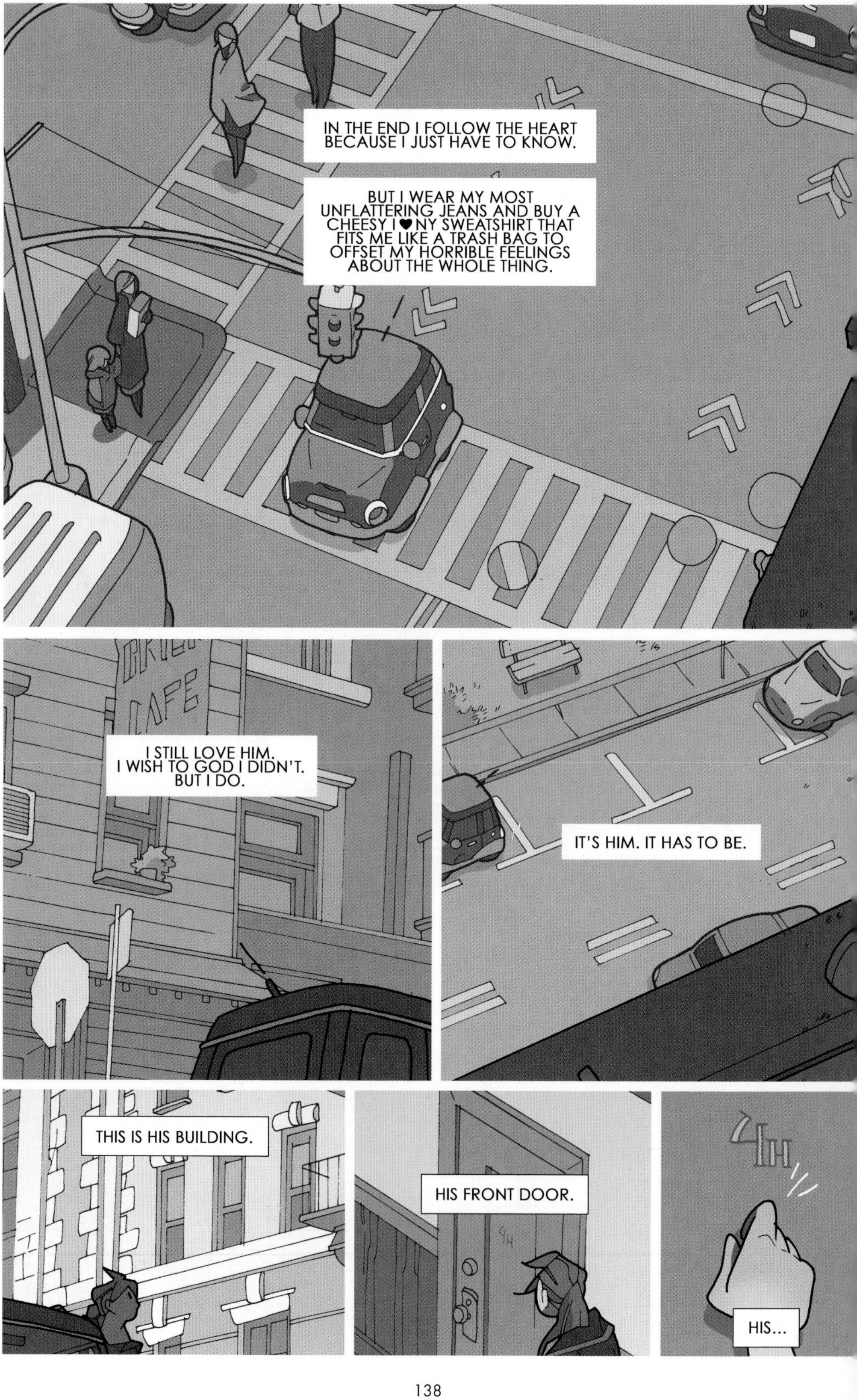
IN THE END I FOLLOW THE HEART BECAUSE I JUST HAVE TO KNOW.
BUT I WEAR MY MOST UNFLATTERING JEANS AND BUY A CHEESY I ♥ NY SWEATSHIRT THAT FITS ME LIKE A TRASH BAG TO OFFSET MY HORRIBLE FEELINGS ABOUT THE WHOLE THING.
I STILL LOVE HIM. I WISH TO GOD I DIDN'T. BUT I DO.
IT'S HIM. IT HAS TO BE.
THIS IS HIS BUILDING.
HIS FRONT DOOR.
HIS...

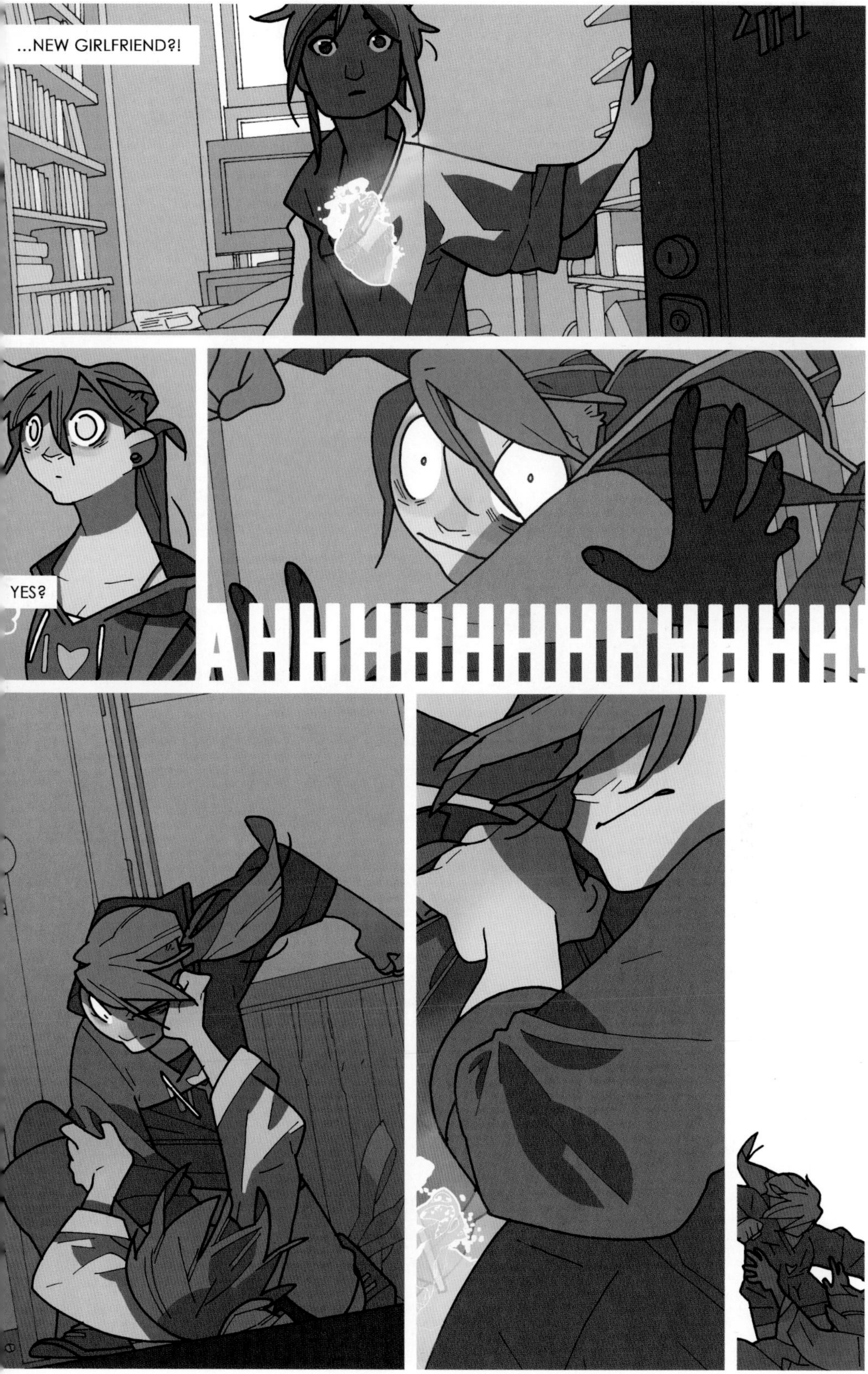
...NEW GIRLFRIEND?!
YES?
AHHHHHHHHHHHH!

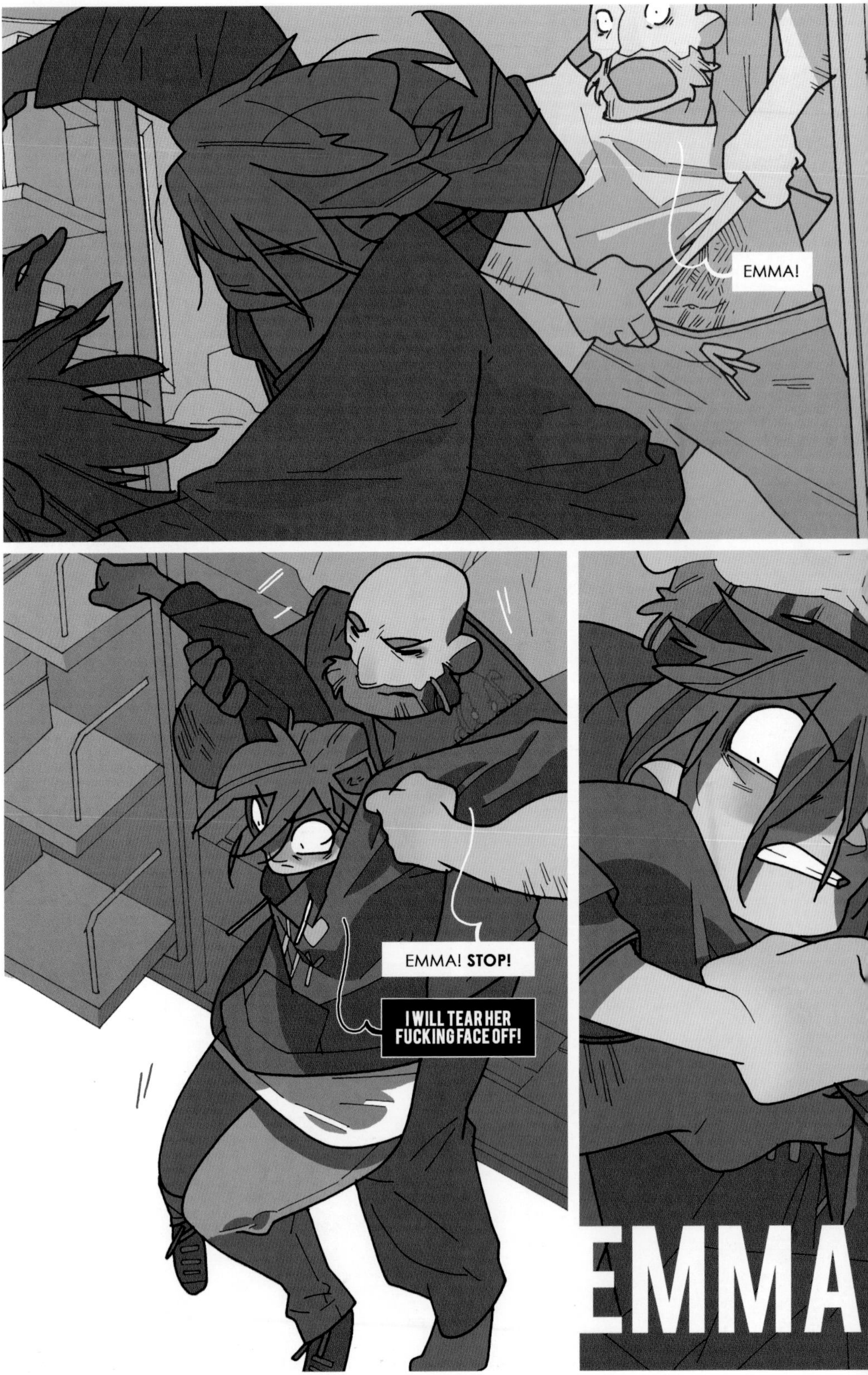
EMMA!
EMMA! STOP!
I WILL TEAR HER FUCKING FACE OFF!
EMMA

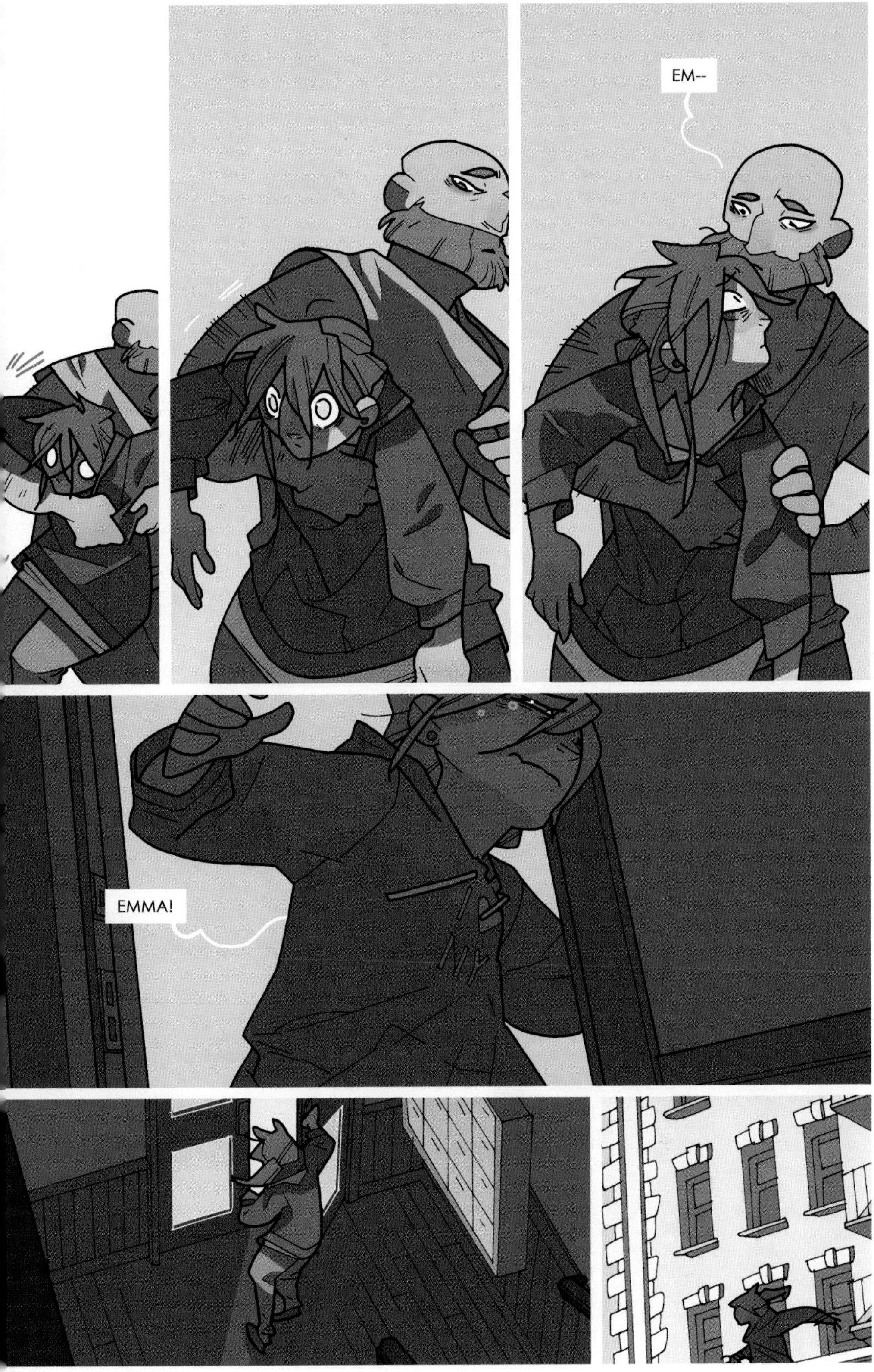
EM--
EMMA!

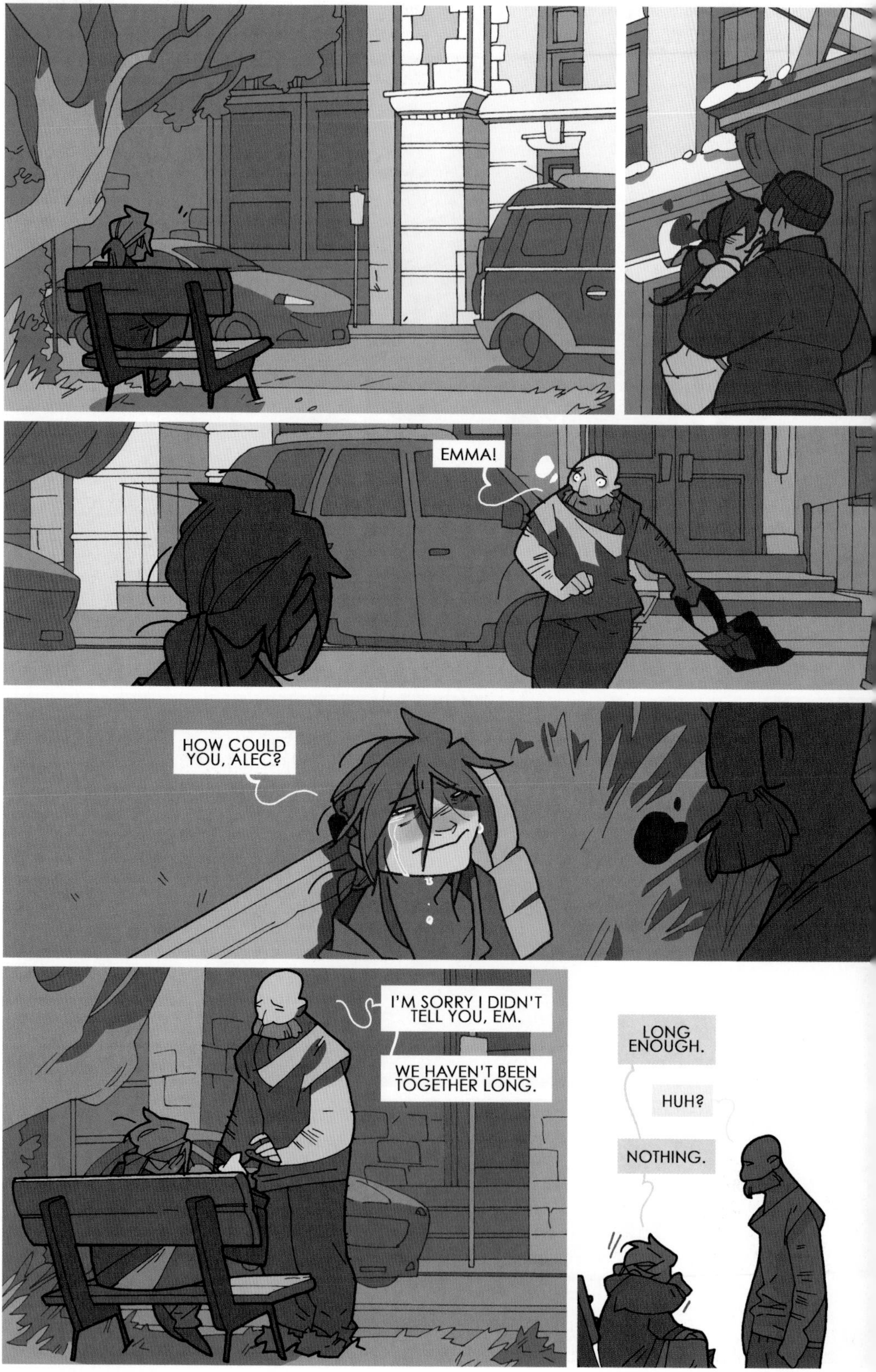
EMMA!
HOW COULD YOU, ALEC?
I'M SORRY I DIDN'T TELL YOU, EM.
WE HAVEN'T BEEN TOGETHER LONG.
LONG ENOUGH.
HUH?
NOTHING.

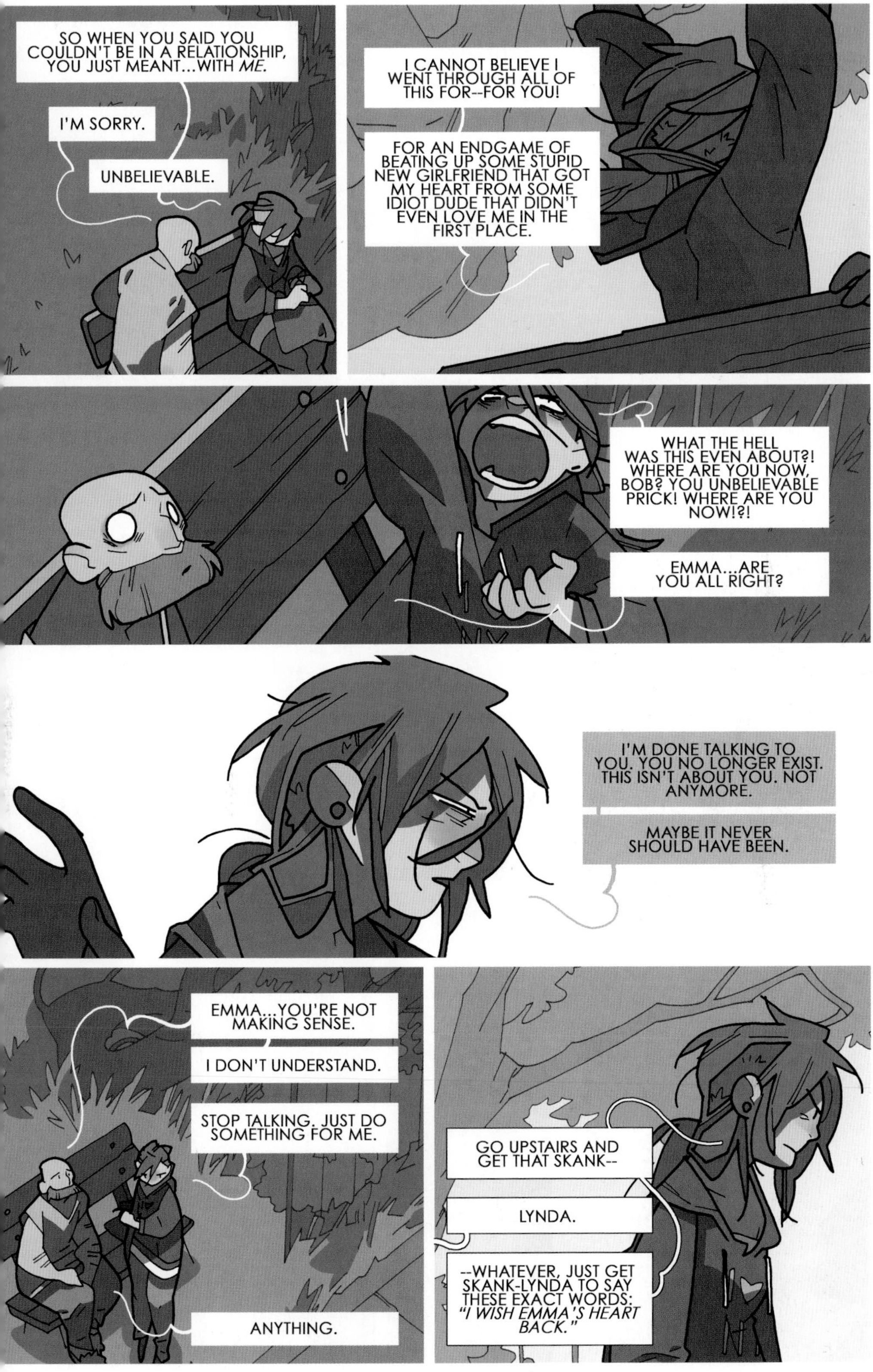
SO WHEN YOU SAID YOU COULDN'T BE IN A RELATIONSHIP, YOU JUST MEANT...WITH *ME.*
I'M SORRY.
UNBELIEVABLE.
I CANNOT BELIEVE I WENT THROUGH ALL OF THIS FOR--FOR YOU!
FOR AN ENDGAME OF BEATING UP SOME STUPID NEW GIRLFRIEND THAT GOT MY HEART FROM SOME IDIOT DUDE THAT DIDN'T EVEN LOVE ME IN THE FIRST PLACE.
WHAT THE HELL WAS THIS EVEN ABOUT?! WHERE ARE YOU NOW, BOB? YOU UNBELIEVABLE PRICK! WHERE ARE YOU NOW!?!
EMMA...ARE YOU ALL RIGHT?
I'M DONE TALKING TO YOU. YOU NO LONGER EXIST. THIS ISN'T ABOUT YOU. NOT ANYMORE.
MAYBE IT NEVER SHOULD HAVE BEEN.
EMMA...YOU'RE NOT MAKING SENSE.
I DON'T UNDERSTAND.
STOP TALKING. JUST DO SOMETHING FOR ME.
ANYTHING.
GO UPSTAIRS AND GET THAT SKANK--
LYNDA.
--WHATEVER, JUST GET SKANK-LYNDA TO SAY THESE EXACT WORDS: *"I WISH EMMA'S HEART BACK."*

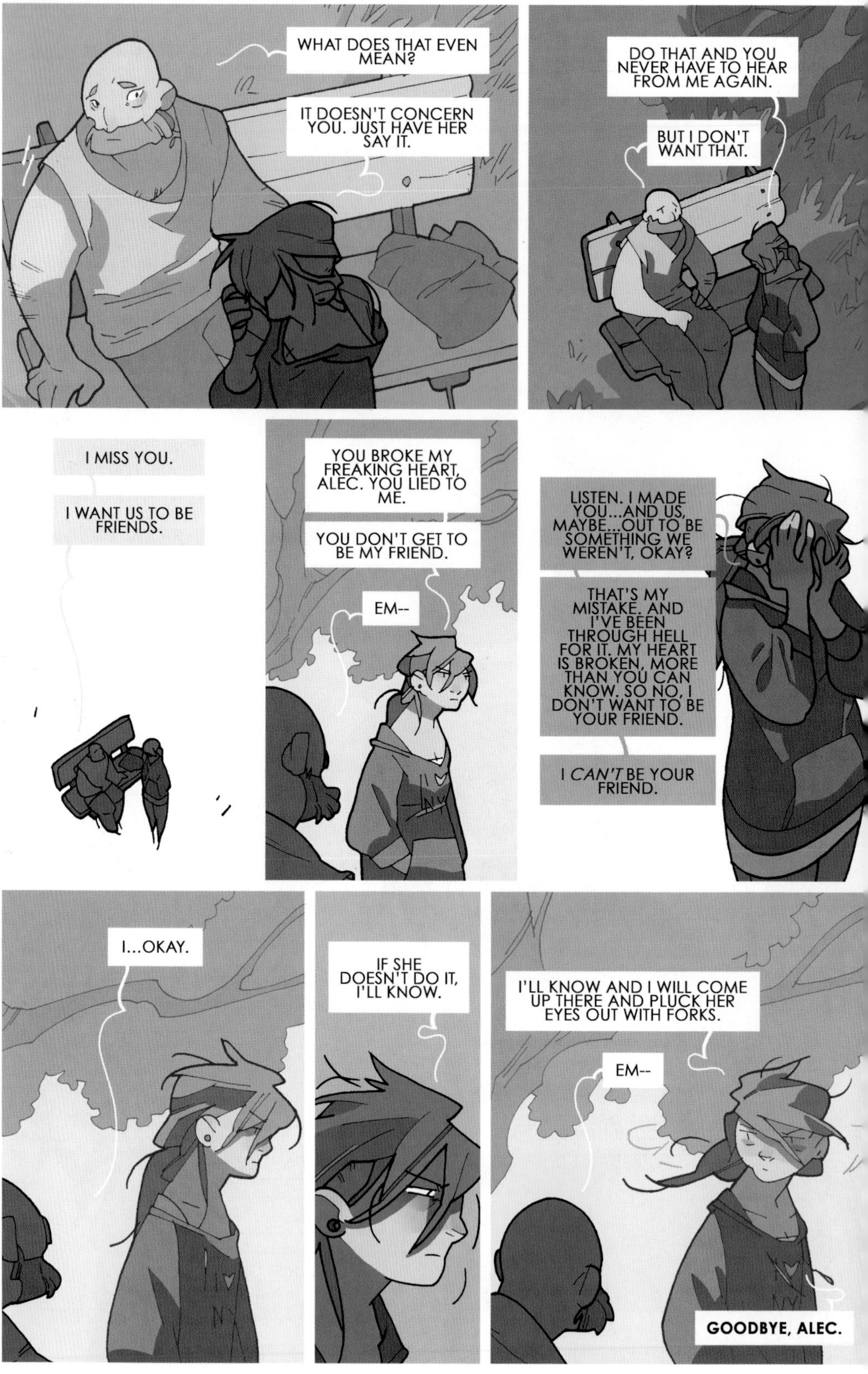
WHAT DOES THAT EVEN MEAN?
IT DOESN'T CONCERN YOU. JUST HAVE HER SAY IT.
DO THAT AND YOU NEVER HAVE TO HEAR FROM ME AGAIN.
BUT I DON'T WANT THAT.
I MISS YOU.
I WANT US TO BE FRIENDS.
YOU BROKE MY FREAKING HEART, ALEC. YOU LIED TO ME.
YOU DON'T GET TO BE MY FRIEND.
EM--
LISTEN. I MADE YOU...AND US, MAYBE...OUT TO BE SOMETHING WE WEREN'T, OKAY?
THAT'S MY MISTAKE. AND I'VE BEEN THROUGH HELL FOR IT. MY HEART IS BROKEN, MORE THAN YOU CAN KNOW. SO NO, I DON'T WANT TO BE YOUR FRIEND.
I *CAN'T* BE YOUR FRIEND.
I...OKAY.
IF SHE DOESN'T DO IT, I'LL KNOW.
I'LL KNOW AND I WILL COME UP THERE AND PLUCK HER EYES OUT WITH FORKS.
EM--
GOODBYE, ALEC.

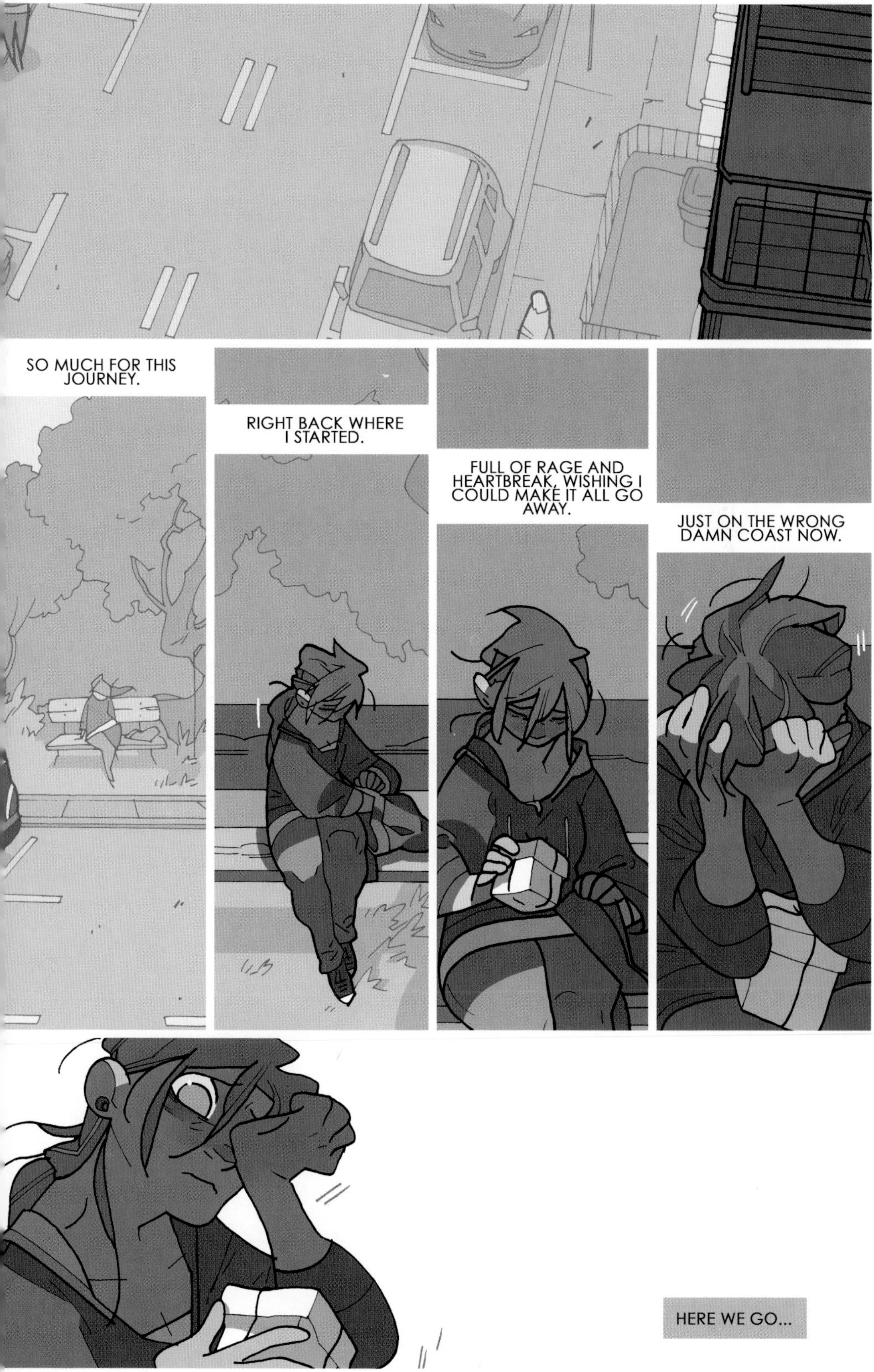
SO MUCH FOR THIS JOURNEY.
RIGHT BACK WHERE I STARTED.
FULL OF RAGE AND HEARTBREAK, WISHING I COULD MAKE IT ALL GO AWAY.
JUST ON THE WRONG DAMN COAST NOW.
HERE WE GO...

PIECE no. 7

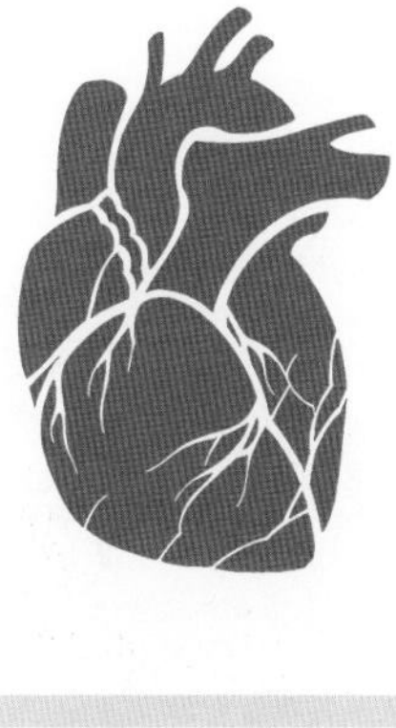

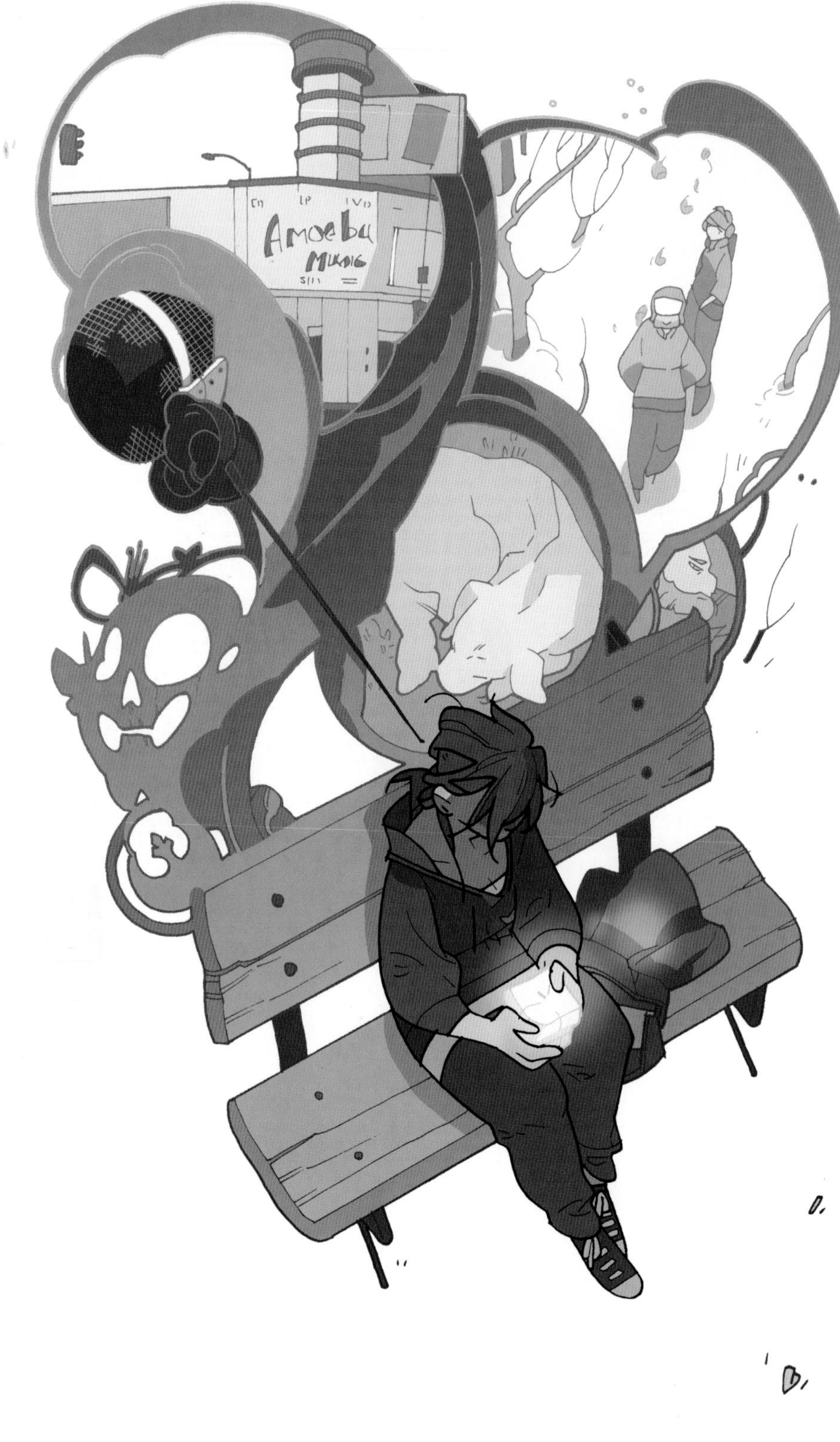
LP
Amoeba

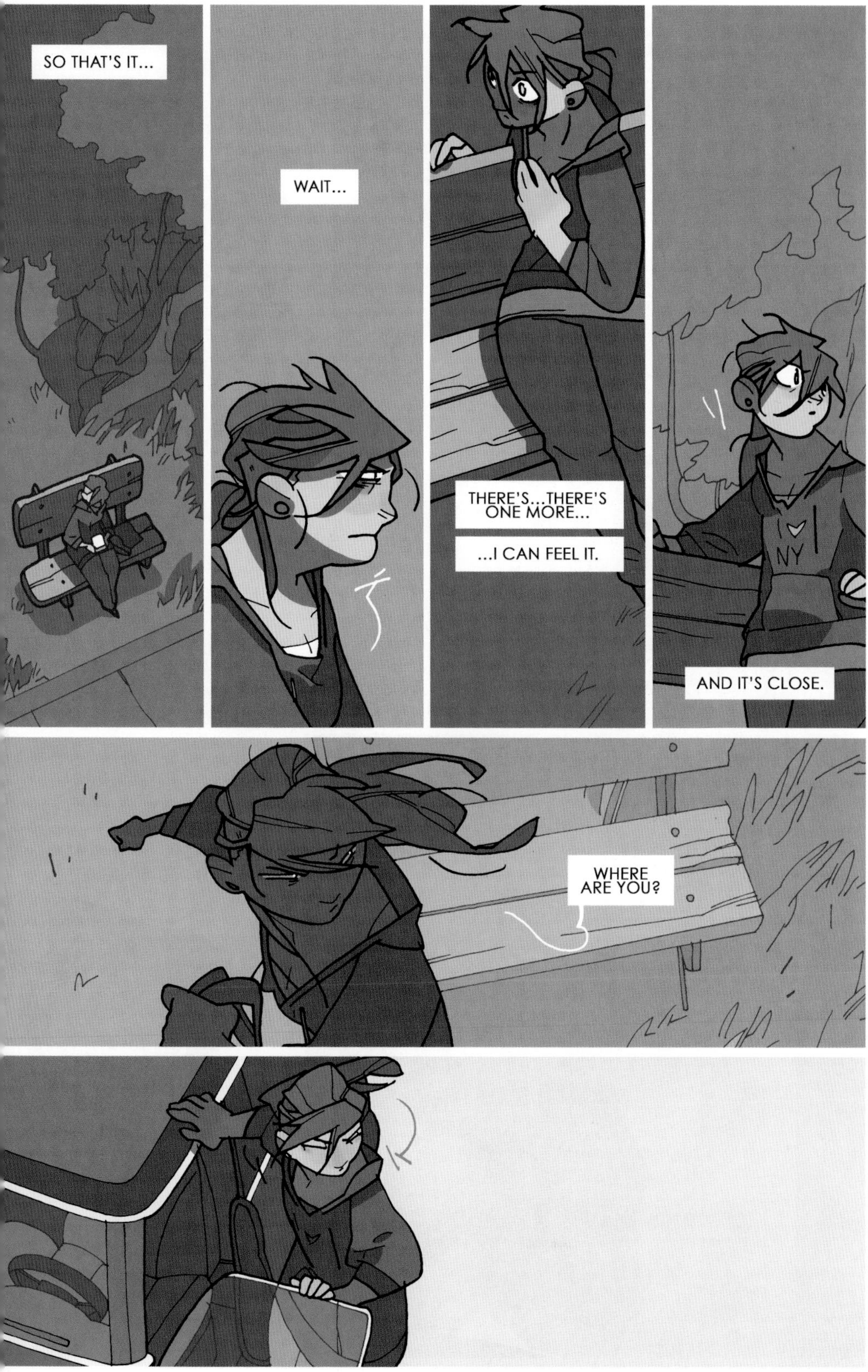
SO THAT'S IT...
WAIT...
THERE'S...THERE'S ONE MORE...
...I CAN FEEL IT.
AND IT'S CLOSE.
WHERE ARE YOU?

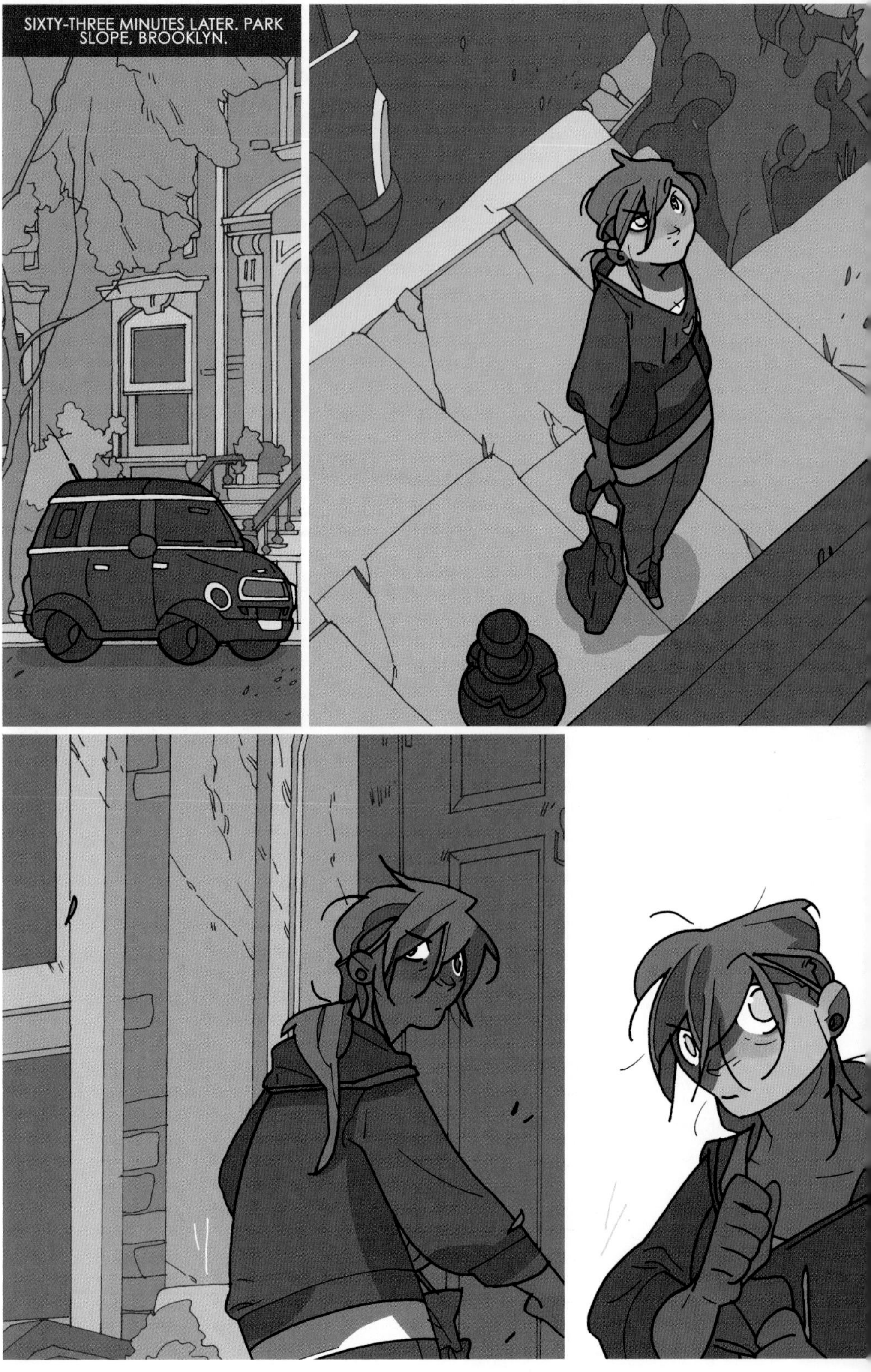
SIXTY-THREE MINUTES LATER. PARK SLOPE, BROOKLYN.

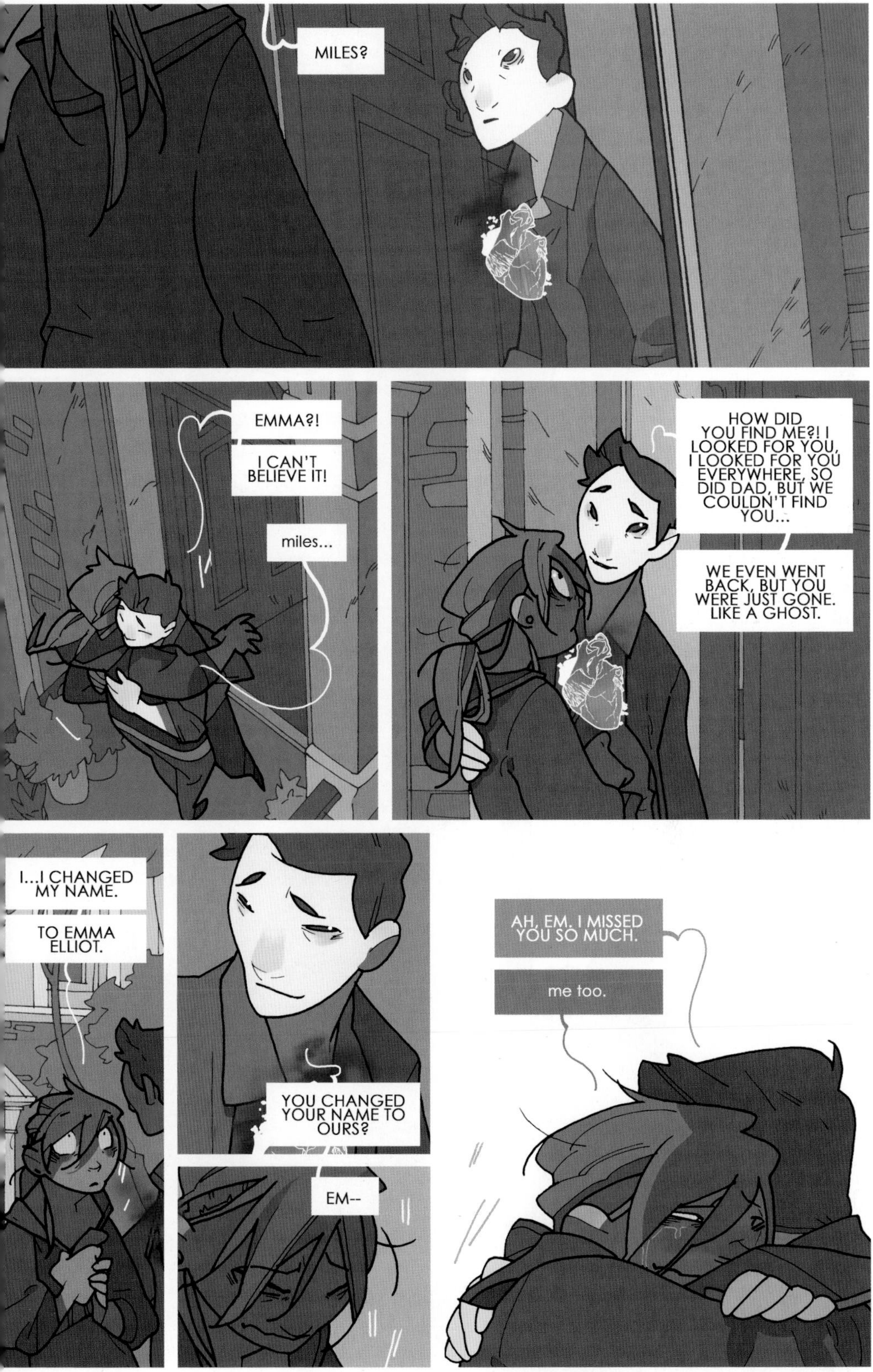
MILES?
EMMA?!
I CAN'T BELIEVE IT!
miles...
HOW DID YOU FIND ME?! I LOOKED FOR YOU, I LOOKED FOR YOU EVERYWHERE, SO DID DAD, BUT WE COULDN'T FIND YOU...
WE EVEN WENT BACK, BUT YOU WERE JUST GONE. LIKE A GHOST.
I...I CHANGED MY NAME.
TO EMMA ELLIOT.
YOU CHANGED YOUR NAME TO OURS?
EM--
AH, EM. I MISSED YOU SO MUCH.
me too.

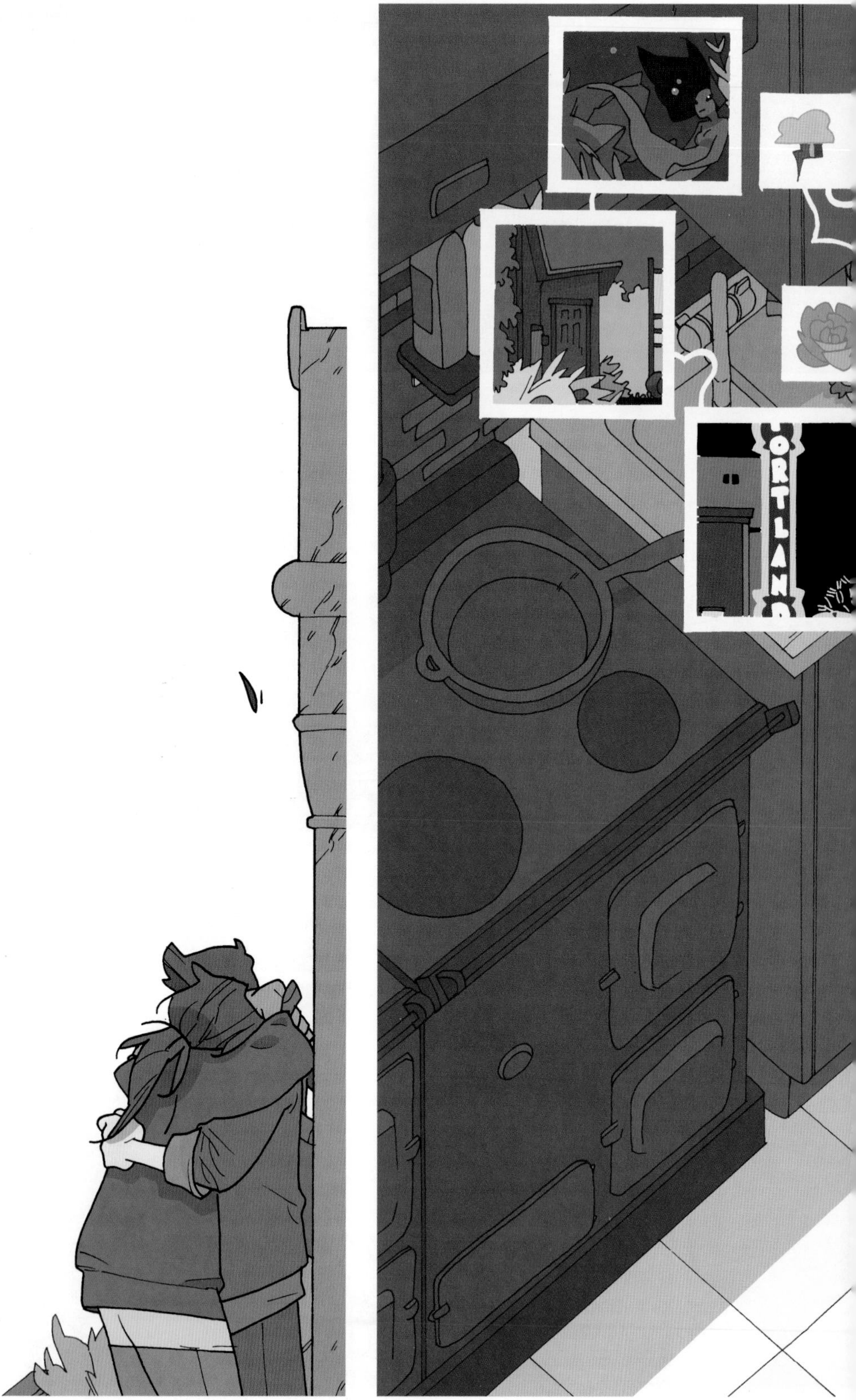
ORTLAND

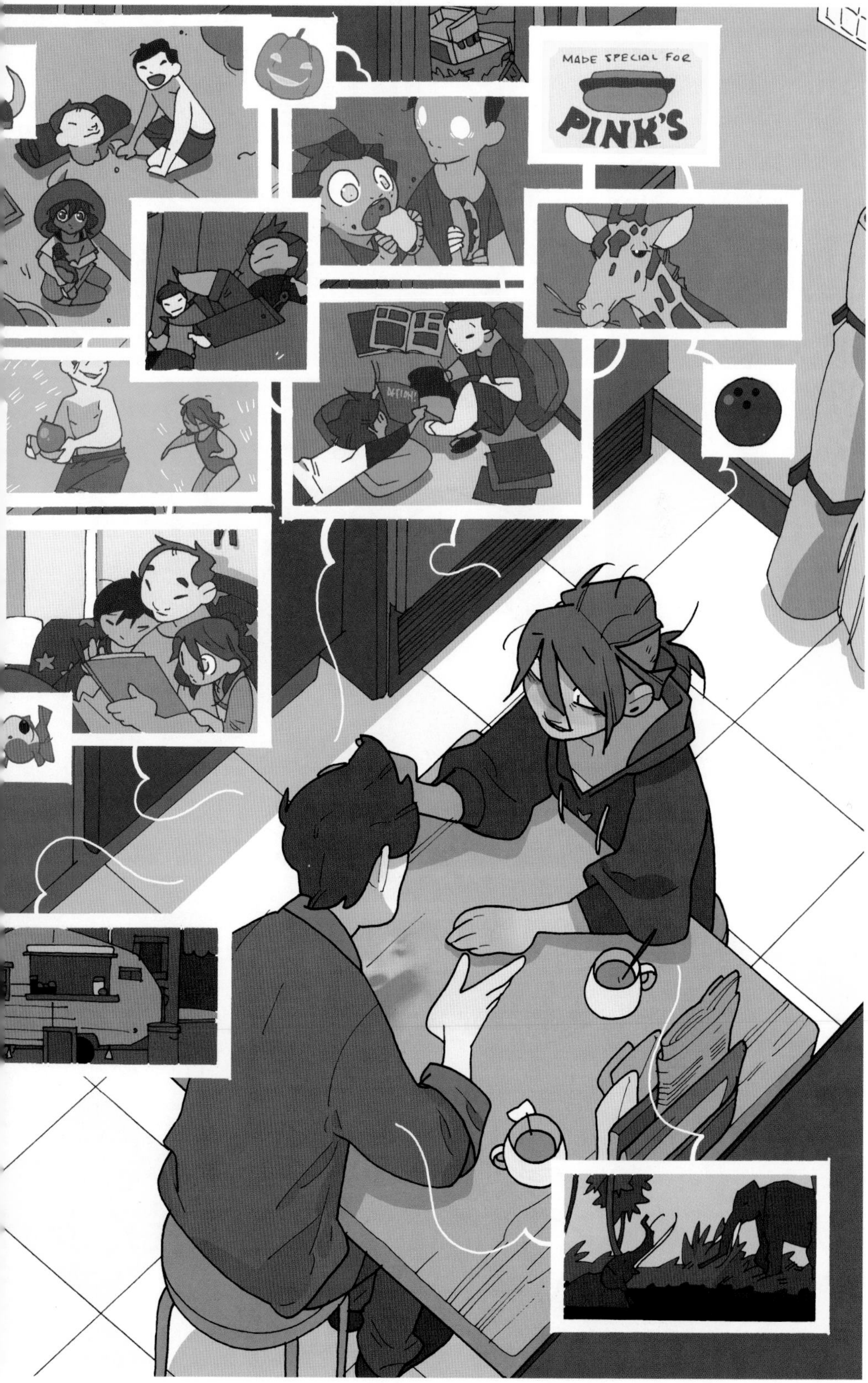
MADE SPECIAL FOR
PINK'S

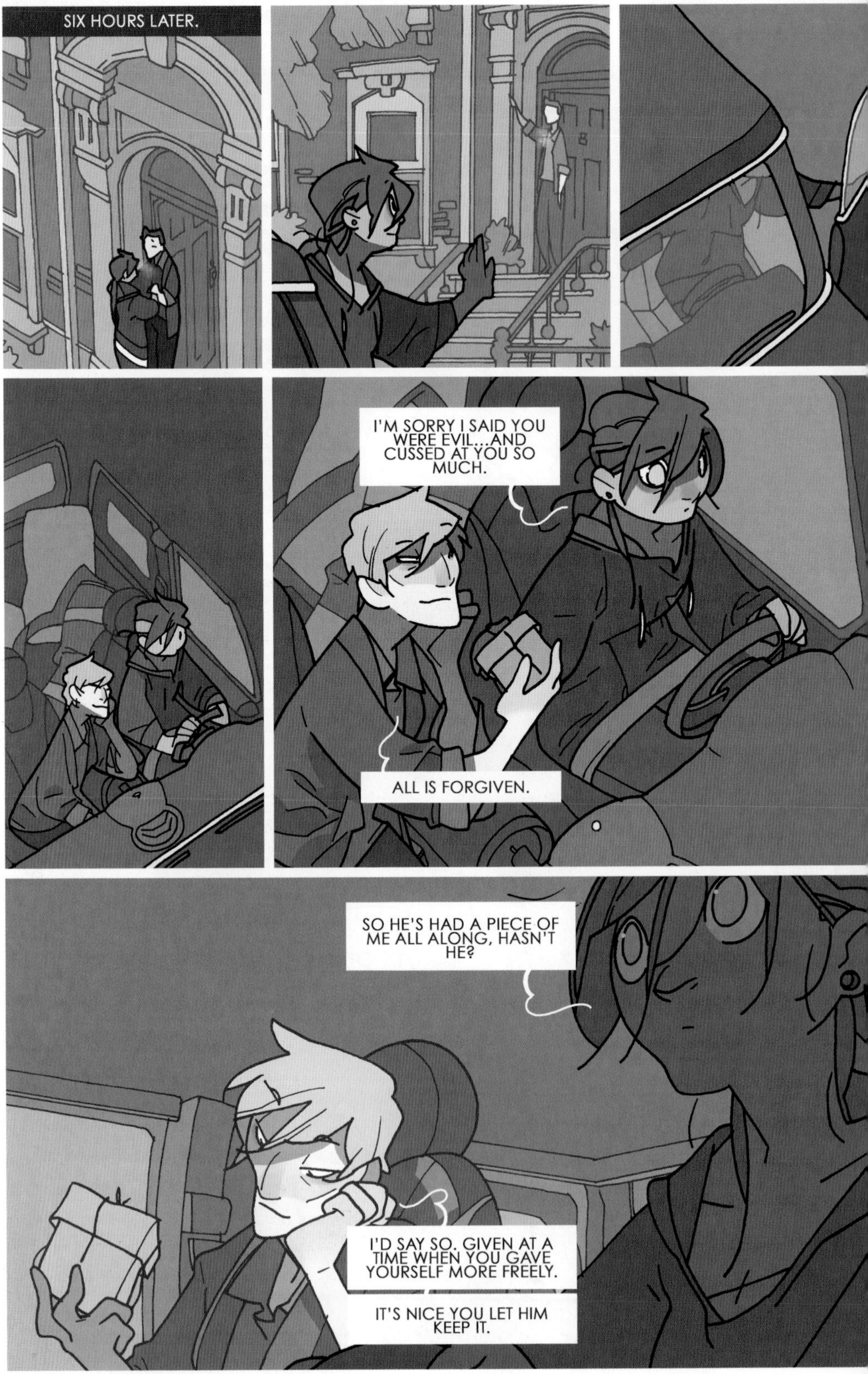
SIX HOURS LATER.
I'M SORRY I SAID YOU WERE EVIL...AND CUSSED AT YOU SO MUCH.
ALL IS FORGIVEN.
SO HE'S HAD A PIECE OF ME ALL ALONG, HASN'T HE?
I'D SAY SO. GIVEN AT A TIME WHEN YOU GAVE YOURSELF MORE FREELY.
IT'S NICE YOU LET HIM KEEP IT.

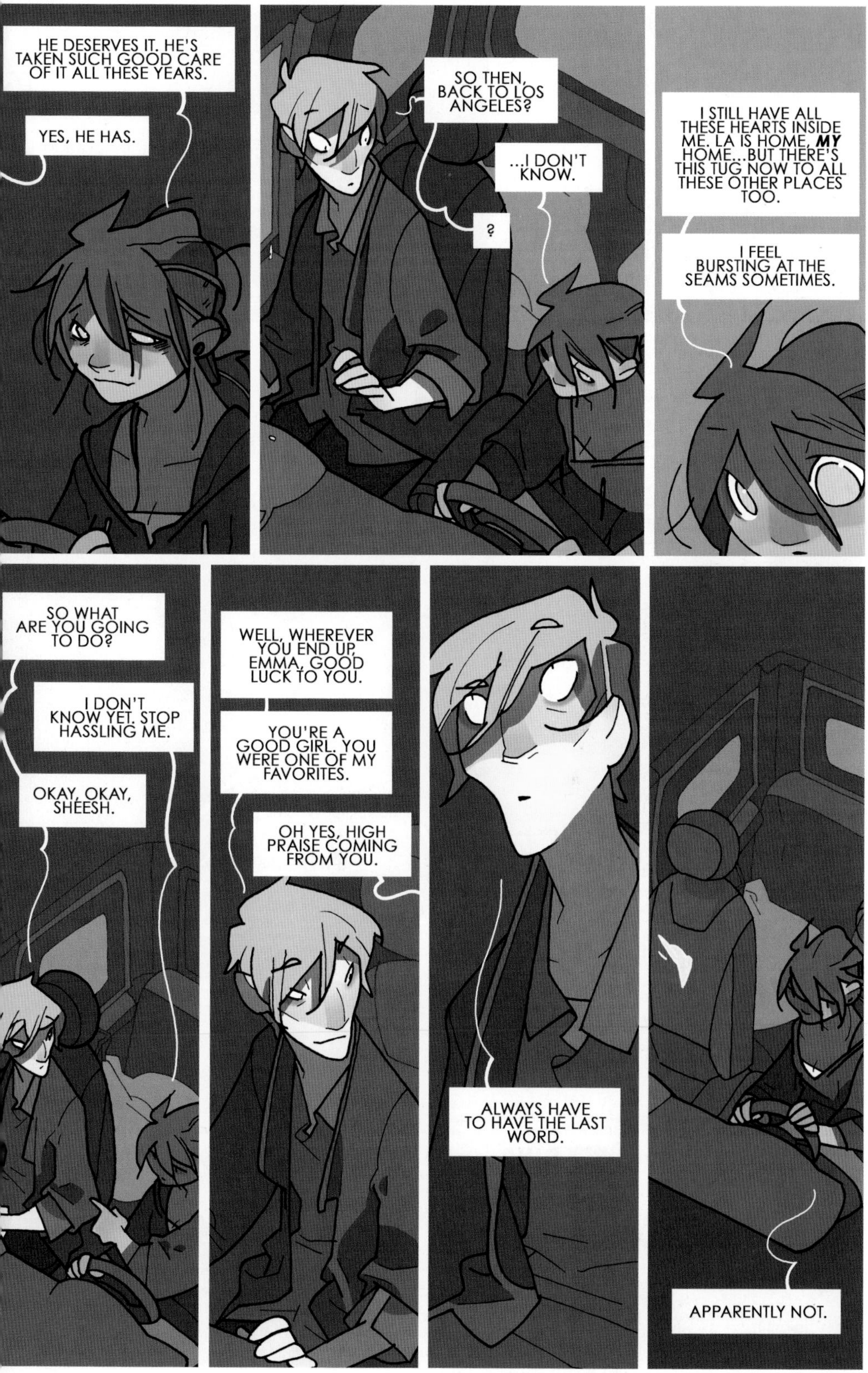
HE DESERVES IT. HE'S TAKEN SUCH GOOD CARE OF IT ALL THESE YEARS.
YES, HE HAS.
SO THEN, BACK TO LOS ANGELES?
...I DON'T KNOW.
?
I STILL HAVE ALL THESE HEARTS INSIDE ME. LA IS HOME, **MY** HOME...BUT THERE'S THIS TUG NOW TO ALL THESE OTHER PLACES TOO.
I FEEL BURSTING AT THE SEAMS SOMETIMES.
SO WHAT ARE YOU GOING TO DO?
I DON'T KNOW YET. STOP HASSLING ME.
OKAY, OKAY, SHEESH.
WELL, WHEREVER YOU END UP, EMMA, GOOD LUCK TO YOU.
YOU'RE A GOOD GIRL. YOU WERE ONE OF MY FAVORITES.
OH YES, HIGH PRAISE COMING FROM YOU.
ALWAYS HAVE TO HAVE THE LAST WORD.
APPARENTLY NOT.

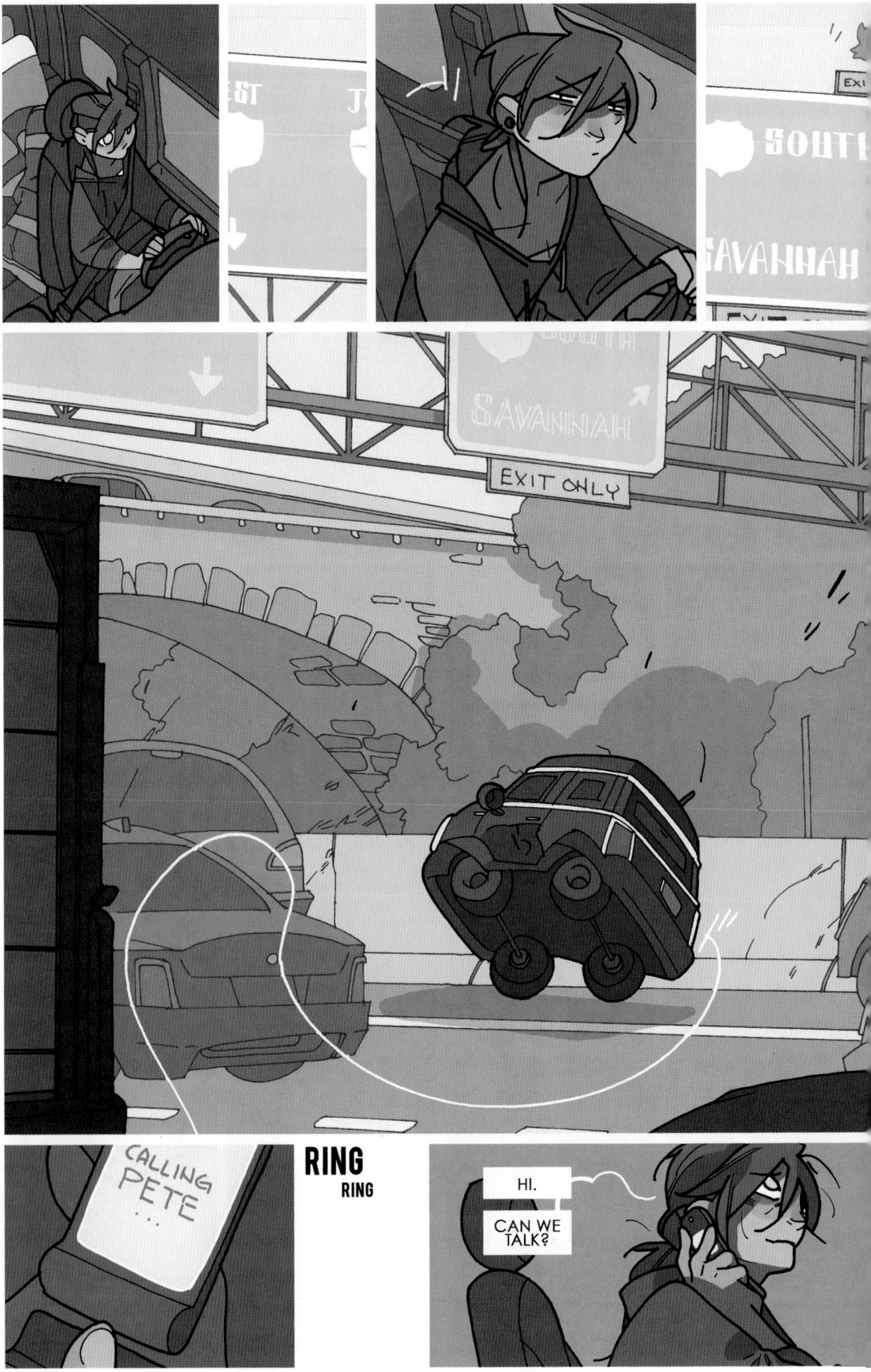
EST
SOUTH
SAVANNAH
EXI
SAVANNAH
EXIT ONLY
CALLING PETE . . .
RING
RING
HI.
CAN WE TALK?

ABOUT THE AUTHORS

KELLY THOMPSON's ambitions are eclipsed only by her desire to exist entirely in pajamas.

Fortunately pajamas and writers go hand in hand (most of the time). Kelly has a fancy degree in sequential art from the Savannah College of Art & Design and has published two novels (*The Girl Who Would Be King* and *Storykiller*). She's currently writing the *Jem and the Holograms* comic from IDW and is cowriting Marvel's *Captain Marvel and the Carol Corps*. Please buy all her stuff so that she can buy (and wear) more pajamas.

You can find Kelly all over the Internet, where she is generally well liked, except where she's absolutely detested.

MEREDITH McCLAREN is just here to eat.

She only started doing comics in an effort to make the time between lunch and dinner go faster.

That this has, in fact, resulted in a career in comics completely baffles her.

Some of her webcomics (*Hinges* and *Scraps*) have even been printed.

Life is funny that way.

ALSO BY KELLY THOMPSON

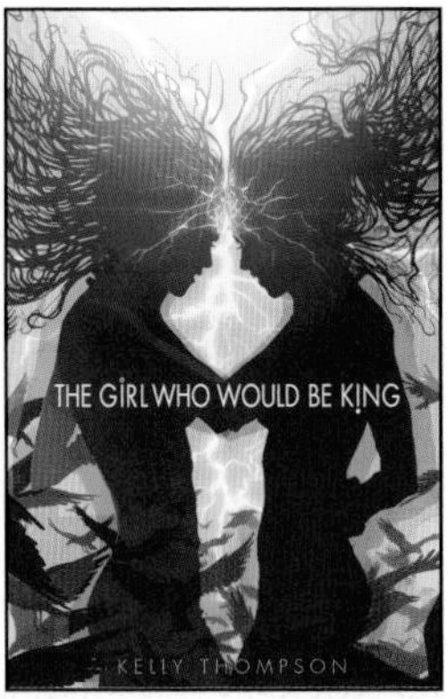
THE GIRL WHO WOULD BE KING
KELLY THOMPSON

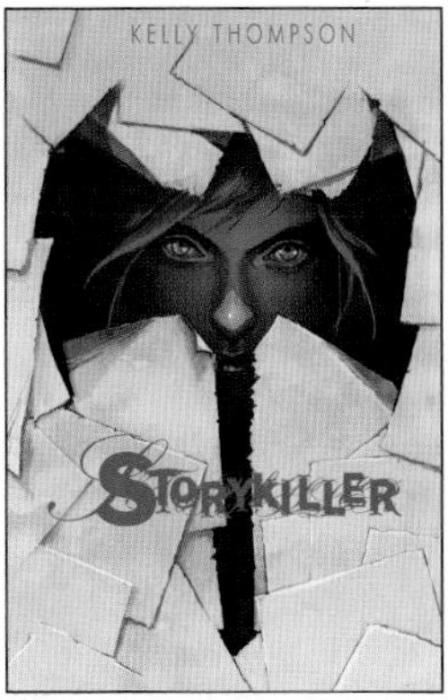
KELLY THOMPSON
STORYKILLER

The Girl Who Would Be King
$14.99 | 978-0-98826-973-6

Storykiller
$14.99 | 978-0-99164-926-6

ALSO BY MEREDITH McCLAREN

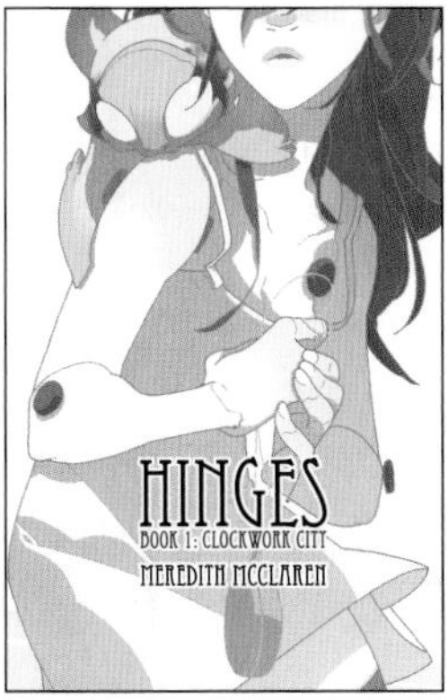
HINGES
BOOK 1: CLOCKWORK CITY
MEREDITH MCCLAREN

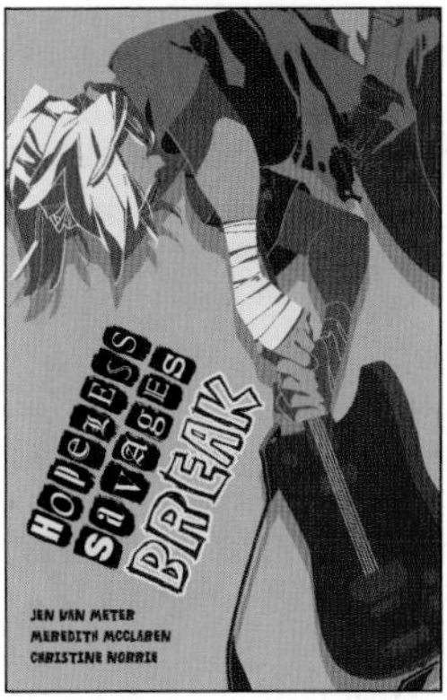
HOPELESS SAVAGES BREAK
JEN VAN METER
MEREDITH MCCLAREN
CHRISTINE NORRIE

Hinges Book 1: *Clockwork City*
$15.99 | ISBN 978-1-63215-253-4

Hopeless Savages: Break
Jen Van Meter, Meredith McClaren, and Christine Norrie
$17.99 | ISBN 978-1-62010-252-7

CREATIVE GIANTS!

GET YOUR FIX OF DARK HORSE BOOKS FROM THESE INSPIRED CREATORS!

MESMO DELIVERY SECOND EDITION - Rafael Grampá

Eisner Award–winning artist Rafael Grampá (5, *Hellblazer*) makes his full-length comics debut with the critically acclaimed graphic novel *Mesmo Delivery*—a kinetic, bloody romp starring Rufo, an ex-boxer; Sangrecco, an Elvis impersonator; and a ragtag crew of overly confident drunks who pick the wrong delivery men to mess with.
ISBN 978-1-61655-457-6 | $14.99

SIN TITULO - Cameron Stewart

Following the death of his grandfather, Alex Mackay discovers a mysterious photograph in the old man's belongings that sets him on an adventure like no other—where dreams and reality merge, family secrets are laid bare, and lives are irrevocably altered.
ISBN 978-1-61655-248-0 | $19.99

DE:TALES - Fábio Moon and Gabriel Bá

Brazilian twins Fábio Moon and Gabriel Bá's (*Daytripper*, *Pixu*) most personal work to date. Brimming with all the details of human life, their charming tales move from the urban reality of their home in São Paulo to the magical realism of their Latin American background.
ISBN 978-1-59582-557-5 | $19.99

THE TRUE LIVES OF THE FABULOUS KILLJOYS - Gerard Way, Shaun Simon, and Becky Cloonan

Years ago, the Killjoys fought against the tyrannical megacorporation Better Living Industries. Today, the followers of the original Killjoys languish in the desert and the fight for freedom fades. It's left to the Girl to take down BLI!
ISBN 978-1-59582-462-2 | $19.99

DEMO - Brian Wood and Becky Cloonan

It's hard enough being a teenager. Now try being a teenager with *powers*. A chronicle of the lives of young people on separate journeys to self-discovery in a world—just like our own—where being different is feared.
ISBN 978-1-61655-682-2 | $24.99

SABERTOOTH SWORDSMAN - Damon Gentry and Aaron Conley

When his village is enslaved and his wife kidnapped by the malevolent Mastodon Mathematician, a simple farmer must find his inner warrior—the Sabertooth Swordsman!
ISBN 978-1-61655-176-6 | $17.99

JAYBIRD - Jaakko and Lauri Ahonen

Disney meets Kafka in this beautiful, intense, original tale! A very small, very scared little bird lives an isolated life in a great big house with his infirm mother. He's never been outside the house, and he never will if his mother has anything to say about it.
ISBN 978-1-61655-469-9 | $19.99

MONSTERS! & OTHER STORIES - Gustavo Duarte

Newcomer Gustavo Duarte spins wordless tales inspired by Godzilla, King Kong, and Pixar, brimming with humor, charm, and delightfully twisted horror!
ISBN 978-1-61655-309-8 | $12.99

SACRIFICE - Sam Humphries and Dalton Rose

What happens when a troubled youth is plucked from modern society and thrust though time and space into the heart of the Aztec civilization—one of the most bloodthirsty times in human history?
ISBN 978-1-59582-985-6 | $19.99

AVAILABLE AT YOUR LOCAL COMICS SHOP OR BOOKSTORE
To find a comics shop in your area, call 1-888-266-4226. For more information or to order direct: ON THE WEB: DarkHorse.com E-MAIL: mailorder@darkhorse.com / PHONE: 1-800-862-0052 Mon.–Fri. 9 a.m. to 5 p.m. Pacific Time.

Mesmo Delivery™ © Rafael Grampá. Sin Titulo™ © Cameron Stewart. De:Tales™ © Fábio Moon & Gabriel Bá. The True Lives of the Fabulous Killjoys™ © Gerard Way & Shaun Simon. DEMO™ © Brian Wood & Becky Cloonan. Sabertooth Swordsman™ © Damon Gentry and Aaron Conley. Jaybird™ © Strip Art Features, www.safcomics. com. Monsters!™ © Gustavo Duarte. Sacrifice™ © Sam Humphries & Dalton Rose. Dark Horse Books® and the Dark Horse logo are registered trademarks of Dark Horse Comics, Inc. All rights reserved. (BL 5018)

DARK HORSE BOOKS